Obadiah Walker

The Benefits Of Our Saviour Jesus Christ

Obadiah Walker

The Benefits Of Our Saviour Jesus Christ

ISBN/EAN: 9783742814333

Manufactured in Europe, USA, Canada, Australia, Japa

Cover: Foto ©Lupo / pixelio.de

Manufactured and distributed by brebook publishing software (www.brebook.com)

Obadiah Walker

The Benefits Of Our Saviour Jesus Christ

Benefits of our Saviour,

JESUS CHRIST,
TO MANKIND.

1 COR. 1. 31, 32.

[Jesus Christ] *is made unto us Wisdom, and Righteous-*
ness, and Sanctification, and Redemption.
He that glorieth, let him glory in the Lord [Jesus
Christ.]

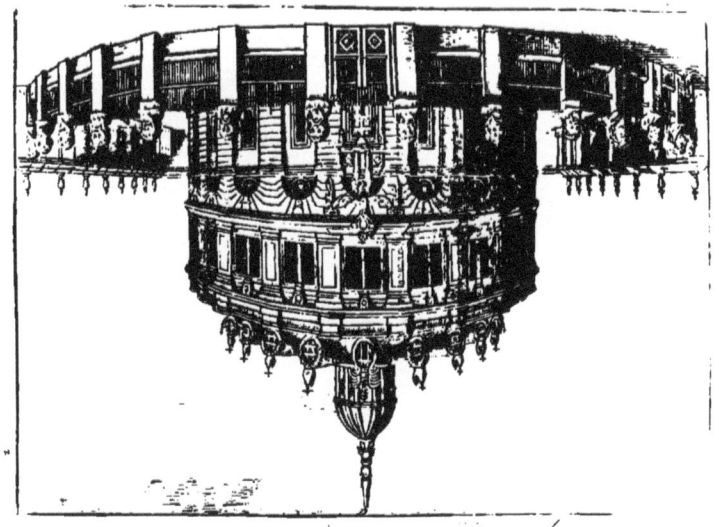

At the THEATER in OXFORD.
MDCLXXX.

PREFACE.

THE chief intention of publishing these discourses is, to suggest to devout persons some few but copious heads for their Meditation. To which purpose it is not amiss to premise:

That in meditating on any action or passion of our Saviour; consider his person doing or suffering it, not as man, but God and Man. Either of which will produce affections in you diverse from the other; both full of Benefit. When you consider him as Man; you will more admire and love, in human infirmity, his innocence, and all his betoical virtues, and merits; and compassionate his indign sufferings; and, these being for you also, in representing to your self such his human weakness, it will render them far more dear unto you; and your gratitude much more to him. As he is man, you will have a more familiar confidence in his goodwill toward you: more interest your self in, and indeavour to imitate, what he did and suffered; and more firmly believe, that it shall be done unto you (if being like him) what was done by God to him.

But again, when you consider him as God; not a word,

PREFACE.

word, not an answer, not a circumstance of any a-
ction of his, passeth without your admiration, and
deep reverence of it; you will be astonisht that such
Majesty and power should so low descend for your
sake; and be infinitely more ready to fear, to
praise, to love, to admire, to sacrifice all you are,
and have, unto him: and then grieve, comparing
it with his, i.e. Gods love to you, that it is so in-
considerable: you will discover new wisdom in e-
very passage of his story: and his sufferings, humility, mildness, it will still gracten to you as his person doth. You will not only make your addresses with
more caution to him; but also more expect strength
and protection from him; and in every thought
of him will bend your soul, to fall down, adore, reverence, and fear such a divinity. And in this
meditation will say; Lord depart from me for I
am a sinful man: as in the former; Lord I will
follow thee whither soever thou goest.

OF THE
CHAPTERS.

CHAP. I. Jesus Christ a Prophet, Lawgiver, Apostle, declaring all Gods will, &c. Pag. 1.
CHAP. II. Jesus Christ the Exemplar and pattern in all obedience to Gods will, and the reward of that obedience. p. 18.
CHAP. III. Jesus Christ the Mediator of the new Covenant. p. 36.
CHAP. IV. Jesus Christ the Sacrifice. p. 45.
CHAP. V. Jesus Christ the Redeemer from sin, the law, death, and Satan. p. 58.
CHAP. VI. Jesus Christ the second Adam. p. 71.
CHAP. VII. Jesus Christ the Melchizedechical High Priest. p. 110.
CHAP. VIII. Jesus Christ the Lord and King. p. 155.
CHAP. IX. The benefits of our Saviour common to all Generations ever since the beginning of the world. p. 175.

(1)
Mans Restitution
BY
JESUS CHRIST.

Jesus Christ sent by the Father a *Prophet*, *Lawgiver*, *Apostle*, declaring all Gods Will, &c.

GO D, who in the begining, writ his Laws in the hearts of all men, (*Rom.* 2. 14, 15. The Gentiles not having the Law of Moses yet *shew the work of the Law written in their hearts, their thoughts accusing, &c.* So *Rom.* 1. 21, 25, 28, 32. *Because when they knew God, they glorified him not as God,* v. 21. *but changed the truth of God into a lie,* v. 25. *tho knowing that they, who commit such things, are worthy of death,* v. 32. *as they did not like to retain God in their knowledge, so God gave them over,* &c. ver. 28) made, besides this, from the begining, many expres revelations by Prophets *Jude* 14. in many particulars concerning his service and worship, to the Church. Therefore find we much of the ceremonial Law practised before Moses, *Gen.* 14, 20. 35, 2. 8, 21. *Exod.* 24, 5. *Gen.* 15, 10. compared with *Lev.* 1, 17. *Gen.* 9, 4. &c.

§ 1.

Jesus Christ the truth, in the fulness of time.

But here, much of these Laws by so ill a Register, and in so long time being more and more defaced and worn out, (for *Moses's Law* was added because of the overflowing of transgressions against the Law *natural, Gal.* 3. 19. *till Christ should come* : The effects of which Law Mosaical among the Jews, the rules of Philosophy (being only the Law of nature revived by the wisest of other nations) in

A   some

The benefits of our Saviour.

some inferior degree wrought among the Gentiles) after more than 2000 years, when the Church very numerous was grown into a State, God published them again unto the world with great solemnity by Moses; and writ them himself in Tables of stone to last the longer; and, doubtless, in these then, added many explications at least to those which formerly were practised, or enjoyned to Adam, *Gen.* 4. 3, 4. or Noah, *Gen.* 9. *1.* &c.

But here again, his Laws being neither obeyed so far as understood; nor understood so far as they obliged; after a long space of his tolerating the unbelief and imperfection of the veiled Jew 2 *Cor.* 3. 13, 14, 16.) and his *winking* at the ignorance and idolatry of the Gentiles; and his *suffering them to go on in their own ways* : *Act.* 17. 30, 14, 16. and he having now sufficiently educated his Church in the pedagogism of the Law and of Ceremonies, after about 2000 years more, in the full and due time *Eph.* 1. 10. 1 *Tim.* 2. 6. *Heb.* 11. 40. and the worlds mature age *Gal.* 4. 3. (therefore the first words of our Saviours preaching are : *The time is fulfilled* *Mark.* 1. 15. -the Gospel retaining much what the same distance from the *covenant* made with *Abraham*, wherein were included any Proselytes of the Gentiles, and the promulgation of the Law; as *these* were from the beginning of *nature* , for he doth all things in number, weight, measure) : He sent his Son *Jesus Christ* the greatest and last Prophet, and the Holy one of God, yet more perfectly and fully to revele and declare to mankind his last, and all, his will, &c. *Mat.* 15. 24. *Jo.* 3. 34. -5. 38.

And Him he then sent into the very middle and Navil, as it were, of the then known world, and there seated him not at *Jerusalem*, but in *Galilee* ; half (as
it

CHAP. I.

it were) amongſt the *Gentiles*; to whom the Church was now to be enlarged, and Salvation to be preached as well to the *Jewes*. Tho to the *Jewes* in the firſt place ſee *Jo.* 4. 40. Sent him at this time, and to this *place*; From which time and place, that which he did and taught, might by the Teſtimony of many *witneſſes choſen before of God.* *Act* 10. 41. deſcend conveniently to all other places and times. This thing being neceſſarily to be effected in ſome determinate age, in ſome particular Nation and Country; unleſs perchance the unreaſonableneſs of our unbelief will have him for our fuller ſatisfaction to act over and over again that great work, in all places; and in each of them too at all times; and that we will not in this one thing allow to as firm *relations*, as poſterity is capable of, (I mean the *Goſpels*) that credit, which wee ſo eaſily yield to the Hiſtories of all other famous actions and paſſages of the world.

Which Relations of theſe four Evangeliſts, and three of them ocular witneſſes, common and uſed in the beginnings of Chriſtianity, are ſhewed to be moſt true. 1. From the converſion of ſo many thouſands to this Faith (which thing cannot be denyed) who lived in the time, when theſe Scriptures were writ; and in the places, where theſe things were pretended to be acted; where any falſity might have been moſt eaſily diſcovered; eſpecially in ſo many famous and publick paſſages related in them, which few could be ignorant of. As; *Herods* murthering the Infants: the darkneſs at the execution of *Jeſus*: *John* Baptiſts preaching: many of our Saviours and the Apoſtles miracles. See 1 *Cor.* 15. 6. 2 From the propheſies of the old Teſtament concerning the Meſſias to thoſe who allow thoſe writings)

§ 3.

1.

2.

tings) exactly agreeing with, and fulfilled in, the History of *Jesus* (even as they were interpreted by the learned Jews before the coming of the Messias) in so many punctualities of his life and death; and especially in the time of his coming; which was to be under the second Temple, *Hagg.* 2. 7, 9. But this Temple was destroyed by *Titus*; And when the Scepter was departed first from the Jewish Nation (for this King was then to be sent when the others failed;) But this happened first in the time of *Herod*, the first stranger King, after both *Davids* and *Levi's* rule deposed; and when also the Roman Empire, under whose yoke the Jewes were now faln, was first perfected and at its height in *Augustus*; in whose times our Saviour came. 3. From the plain prophecies contained in these Relations, as *Matt.* 24. &c. concerning the persecution of the Christian profession; the destruction of *Jerusalem* and Temple; and dispersion of the Jewes; set down in them long before the event. 4. As likewise from those heavy curses which the world hath seen to fall upon all the enemies of Christ, and the primitive Christians; as, upon the Jewes (the desolation of which Nation beareth witness to this day in all Countries to the truth of the Gospel); upon *Herod* the Great; His son *Archelaus*; *Herod* the Tetrarch, *Archelaus's* brother that beheaded *John*; *Herod Agrippa* (*Act.* 12, 23.) that killed *James*; it being observed by *Josephus* (a stranger to this cause) that of *Herods* very numerous race within 70 years none were left, but all extinguished in a most miserable manner; and upon the Roman Emperors, so long as the persecutions endured i. e. till *Constantine's* time, most of whom suffered unhappy ends. 5 From the then, (by the Heathen confessed) cessation of oracles,

CHAP. I.

cles, (see *Plutarch's* treatise of it) and the miraculous propagation of the Christian Doctrine, tho so severe and opposite to flesh and blood, by such mean and unarmed instruments, thro such sufferings; which shews it to be a work of no less then a Divine power. And tho another Religion since it, even that of the great Antichrist, Mahometanism, hath also spread much in the world; yet first both the manner of its growth shews it not to be of God: being both planted at first & since continued by the sword, alwaies destitute of any true miracles: (this being not only the practise but the Doctrine of that great Impostour opposite to Christs, That men are by war to be compelled to the Faith.) And also being tempered with much brutish liberty and sensuality indulged to the flesh, which much easilier enclines mens affections to it. *Nova secta ita tandem se late diffundit, si portam luxuriæ & voluptatibus aperiat.* And again; 2. Its growth never equalled the amplitude of Christianity: nor ever shall so universally overrun it, as Christianity hath, and shall, destroy Heathenism; and also God in all Ages preserveth a place of retreat for his Church, from the face of the Dragon and of the Beast to whom he gives his power. *Apoc.* 12. 6, 14. compare 13, 5. *Dan.* 7, 8. 3 Lastly it never advanceth farther then the sword by violence carrieth it: whereas our Lord 1. by the power of the spirit; 2. and the Testimony of miracles; and 3. by sufferings instead of Arms, as in the beginning, so still shall continue to propagate his truth; and goes on conquering and to conquer Nations remote, whom the sword cannot reach: in every age some new people voluntarily submitting to his Scepter.

All these, and many more justifie sufficiently the
truth

truth of these Relations. So that though our Saviour came but in one appointed time, yet all times, that did not see it, notwithstanding want not the greatest reason that can be had from the evidence of History to beleive it. And he that requires more would leave no place for the exercise and merit of Faith: which otherwise would have been as worthless as that feeling one of St *Thomas*, which suffered a reprehension from our Saviour. But Gods pleasure it is, as well for the trial of our inclinations to heavenly things, as for his greater glorification in our service of him, and advancement of our future reward, to give grounds of belief sufficient, not coactive and uncontradictable; and to make us walk only by Faith here, not by sight: that our adherence might be so much more esteemed, by how much we had less evidence, tho all may have evidence enough. See *Jo.* 20. 29. *1 Pet.* 1. 8. Else, let us also require, that God should also shew his personal presence amongst us; and when he ministers to our necessities, do it by Angels visible; and alwaies present to us a prospect of the Joyes of Heaven, as the Devil did to our Saviour the glories of this lower world; and then let him blame us if we do not reverence, trust in, and serve, him.

§ 5.

Anointed.

Hither therefore *at this time* sent; He, in whom were hid from all eternity *all the treasures of wisdom and knowledge*, *Col.* 2. 3. was first anointed (as Prophets anciently were, *1 King.* 19. 16.) and sealed by the Father to this office *Jo. C.* 27. *Luk.* 4. 18, 22. *Esai.* 11. 2. *Act.* 10. 38. *Act.* 4. 27. Anointed with the holy Ghost and with power; and that visibly at his Baptism; *Jo.* 1: 33. that all might know him to be sent (since none unsent may take such honour. *Heb.* 5. 4.) Yea filled with the holy Ghost which

never

CHAP. I.   7

never man was before him. (*For it pleased the Father that in him should all fulness dwell.* Col. 1. 19. *And God gave not the Spirit by mesure to him,* Jo. 3. 34; but according to mesure he gives it to all men else *Eph.* 4. 7.) see Matt. 3. 16. Luk. 3. 5.

Thus furnished for the many offices to which he was predestined by the Father, He was sent First as *a new Legislator*; being *faithful as Moses.* Heb. 3. 2. but yet more to be observed, being *Master of the house wherein Moses was a servant.* (v. 6.) Therefore *Moses,* when he should come, referred them wholly to him *Deut.* 18. 15. And in this office of his, first a new Legislator in some respects as to the law moral. §. 6. *A new Law-giver. For the law moral.*

First, to rectifie the understanding of the Law, formerly either falsifyed, or mutilated: he expounding it in most things more fully, and in some things also contrary to what had been said of old. *It hath been said of old so, but I say unto you,* Matt. 5, 6, 7, chapters. Jo. 1. 17, 18. -3. 2. -4. 25. 1. *Expounding it.*

2. Again, to exact to this Law thus expounded by him a more true, and inward, and full obedience of all men that would be his Disciples, then ever had been performed before by the strictest Sects of all the Law-zealots; not to let *a title of it pass away* (pass away heaven and earth first) *till all the Law be fulfilled.* (*Matt.* 5. 17, 18, 19, 20. 1 *Cor.* 7. 19. *Gal.* 2. 17. *Jam.* 2. 12.) 2. *Requiring stricter obedience.*

3. To make to such observers of this Law more open and manifest promises of the Kingdome of Heaven *Heb.* 8. 6. and against the breakers of this Law, heretofore winked at, and suffered to walk in their own way, &c. *to revele the wrath of God from Heaven* (as not the joyes of heaven, so neither the paines of Hell before his coming having been so much 3. *Denouncing heavier judgments.*

much talked of) *Rom.* 1. 18. charging men every where to repent *Act.* 17. 30. becaufe a *day is appointed wherein he will judge the world.* v. 31. *Tit.* 2. 11, 12, 13. Therefore he came, faith the Baptift, *with an axe* on his fhoulder; *with a fan in his hand;* to cut down the fruitlefs trees; to purge Gods floor of the chaff; and with a fire made ready to burn them both. *Matt.* 3. 10. &c. He was laid a *ftone for ftumbling; and the fall,*as well *as the rifing again, of many in Ifrael.* (*Luk.* 2. 34.) That *every foul, that hears not this man, who the laft fpeaks from Heaven* (Heb. 12. 25.) *fhould be deftroyed from among the people. Act.* 3. 23. *Ef.* 6. 9, 10, 11. compare with *Matt.* 13. 14. E*fai.* 61. 2. and that none fhould have any way to efcape that turneth away from him. He came for judgment, that they, *who will not fee, might be made blind Jo.* 9. 39. and the laft ages, knowing by him Gods will and not obeying it, fhould *be beaten* (as they are) *with more ftripes* Luk. 12. 48. and *their fin remain for ever.* Jo. 9. 41.

§. 7.
Miniftring the fpirit.

4. He was fent not only the moft perfect and exact Interpreter of the letter; that Gods law and will might be fully known, and an exactor of the obfervance of it in the ftricteft fenfes thereof, upon the moft grievous punifhments to the difobedient (which is all, hitherto, but a fuller miniftration of condemnation and death,) But, as of the exacteft letter, fo he came the *minifter of the fpirit* (2 *Cor.* 3. 6. *Jo.* 1. 16, 17. *Gal.* 3. 14. *Phil.* 4. 13. *Eph.* 1. 23. *1 Cor.* 1. 8. *Act.* 3. 26.) that by the power of this fpirit, the Law, by them that beleived, might be fulfilled. (See *Rom.* 8. 3, 4); which was the miniftration of the foul as it were of the law, and of righteoufnefs and life unto us (2 *Cor.* 3. 7, 8. *Gal.* 2. 19. Διὰ νόμου νόμῳ ἀπέθανον compare with v. 17. and *Rom.* 8. 2. *Jam.*

CHAP. I.

Jam. 2. 12. 1 *Cor.* 9. 21.) Before, the law was writ in the conscience only; as the law of Nature for the Gentile *Rom.* 2. 14, 15; or also more evidently in stone; as the law of *Moses* for the Jew; to bring forth knowledge of sin. But by him it was written with the spirit in the heart, to bring forth obedience to justification. *Jer.* 32. 40. The other brought in the spirit of fear, subjecting our inability to the curse of it; but he gave the spirit of love; out of this love procuring our observance of it 2. *Tim.* 1. 7. *Rom.* 8. 15. 1 *Tim.* 1. 5. 3. Which love keeps it far more perfectly then fear would: as shewing its zeal not only in Negatives (of which is the letter) i.e. in working no ill *Rom.* 13.9, 10. but also in the Affirmatives, (not exprest in the word of the the law) i. e. in doing all good, to all, to the highest degree. Therefore this love, the greatest of all gifts 1 *Cor.* 13. is called Chrifts *new commandment Jo.* 13. 34. -15. 12. 1 *Jo.* 2. 8. 2 *Jo.* 5. had only from the beginning of the Gospel, i.e. from Christ: and belonging only to the sons thereof; (tho this Gospel hath had such sons from the beginning) who are said 1 *Thess.* 4. 3. to be *taught of God*, that is by his spirit 1 *Jo.* 4. 7, 8. 16. as the spirit also the only Author of love, and which is love, was his new gift, by which love, he faith, his disciples should be discerned from the disciples of the law. *Jo.* 13. 35.

By which ministration of the spirit and of love § 8. (the proper fruit thereof) by Christ we now so easily understand and do the things commanded by the law; that the letter of the law is said to become as *Abrogating* it were void and useless to us by the coming of the *the letter.* promised seed; and the Schoolmastership thereof to be outdated by Christ, not *because we are now without law* 1 *Cor.* 9. 21. but because we have it superabundantly

abundantly written in our hearts by the spirit; and the works thereof continually brought forth by love, thro the efficacy of the last law-giver Jesus Christ. 1 *Tim.* 1. 5, 9. *Gal.* 5. 23.-3. 19. *Rom.* 8. 15. Therefore called the law of liberty, *Jam.* 2.12. This for the law moral; which, in some sense our Saviour is said to abrogate *Gal.* 3. 25. *Col.* 2. 14. that is according to the former use thereof, (namely as only giving knowledge of sin *Rom.* 3. 20. being a letter of condemnation, and *working wrath* (*Rom.* 4. 15. 2 *Cor.* 3. 7, 9.) and keeping us in slavery and bondage *Rom.* 8. 15. Tho this abrogation is done, not by absolving us from any more observance of it, but by enabling us to keep it; and by making this observance now also voluntary.

§ 9.
For the law ceremonial. Cancelling it.
But next for the law Ceremonial; he was sent yet more properly to annul and cancel it; and to appoint new Ceremonies at pleasure instead of it. He being the substance and body *Col.* 2. *17.* of which it was a type and shadow; *when that which is perfect was come, the imperfect being to be done away.* He was sent therefore to reform or perfect the worship of God, from those many exterior rites so strict and burthensome (see *Act.* 15. 10. *Heb.* 13. 9. *Col.* 2.14.) to that of the spirit and of truth. *Jo.* 4. 23. As also to reform many liberties and indulgences under the law (see *Matt.* 5. 31, 34. -19. 8.) Therefore his times by the Apostle are called the *times of Reformation Heb.* 9. *10.* For as he took away hardness of heart by the ministration of the spirit; so it was correspondent to this, that He should take away all remissions and abatements of any part of righteousness, which were permitted only because of such hardheartedness, *Matt.* 19. 8.

§ 10.
Thus anointed *Luk.* 4.18. a little before he began
to

CHAP. I.

to preach, by the Father, and publickly proclaim- ed alſo by a voice from Heaven to be the ſon of God at the ſolemn time of *Johns* miniſtration of Baptiſm *Act.* 10. 37. who, as likewiſe all the people, then called out into the wilderneſs unto him, by this unction of the ſpirit, the third Perſon in the deſcent of a Dove, and the teſtimony of the firſt perſon in the deſcent of a voice from Him, (the greateſt appearance of the ſacred Trinity that hath been upon earth) were to know and diſcern him, whom the Father had ordained, to be the light of the world baptizing with the holy Ghoſt. And of whoſe coming *John* was ſent before to give them notice *Jo.* 1. 33. *Anointed thus with the Holy Ghoſt and with power Act.* 10. 38. *Jo.* 3. 34. He was, in the next place, ſent from God as *an Apoſtle Heb.* 3. 1. of the Chriſtian profeſſion; or of the Goſpel. To whom God committed firſt, and ſo he to others the *word of reconciliation* 2 *Cor.* 5. 19. In which reſpect he is called *the great Shepheard* or *Paſtor* by St *Paul Heb.* 13. 20. *Paſtor and Biſhop of our ſouls* by St Peter 1 *Pet.* 2. 25. διδάσκαλϛ *Jo.* 13. 13. διάκονϛ *Rom.* 15. 8.

2 *An Apoſtle of the Goſpel.*

In which miniſtry, he was not only to expound the old, (ſpoken of before); but alſo to deliver ſome new, meſſages from the Father; *To bring life and immortality to light thro his Goſpel* 2 *Tim.* 1. 10; to revele the great myſtery of ſalvation, which God had decreed from all Eternity, and ſhadowed under types to all former ages; but yet (for the open manifeſtation of it) *kept ſecret ſince the beginning of the world* Rom. 16. 25. and hid from former generations *Col.* 1. 26. till this time, (notwithſtanding ſo much longing after it of ſo many Prophets and Righteous men, yea and of the

§. 11. *Preaching it*

Angels

The benefits of our Saviour.

Angels themselves. (See *Matt.13.17.* 1 *Pet.* 1.10, 11. *Eph.* 3. 9. *Matt.* 11. 11. 1 *Cor.* 2. 9.) When the Son, who only knew the Father, was sent out of his bosome to declare him *Jo. 1. 18. Heb. 1. 1. Matt. 11. 27. Esai. 11. 3. Col. 2. 3. to preach the Gospel to the poor, deliverance to the captives, the acceptable year of the Lord Luk.* 4. 18, 19. The time of his good will towards men ; *to preach peace Act. 10. 36.* and salvation, and remission of sin (for which Baptism was then also instituted): and the fulfilling of the promise of God to the Jew, that was made unto their fathers, but likewise of his new mercy to the Gentiles, that the *Gentiles too should glorifie God for his mercy Rom. 15. 8, 9.* And all this to be performed to the world through himself that taught it: for, as he was the text and subject that was preached of, so also was he the preacher *Psa.2.7.-40. 9, 10. Jo. 14. 6.* and none could see that light, but by the light of it: which though it much stumbled the Jews, that he should *bear record of himself*; and He as the truth preach himself as the life *Jo. 8. 13.* yet both the witness of *John*, besides that of all the Prophets, and of his Father from Heaven at his Baptism, &c. and that of his miracles ; (all which he quoted to them to justify his Commission,) were abundantly satisfactory.

§. 12.
Remitting sins ; giving the Holy Ghost; admitting into the kingdom of Heaven.

And, as this Apostle came to preach the Gospel, so received he power, to remit, and absolve from sin *Matt.* 9. 2, 6, 11. and that here on earth as man, see v. 8. and, as Priest *Heb. 8. 6* ; to *justify the ungodly Rom.* 4. 5. *Act.* 5. 31 ; and to make *sons of God Jo.* 1. 12. and admit into the Church and the kingdom of Heaven, by the new ceremony of Baptism (which he did ordinarily by his Disciples *Jo.* 4. 2 ; but yet some conjecture from the practice *Act. 19.5. Jo.3.22.*
that

Chap. I.

that he himself first baptized some of his Disciples at least; and so accordingly afterward he ministred the Eucharist).To admit I say into the Church all those, who repented i. e. confessed their sins, and promised amendment of life. *Matt. 3. 8.* And who beleeved in him, that he was the Son of God *Act. 8. 37. -19. 4. Jo. 3. 18.* and in his word, that it was truth, and he the last teacher sent from God, &c. and who rejected not the counsel of God sent to them by him *Luk. 7. 30. Jo. 5. 24. -8. 31. -12. 48.* Lastly to give the holy Ghost *Jo. 20. 22. Act. 2. 33, 38. Eph. 4. 7. 2 Cor. 3. 8.* by which to seal his converts unto glory. In which respect also he is said to *give eternal life to as many as receive him Jo. 17. 3.* and to *have the key of David,* as the chief Oeconomist and officer in that family, opening and shuting as, and to whom, he pleased, *Rev. 3. 7. Esai. 22. 22. Rev. 1. 18. and all judgment to be committed unto him.* Jo. 5. 22. *Christus, ut homo, remittit peccata, dat spiritum sanctum, vitam æternam, &c. potestate tantum communicata & delegata, sed modo excellentiori quam ministris ejus concessum est. Ut homo ad has actiones concurrit tantum instrumentaliter & meritorie, non efficienter; sed tamen ut instrumentum efficienti conjunctum & singulare; non separatum & commune, qualia sunt instrumenta Apostoli, & Prophetæ.* So the Schoolmen. And in all this at first he became the Minister of the Circumcision only, i. e. of the Jews *Rom. 15. 8. Act. 10. 36.* (and, according to his own commission, for a certain time, he limited his Disciples *Matt. 10. 5, 6.*) and began there also in *Galilee* amongst the meaner sort of the people, and remote from the chief Citty the least to provoke the envy of those in power till the appointed time of his passion approached, and preached

preached here moſtwhat in parables; for ſo it pleaſed God, that till his ſufferings were accompliſhed, the peoples ignorance ſhould not be quite diſpelled, and that this light ſhould riſe upon the world by degrees, and not all at once *Matt.* 13. 11. 1 *Cor.* 2. 8. But when the time drew near of his offering up, *Jo.* 7. 8. He preached more frequently in *Jeruſalem*, and in the Temple (tho uſually not lodging in the City *Jo.*8.1. *Lu.*21.37.) and there at the Feaſts of the greateſt reſort, and profeſſed more clearly and openly who he was, and did his greateſt Miracles *Jo.* 11. and accordingly multiplied exceedingly his Diſciples and followers *Jo.* 12. 19. Upon which the rage of his enemies now heightned to extremity, and after three years preaching *Lu.* 13. 7. and the daies of his Miniſtry accompliſhed, in the laſt place he laid down his life, and died a Martyr for the Truth he had taught. 1 *Tim.* 6. 13. *Rev.* 1. 5. -3. 14. ὁ μάρτυς ὁ πιςὸς.

§. 13.   Now, after his reſurrection from the Dead by the Divine power, in Juſtification alſo of the truth of doctrine, He being to return to God from whence he came, and the ſame truth being neceſſary to be preached, ſins remitted, Sacraments adminiſtred, the Holy Ghoſt conferred, &c. to the end of the world, to one Country after another; and, in them, *Before his departure ordaining others.* to one generation after another; the laſt thing he did here on Earth was the ordaining ſome others for theſe offices in his name, after he had now finiſhed the work of our Redemption, which was to be the ſubject of their preaching. For his former miſſion of them was only preparatory *Matt.* 10. to tell men that the Kingdome of Heaven was near at hand, which now after his conqueſt of Sathan, and of death by his death was fully

CHAP. I.

ly come, erected, and compleated *Jo. 12. 31. Jo. 19. 30.* At which time also he was to receive, as he had before in his own person, so now the promise of the Father so long expected, the effusions of the Holy Spirit upon his seed, even the whole Church. but these especially upon his Apostles. A type of which was *Moses's* spirit, taken part of it and put upon the 70 Elders, *Num. 6. 11.* which Apostles were to minister this spirit to others *Gal. 3. 2, 5.* The solemnity of whose Ordination and Commission we find *Jo. 20. 21, 22, 23. Matt. 18. 19, 20. Mark. 16. 15. Luk. 24. 47.* Therefore is our Lord named for the Author of administrations and offices, as the Father of miracles, and the Holy Ghost of gifts. 1 *Cor. 12. 4, 5, 6.*

§. 14. *Transferring his authority to them.*

To these, as his Vicegerents, he derived the Doctrine, the Authority, the Spirit, the anointing himself had received of the Father. (See *Jo. 15. 15. -17. 8, 18. Eph. 3. 9, 10.* 1 *Cor. 2. 10, 13. Eph. 4. 7, 8. Act. 2. 33. Phil. 4. 13.* 2 *Cor. 1. 21.*) Concerning whom also he left this Testimony to the world; as the Father had done of him, *He that heareth you, heareth me* (*Matt. 10. 40. Luk. 10. 16. Matt. 17. 5.*) *and as the Father sent me, so I you.* Jo. 20. 21. -17. 18. Hence also are his own attributes frequently communicated to them. They called *foundations Matt. 16. 18.* compared with 19. 24. *Eph. 2. 20. Rev. 21. 14.* And they also said to *save* men *Jude 23. Rom. 11. 14.* 1 *Tim. 4. 16. Job. 33. 24.* and at the last day to sit on a Throne as He; to judge men as he, See *Jo. 5. 22. Matt. 19. 28. Luk. 22. 30.* 1 *Cor. 6. 3.* To these he gave power to Baptize, i.e. admit into the Church those they saw fit; which implies their power also to refuse the unfit, (see *Act.* 10. 47, 48. the Apostle ordering and others ministring Baptism).

The benefits of our Saviour.

ptifm). And this again infers power to exclude out of the Church the backsliding, and thofe not obferving the conditions upon which they were admitted. To thefe he gave power to preach, and to declare to the world all the counfel of God, which he had manifefted to them; and to be Ambaffadors to men about their reconciliation to God for Chrift, and in his ftead, *2 Cor.* 5. 18, 19, 20. *Act.* 20. 27. *2 Cor.* 10. 8. *Gal.* 4. 14. Therefore they are faid to *fpeak in Chrift.* 2 *Cor.* 2. 17. To be received as Angels of God, and *as Chrift Jefus Gal.* 4. 14. and in their miniftry to be *a fweet favour of Chrift unto God 2 Cor.* 2. 15. He Authorizing them to make Ecclefiaftical Laws, and to order all the affairs of the Church. See 1 *Cor.* 11. 34.-14. *chap.* 1 *Cor.* 16. 1. *Act.* 15. 1 *Tim.* 5. 14. 1 *Cor.* 4. 17.

§. 15.   To thefe alfo he committed his keyes of the Kingdome of Heaven, to take confeffions and fubmiffions;to bind and abfolve;to remit fin or revenge it; and that by his power and in his perfon *Matt.* 18. 18. 1 *Cor.* 5. 4. 2 *Cor.* 2. 10. 2 *Cor.* 10. 6. 2 *Cor.* 13. 10. 2 *Cor.* 8.23. called *the glory of Chrift*, i. e. His reprefentation and image, fee 1 *Cor.* 11. 7. To continue the difpenfation of his facred Body and Blood to the worlds end 1 *Cor.* 11. 26. which his Sacred hands firft adminiftred to them, to all the Faithful: and as to admit the worthy, fo to exclude the unworthy from that holy Communion 1 *Cor.* 5. 7, 8. fee 1 *Cor.* 10. 16. *Act.* 20. 11. *Luk.* 22. 19. The [*Hoc facite*] having been alwaies underftood to have fpecial reference to the Apoftle's and their fucceffours, confecrating, or bleffing, breaking, and delivering it, as well as to others receiving it. To intercede for the people and procure remiffion of their fins from God by their prayers *Jam.* 5. 14, 15. 1 *Jo.* 5. 16.

CHAP. I.

5. 16. *Job* 42. 8. *Gen.*20.7. 1 *Tim.* 2. 1. And the promises of hearing their requests *Matt.* 18. 19, 20. *Jo.* 16. 23. seem to be made to them not in general as Christians, but more especially as Gods Ministers and Apostles, and that both for binding and loosing the people from their sins. So see the Presbyters in the description of the Church triumphant holding in their hands the prayers of the Saints *Rev.* 5. 8. to be offered up to him that sitteth on the Throne, as Incense is.

§ 16.

These He enlightned with the spirit (tho others also, see *Jer.* 31. 34. *Jo.* 6. 45.) yet them extraordinarily, for knowledge of the truth. For I imagine those expressions *Jo.* 16. 13, 25. comp: with *Jo.* 15. 16, 20, 26, 27. like to which are those. 1 *Jo.* 2. 20, 27. to belong to the Apostles specially as Christs ministers. Therefore the stile of their whole Body in a Council runneth; It seemed good to the Holy Ghost and to us. See *Act.* 15. 28. -5. 3. -7. 51. 2 *Cor.* 6. 4, 6. As also those extraordinary gifts of the Spirit at or after Baptism bestowed by laying on of the Apostles hands were not onely for Sanctification of the person; see *Matt.* 7. 22. 1 *Cor.*13.1. but also for the publick benefit & further edification of the Church by them. *Rom.* 12. 6, 7. 1 *Cor.* 12. 7. And enabling them by it (that which all humane wisdom is too weak to effect see 1 *Cor.* 5. 10, 12, 13. -4. 19.) to convince mens consciences; convert their minds; cast down throughout the world imaginations and every high thing that exalteth it self against the knowledge of God, and bring every thought into captivity to the obedience of Christ: and with terrors of conscience, with Sathan himself to revenge all disobedience: and this by the power of Christ who speaketh and acteth in them.

C

2 *Cor.*

2 *Cor.* 13. 3. See 2 *Cor.* 10. 2, 3, 4, 5. &c. -13. 2, 4, 10. *Jo.* 16. 8. 1 *Cor.* 14. 24, 25. *Act.* 2. 37. *Matt.* 10. 20. 1 *Cor.* 4. 21. 3 *Jo.* 10. 2 *Jo.* 10. *Tit.* 3. 11. 1 *Tim.* 1.20. 1 *Cor.* 5. 5.   On the other side to minister the Holy spirit to others by their preaching, by prayer, and laying on of their hands, as he had before to them. [The same Ceremony being used also by *Moses* to his Successour under the Law. See *Deut.* 34.9. *Num.* 11. By *Elijah* to *Elisha* in the Prophets. See 2 *King.* 2. 15.] *Gal.* 3. 2 , 5. 2 *Cor.* 3. 6. *Act.* 8. 15 , 19. Subjecting evil spirits unto them, and giving them security from, and power over, all the power of the enemy. See *Luk.* 10. 18, 19, 20. *Behold I give you power over all the power of the enemy;* where note that the mission and Authority given to the Apostles before or after our Saviours death are the same, only spoken of before as it were by Anticipation and promise which were compleated afterward. See *Matt.* 16. 19. comp. with *Jo.* 20. 23; Enabling them to do the same Miracles, as he, for confirmation of their doctrine; and, because their commission was enlarged to all Nations, furnishing them with the gift of Tongues.

§. 17.
Assisting them from Heaven.

Lastly, as himself worketh in these his missioners by the spirit ; so also he cooperateth and worketh with them in others by the same spirit; working by them 2 *Cor.* 5. 20. and yet working together with them too. 2 *Cor.* 6. 1. By whose power only their ministry becomes efficacious over the world 1 *Cor.* 3. 7, 9. *Mark.* 16. 20. 1 *Tim.* 1. 12. where they plant and water he giving increase, 1 *Cor.* 3. 9 ; where the spirit from them pricks the heart *Act.* 2. 37. the same Spirit from him opening it. *Act.* 16. 14. where they take the impotent by the hand, he making him to walk *Act.* 4. 10. *Mark.* 16. 20. see §. 20.

§. 18.

And it is not to be past by unobserved that our
Saviour

CHAP. I.

Saviour delegated this his Authority to others, not with a parity unto all, but with a superiority of some above the rest; who, as they gave licenſe of some miniſtrations to others found qualified for them, See *Act.* 10. 48. ſo they retained ſome other miniſtrations to themſelves. For we find laying on of hands, (which is named, *Heb.* 6. 2. amongſt the principles of the doctrine of Chriſt, [both that at, or after, Baptiſm, uſed to all for receiving the more extraordinary gifts of the Holy Ghoſt, from whence the cuſtome ſince of Confirmation by the Biſhop, and that which was uſed in ordaining Presbyters and ſetting men apart for the Miniſtry of the Goſpel. This impoſition of hands being a more ſolemn interceſſion for them, and a powerful recommendation of them to the grace of God, for the work which they are called to, and are to fulfil] See *Act.* 13. 3. comp. with 14. 26. See St *Paul* himſelf receiving the firſt *Act.* 9. 17. the ſecond *Act.* 13. 3.) wee find I ſay this impoſition of hands, or power of Ordination and Confirmation to be appropriated to the Apoſtles and Apoſtolical men, not common to all. See *Act.* 6. 6. -8. 17 -19. 6. -20. 28. -13. 3. *Eph.* 1. 13. 1 *Tim.* 5. 22. *Tit.* 1. 5. *For this cauſe left I thee in Crete that thou ſhouldeſt ordain Presbyters,* &c. where doubtleſs were many other Presbyters, to whom the ſame office was not permitted; or not permitted to them alone, but as aſſiſtants to *Titus*. See 1 *Tim.* 4. 14. comp. with 2 *Tim.* 1. 6; as alſo a conſent and approbation, or alſo nomination or election of perſons, whom they thought fitting, was permitted to the Chriſtian Aſſemblies, and the whole Church. *Act.* 6. 3. comp. with 6. 2 *Cor.* 8. 19. (tho χειροτονηθεὶς implies not neceſſarily common votes. See *Act.* 10. 41. -14. 23.)

C 2   the

the people being present at the publique acts of the Clergy and assisting them at least with their prayers. See *Act.* 21. 22. -15. 22. 2 *Cor.* 2. 10.

§. 19.
Those ordaining others to the end of the world.

Nor did this Apostolical office of our Lord expire with the Apostles (as some may think that there was no need of continuing such a selected Body of Teachers after Christianity planted, and four Gospels, and so many Epistles written, yet what would not the same men give for such an Apostle at this day as could decide so many controversies which are in Religion, whilst they say they need them not?) But he, who lives for ever and hath the keyes, &c. *Rev.* 1. 18. and who ascended from hence on high to receive these very gifts for, and to bestow then on, men *Eph.* 4. 7, 8. continues for ever also this office of ordination, by his Servants laying on their hands, and his *own breathing* upon, and giving the spirit unto them, to those that have succeeded the Apostles and that shall succeed to the end of the world. Therefore as he gave the Apostles, so 'tis said also he gave the Pastors and Teachers (according to the measure of the gift he thought fit) that were made by the Apostles *Eph.* 4. 11, 8. *Rom.* 10. 15. 2 *Tim.* 1. 14. *Matt.* 23. 24. And *Act.* 20. 28. the Holy Ghost (descending from Him) made the Overseers of the Church of *Ephesus.* And *how can they preach unless they be sent?* *Rom.* 10. 15. *sent* i. e. by God, *Heb.* 5. 4. (For this honour especially of ministring the spirit, remitting sins, &c. never any man might take to himself, but only give, what he first received. If he do otherwise, he is in a worse condition then *Simon,* who at least would have bought the giving it.) *Sent by God* I say, else is their preaching to no purpose, the effect of which for ever consists, not in the

CHAP. I.

the wisdom of men, which works contrary to it, as thought foolishness; but in the power of God 1 *Cor.* 2. 5. see 1 *Cor.* 12. 3. *Matt.* 16. 17. 1 *Jo.* 4. 2. *Luk.* 18. 34. *Act.* 10. 14. *Jam.* 1. 5, 17. -3. 15, 17. *Eph.* 3. 5. Therefore St *Paul* calls his Apostleship *a Grace*; and those, whom the Apostle, as well as whom our Saviour ordained, received in such Ordination a gift from our Lord, see 1 *Tim.* 4. 14. 2 *Tim.* 1. 6.

§. 20. *He assisting a their Successors for ever.*
And the same form of Doctrine was kept in the Apostles successours by the same Holy Ghost. 2 *Tim.* 1. 14. Neither is Christs assistance promised only to the Apostles, but to their Successours to the end of the world *Matt.* 28. 20. *Jo.* 14. 16. παράκλητον εἰς τ̄ αἰῶνα, i. e. an assistant to you for ever. *Matt.* 18. 20. comp. *Col.* 2. 5. The Church alwaies the pillar and ground where truth is to be found. 1 *Tim.* 3. 15. 2 *Tim.* 2. 19. comp. 16, 17. *Heb.* 12. 25. Tell the Church, saith our Lord, for whatsoever they shall bind, &c. *Matt.* 18. 17, 18; And the gates of Hell shall never prevail against those to whom I give the keyes, &c. *Matt.* 16. 18, 19. Therefore our Saviour after all the Apostles times, except *Johns*, is described *Rev.* 1. 13, 16. tho in glory, yet walking in the midst of the golden Candlesticks; i. e. the Churches of *Asia*; and holding the Stars i. e. the Angels of those Churches in his hands. And see our Lord still acting *Act.* 3. 26. *Act.* 5. 31. *Phil.* 4. 13. *Jo.* 15. 5.

§. 21. *The Apostles also delegating to them the authority received from Him.*
Therefore also we find the Apostles, being to go away, by vertue of the perpetual continuation of the assistance and influence of the great Bishop of the Church, our Lord, transferring their Commission again to others (as namely St *Paul* to *Timothy* and *Titus*); and this also as themselves received it 2 *Tim.* 1. 6. Giving them also the name of Apostles 2 *Cor.* 8. 23. and *Phil.* 2. 25. ἡμῶν δὲ ἀπόστολον. *Act.* 14. 4, 14. where

(where *Barnabas*, ordained by the Church, is called an Apostle) investing them with authority not only of preaching and administring the Sacraments; but of holding Ecclesiastical Courts; receiving accusations; and that against Presbyters as well as others; and providing more plentifully for the more industrious amongst them. 1 *Tim.* 5. 17, 19, 21. 1 *Cor.* 5. 12, 13. *Rev.* 21. 2. agreeable with that of *Matt.* 18. 17. Of correcting, and that publickly in the Court. 1 *Tim.* 5. 20. Of silencing, and separating the refractory. 1 *Tim.* 1. 3. *Tit.* 1, 5, 11.-3. 10. compare 2 *Tim.* 2. 21, 19. [*from iniquity*] i. e. such error, comp. 17, 18, 20. 1 *Tim.* 6. 5. 2 *Tim.* 3. 5. 1 *Tim.* 5. 11. Of absolving and forgiving 2 *Cor.* 2.-7,10. Above all, transmitting to them the charge (tho no doubt the Church had then some of the Gospels at least, and perhaps more of St *Pauls* Epistles, which he took order might be made common, then now we, because by those that remain we perceive some are lost) of keeping the form of Doctrine they had learnt of them; and of preserving the Commandement that was committed unto them without spot 1 *Tim.* 6. 14, 20. 2 *Tim.* 1. 13, 14. *John* to the Angel of *Sardis Rev.* 3. 3. *Remember therefore how thou hast received and heard and hold fast.* And lastly the charge of ordaining others and giving them in charge the same doctrines till the coming of the Lord Jesus. *Tit.* 1. 5. 1 *Tim.* 5. 22. -1. 3. -6. 14. Such Ecclesiastical government was then ordered by them in *Ephesus* and in *Crete*, &c. Therefore we may presume the same was established every where else; first both because of the Apostles special endeavour of uniformity in Churches 1 *Cor.* 4. 17. -7. 17. -11. 16. Secondly, and because we find in the Church-History the same government *de facto* to have been in all the rest,

Chap. I.

rest, as it was in that of *Ephesus*, where *Timothy* resided; & in *Crete*, where *Titus*; and also find every where the like Catalogues of their Bishops; and so, in the *Revel*. the Angel of *Ephesus* the Church, wherein *Timothy* was placed by St *Paul*, no way differing from, or more single then, the rest of other Churches. Thirdly, and again because we find such Government without the mention of any opposition; (which must needs have been in the purity and fresh memory of those times, upon any innovation; especially so universal; and in this case of some mens usurping preeminence, sooner then in any other:) without the mention I say of any opposition either of the inferiour Clergy, or of the superior Apostle; St *John*, living some time after the settlement of these Episcopal Governments. The continuation of which Government so uninterruptedly ever since, as well in the most adverse, as the most prosperous, times of the Church, is the greatest argument that can be: that it hath our Lords protection; and that it was his first institution; and that it shall continue yet longer, even till the end.

Now the Authority of this our Lord's Legislatorship, and Apostleship; and the Truth of his Revelations and doctrines newly manifested to the world Our Saviour confirmed and shewed to come from God (a question the Jews often asked him): First by the Testimony of the writings of the old Testament; those of *Moses Jo.* 5. 45, 46. and those of the Prophets *Rom.* 16. 26. *Luk.* 24. 47. *Matt.* 22. 32. And by the Testimony of *John* the Baptist, who succeeded these, and was more then a Prophet *Jo.* 5. 32, 33. 2ly, By an irresistible power of the spirit, accompanying him teaching, &c. *He delivering this Gospel with great authority, not like others,* Matt. 7.

§. 22.
The truth of our Saviours doctrines, &c. attested by,

1.
Scripture.

2.
Spirit.

The benefits of our Saviour.

29; *never man speaking like Him.* Jo. 7. 46: *to the astonishment of all the people, crying out, what wisdome is this,* Mark 6. 2. *and no man being able to answer Him a word,* Matt. 22. 46. 3dly, By miracles of all sorts, *Jo. 5. 36. -10. 38. Act. 2. 22. Jo. 3. 2.* 4ly, By undergoing all sufferings; and at last by laying down his life for the truth, and being martyred rather then recant it; witnessing before *Pilate a good confession* 1 Tim. 6. 18. and telling the unjust Judge that he came for this end into the world *to bear witness* (to the uttermost) *unto the truth Jo.* 18. 37. and therefore called *the faithful Martyr Rev.* 1. 5, Where note; that as our Lord used great silence as to the vindicating of his innocency before persons self-convinced, and (as he told them, *Luk.* 22.68.) that would upon no account absolve him; yet no way to betray the Truth: Which upon all occasions he most freely confessed, tho upon this his Confession they grounded, and he foreknew it, the taking away of his life. Thus, on Thursday night in the Garden he went forth, and met those who sought for him *Jo.* 18. 4. and freely told them who He was without their need of a *Judas* to disclose him; and, when they were startled and recoiled upon it, a second time he told them it. *Jo.*18.8. Brought before the High Priest and Council, and there examined concerning his Doctrine, he told them, he had ever publickly declared it in their Synagogues, in the Temple, and that they could not want witnesses enow, if any thing were condemnable therein. *Jo.* 18. 20. When asked again more particularly (not to inform their Faith, as he well knew *Luk.* 22. 68. but, as they used formerly, to intrap him for his life,) whether he was the Messias? Whether the Son of God? *Matt.* 26. 64. *Mark.*

3. *Miracles.*

4. *Death.*

CHAP. I.

Mark. 14. 61. He now referred them not to witnesses, nor asked them a counter-queſtion, but anſwered plainly; *I am Mark. 14. 62.* and foreſeeing that day of retribution, that would be ſo terrible to them, when he ſhould ſit on the Throne, and they ſtand trembling at his Barr, in great compaſſion adds further, that [whatever he then appeared] neverthelefs they ſhould *ſee him* hereafter *ſitting* [as David had foretold *Pſal. 109. 1.*] *on the right hand of the power of God* and *coming in the Clouds of Heaven* [to judge the world, and, among the reſt, them, his Judges;] ſhewing alſo in this, that he retained a magnanimity ſutable to his perſon, and that he kept his eye fixed on the future glory in the midſt of theſe his Humiliations. Upon this his confeſſion, which they thought ſufficient to diſpatch him, being brought by them before *Pilat* the Judge to receive his ſentence; and there, upon their accuſation, asked again; whether he was the King of the Jews? which was a Title equivalent to the Meſſias, or Chriſt, but ſomewhat more odious, they conceived, to a Roman Governor: Here our Lord both freely profeſſed to him, that he was ſo: *Matt. 27. 11.* and alſo informed Him, to prevent miſtakes, of what nature his kingdome was; *Viz.* that it contained nothing in it prejudicial to any terrene or temporal *Monarchy*; *as clearly appeared*, in that he had no humane forces or Servants to fight for Him that he ſhould not have been delivered into the hands of the Jews, i. e. the chief Prieſts, Scribes and Phariſees. *Jo. 18. 36.* Yet asked by him a ſecond time; whether, tho his Kingdom not of this world, yet he was a King? He again profeſſed it; and told him, that to this end he *was born and for this cauſe came into this world* [for this

D   end

The benefits of our Saviour.

end defcended from Heaven and was Incarnate, to bear witnefs to the Truth. *Jo.* 17. 37. After which *Pilat*, upon his wonderful filence and not pleading for Himfelf, nor vouchfafing further to acquaint him with his divine Originals *Matt.* 27. 14. *Jo.* 19. 9. minding him before whom he ftood and that he had the power in his hands to abfolve or condemn Him (which fhews that our Lord ftood before him in the midft of fuch heavy and falfe accufations, faying that he made a Sedition in *Galilee*; forbad paying tribute to *Cefar*; faid he would deftroy the Temple made with hands, and raife another made without hands, &c. *Luk.* 23. 5. *Luk.* 23. 2. *Mark.* 14. 58. as one altogether unmov'd and as it were unconcerned therein) our Lord freely admonifhed him of the Original of his power, which indeed was Himfelf, that *he could have no power againft Him except what was given him from above*, *Jo.* 19. 11. i. e. from Himfelf King of Kings, by whom, God his Father governeth the world; and therefore that their fin was the more intolerable, who had thus bound and delivered him up to be judged by thofe his Officers, who from Him hold their power, and by whom they Rule. *Jo.* 19. 11. Thus (as the Apoftle 1 *Tim.* 6. 15.) he witneffed before *Pilat* a good and free Confeffion, and that with fo much power and Majefty, as that the Governor feems to have been in fome manner perfwaded of the truth of what he faid; and became much affraid; *Jo.* 19. 8, 9. and would have queftioned further with him concerning his Divine Original; but that this meek Lamb of God having faid what was fufficient, and intent upon his fufferings, thought fit to put no obftruction thereto by a further declaration to this *Gentile* of his Parentage. *Jo.* 19. 9. But fo much was already faid,

CHAP. I.

said, as that the Governor both professed his Innocence, and washed his hands, *Matt.* 27. 24, 25. and sought all means to release Him, *Jo.* 19. 12. even by exercising some cruelties on him himself to have preserved him from greater, *Jo. 19. 1, 4.* and after this when out of the surprisal of a contrary fear, he most unworthily and cowardly pronounced sentence upon him, or rather yeilded him up to the sentence of the Jews: *Matt.* 27. 24. *Mark* 15, 15. *Luk.* 23. 24. Yet He resolutely maintained his Title of a King, nor would upon any their solicitation change it. Answering them only *Quod scripsi, scripsi. Jo.* 19. 21. &c.

And God the Father likewise confirmed both this his Office and his Doctrine, first by (several times) speaking from Heaven: thrice by Thunder; these voices *coming for our sakes. Jo.* 12. 30. And by charging the people immediately by himself to hearken unto him. This is, &c. *Hear ye him Matt.* 17. 5. Secondly, by justifying his Innocence and Righteousness, and all that he had said and done, by his raising him again from the dead (after he had been murdered by injustice) and giving him glory 1 *Pet.* 1. 21. and by taking him up into Heaven, *by this did God give assurance unto all men.* Act. 17. 31. *And declared him now to be his Son with power.* Rom. 1. 4. By this resuscitation of him by the Spirit of the Father was He justified, against all calumny of the world, to be the Son of God, and ever since, in the world, beleeved on 1 *Tim.* 3. 16; And by this his Ascention the Holy Ghost now and for ever convinceth the world of his righteousness. *Jo.* 16. 8, 10. Amen.

§. 23.

And a resurrection.

CHAP. II.

The way.

Jesus Christ the Exemplar, and Pattern, in all obedience to the Divine will; and in the reward of that obedience.

O quantas tibi gratias tenemur Domine referre, quod viam rectam dignatus es ostendere! Nisi tu nos præcessisses, quis sequi curaret? Heu Quanti longe retro manerent, nisi tua præclara exempla respicerent. Ecce adhuc tepescimus, &c. Kemp. Imitat. Christi lib. 3. cap. 13.

§ 1.
Christ an Example.
1 *In doing the work.*

BOTH the whole world being deficient in former obedience, see *Rom.* 3. 9. &c. And now stricter obedience being exacted by God, then formerly. Next, God sent his Son, assuming first the same infirm nature we bear, to become an example also of that perfection, he proposed; to be, as *the truth,* so *the way;* to walk first himself in these paths, wherein he directed others; and to beat the ways, that we might follow him: to perform first Himself clothed with our weak flesh, the hard tasks that he set us: least he might seem, with the *Pharisee,* to *lay heavy burdens on other mens shoulders,* and *not to touch them with one of his own fingers.* That this was a chief end of his coming, see 1 *Pet.* 2. 21. *For even hereunto were we called, Christ leaving us an example, that ye should follow his steps.* 1 Jo. 2. 6. *He that saith, he abideth in him, ought himself also to walk, even as he walked.* Jo. 13. 12, 15. *Know ye what I have done to you,* and, *I have given you an example, that ye should do as I have done to you.* Jo. 17. 19. *For their sakes I sanctify my self, that they also might be sanctified, &c.* Matt. 11. 29. *Learn of me* [by my example] *for I am meek,*

In all obedience to Gods commandements.

CHAP. II.

meek, &c. Therefore, in all thofe ways of God he pointed out unto us, he never faid: *Let him take up his Crofs* and *Go* ; but *follow* Luk. *9. 23.* And *Jo. 10.* This Shepheard followed not but led his Sheep. He danced firft after his own Pipe ; and for every rule gave his Scholars an Example ; an example in himfelf, to all thofe hardeft leffons in his Sermons. According to his Doctrine *Matt. 5. 18,* kept all both the leaft and greateft Commandements, left *Moral.* not a title unfulfilled ; for *none could accufe him of fin. Jo. 8. 46.* fee *Heb. 4. 15.* According to his Doctrine *Matt. 5. 39. &c.* He *refifted not evil :* fee 1 *Pet. 2. 23. who when he was reviled* he *reviled not again* ; *when he fuffered he threatned not.* But *when they fmote him on the right cheek he turned to them the other alfo.* Matt. 27. 29. *When they took away his Coat he let them take away Cloak. alfo,* Jo. *19. 23. &c.* tho he could have commanded Myriads of Angels for his affiftance yet, *as a Lamb dumb before the Shearer, fo He opened not his mouth.* Matt. *27. 14.* According to *Matt. 5. 44.* He fuffered death it felf for his enemies, that he might fhew the greateft love that could be to them ; He *prayed for thofe that defpitefully ufed him. Father forgive them* Luk. *23. 34.* He *returned good for evil* continually ; and ·efpecially in that eminent example of reftoring his eare to the High Priefts Servant. According to *Matt. 6. 3.* In fo often hiding his Miracles, he endeavoured, that *his left hand might not know, what his right hand did,* fee *Mark 1. 44. Matt. 17. 9. Luk. 9. 21. Mark 7. 36.* So when he grew famous in *Judea,* and preferred before the Baptift, either not to prejudice *Johns* Miniftry, or to avoid vain popular concourfe and applaufe, he removed prefently out of the Country. See *Jo. 4. 1, 3.* According to *Matt. 19. 21, 24.*
Luk.

Luk. 12. 31, 33. He made an election of the state of poverty, leaving all his friends for the service of God; travailing up and down the Country on foot see *Jo.* 4. 6. Receiving alms from others *Luk.* 8. 3. and enjoyning the same to his Disciples Matt. 10. 9. *the Labourer being worthy of his meat* from those he labours for, verf. 10. According to *Matt.* 6. 6. he hid his Devotions with Wildernesses, Mountains, Nights, *Luk.* 5. 16. -6. 12. According to *Matt.* 5.29. *Luk.* 14. 26. He forsook his reputed Father, and his Mother, and Kindred when they might have hindred him in his Service to God. See *Luk.* 2. 48. *Matt.* 12. 47, 48. According to his Doctrine *Matt.* 6. 25. *&c. He laid up no treasure upon earth: took no thought for* his life or for *the morrow*; not so much as for his next nights lodging, not having many times where to lay his head *Matt.* 8.20. But all these things were by Gods providence, by some that followed him, ordinarily, *added unto him Luk.* 8. 3. According to his Doctrine *Matt.* 20. 26. He made himself inferior to the lowest of his inferiors, even to the Servant that he then knew would betray his life; even to the stooping to wash and wipe their feet. *Jo.* 13. 15; And did this for this very reason; to give them a good example. *The chief among you let him be your servant. Even as the Son of Man, &c. Matt.* 20. 28. So in his very triumph when all saluted him King; and covered his way with garments, his lowliness made choice of an Asse to carry him, a little young Asse *Matt.* 21. 5. to shew humility. According to his Doctrine *Matt.* 6. 33. He prosecuted all Righteousness with such zeal and diligence that he scarce allowed himself time to eat on the day time, for doing good to men. See *Jo.* 4. 31, 34. *Mark.* 6. 3. 31. or to sleep in the night, for following his Devoti-

ons

CHAP. II.

ons to God *Mark. 1. 35. Luk. 6. 12.* Laftly, as the Apoftle obferved, Chrift *pleafed not himfelf Rom. 15. 3.* but fought the good of others; and this for our learning. *Ver. 4.*

And as for the Moral, fo for the Ceremonial law: §. 2. very punctual he was in all obedience, tho ufelefs *Ceremonial.* and non-fignificant in him, as it related to remiffion of fin, &c. yet *coming* (at beft) *in the likenefs of finful flefh Rom. 8. 3.* he was circumcifed; was baptized with the Ceremony of the defcent of the Holy Ghoft; celebrated the Paffover, the Eucharift; tho alwaies full of the Holy Ghoft, and free from fin, he needed no cleanfings nor expiations fignified by the one; nor had this Redeemer received any redemption fignified by the other. Kept the folemn Feafts and the Sabbath (whatever they falfely alledged againft him) exactly, tho he was abfolute Lord of it *Matt. 12. 8.* was obedient to every human ordinance; To *John* the Baptift wondring at this his humility; to his Parents; to his Governors; tho he the Creator of them, and Governor at that very time of all things, to whom all things in Heaven and Earth ought to bow: paid tribute patiently, tho free, leaft the ftanding on his right might be any way offenfive *Matt. 17. 27.* Fafted 40 days together; tho his flefh was conftantly obedient to the fpirit, to fhew to others that excellent way of conquering temptation: fought by prayer, what he might command *Luk. 22. 32.* prayed whole nights together, tho he knew his Father heard him alwaies *Jo. 11. 42*; to teach us by his example the leffon *Luk. 18. 1.* fuffered fuch anguifh and affliction for our fins in the Garden, to teach us what we ought to practife for them our felves in repentance. For thus it became him to fulfil

all

all that, being our Leader, the doing of which was neceſſary righteouſneſs and obedience in his followers *Matt*. 3. 15.

§ 3.
2 *In all ſufferings for righteouſneſs ſake.*

Thus God ſent his Son to be an Example to us, and a forerunner in all holy obedience to his commands. God again decreeing that all that yeild this obedience *ſhall in this world ſuffer perſecution*, 2 *Tim*. 3. 12. that they that *receive good things* hereafter ſhall *now receive evil*. *Luk*. 16. 15. *Luk*. 6.21, 24. that they that ſhall *laugh hereafter* ſhall *now mourn*, as they alſo that laugh now ſhall mourn hereafter. (And indeed it cannot otherwiſe be, as long as there are more evil men then good, nor this to have more men evil be otherwiſe; as long as men have free-will to evil, which is any deviation whether in exceſs or defect from good ; and therefore (*bonum* being *unum*, and *malum multiplex*) much eaſier then good : nor again can this be otherwiſe, i. e. that men ſhould not have free will; unleſs we, wiſer then God, would have the world new moulded without containing any free-will-agent in it, and what is this but having in it a great imperfection and defect.) That there may be a viciſſitude in all things, ſent his Son to be a pattern to the reſt of his Servants of all ſufferings : *For it became him*, (ſaith the Apoſtle) *by whom, and for whom are all things*, in his ſacred purpoſe of *bringing many Sons* thro mortality and affliction *unto glory*, to *make* alſo the *Captain of their Salvation perfect thro ſufferings*. *Heb*. 2. 10. That ſo he alſo might firſt found the depths of human miſeries; and being juſt of our pitch, might wade before us thro them all, and ſhew them eaſily paſſable; that we might follow him with cheerfulneſs and courage, and not expoſtulate with the Almighty, if here perchance he

CHAP. II.

he useth us no better (yet whom doth he not so?) then he did his only Son; his Son *in whom he was alwaies so well pleased Matt.* 3. 17. that never sinned against him. And thus in obedience to his Father first clothed with all the (innocent) infirmities of our nature, and indulging himself none of the contents thereof: *Rom.* 15. 3. But exercising a perfect abnegation of himself, and of his own will (tho he had also his natural affections after things agreeing to it. See ε *Jo.* 5. 30. *Matt.* 26. 39. *In all things made Heb.* 2. 17. *and tempted Heb.* 2. 18. *like unto his Brethren*; undergoing temptations from Sathan more then once *Luk.* 4. 13. and so far as to be carried up and down by him *Matt.* 4. 5. and that unclean spirit the most cursed of all the creatures of God to be suffered to take his onely Son in his arms. From the world; having all the glory of it presented to him *Matt.* 4. 9. a Kingdom offered him *Jo.* 6. 15. From the often necessities and natural inclinations of the flesh; as may be sufficiently discovered in that passionate sad, blood-sweating, prayer, (many times iterated) to be freed from death which he so resignedly concluded; with *not my will, but thine be done*) for our example, as if himself would have *learnt patience by the things which he suffered.* *Heb.* 5. 8. He voluntarily *became of no reputation Phil.* 2. 7; *A man of sorrows Esai.* 53. 3. put himself in the worst condition of life; that those in the worst condition may neither complain, nor boast, that their sufferings are gone below the Son of God; and then ended it in the most ignominious death; upon a Gibbet; naked among theeves; a death inflicted on no free man; particularly cursed by God. *Gal.* 3. 13. *Deut.* 21. 23. commanded and executed under the Law only in the

E .   most

The benefits of our Saviour.

most horrid crimes, (as in the Israelites idolatry with *Moab*. The perjur'd murthers of *Saul*: the Kings of the curfed *Canaanites*) to appeafe Gods extraordinary wrath, where Famine or Plague broke out upon the people: therefore is it ftiled *hanging them up before the Lord*. And fo oathfome a fpectacle was enjoyned again to be taken down and buried the fame day (as our Saviour was) as it were out of his fight. See *Deut.* 21. 22. *Numb.* 25. 4. *Joſh.* 10. 26. 2 *Sam.* 21. 6. This fuch a death he underwent (*defpifing the fhame Heb.* 12. 2.) that in the greateft ignominy of their end alfo, all his Sons might fee before them a Divine precedent. And fuffered being perfectly innocent that none hereafter might think much to fuffer for innocency, all being fome other way perfonally guilty. For our example he became lowly and meek, and ftooped his neck unto the yoke that we might learn of him to be fo too: *Mat.* 11. 29. and put his fhoulder under the heavieft crofs that ever man bare; that we might take up our lighter ones and follow him. *Luk.* 9. And thus he fuffered, and thus he dyed not only before us, but alfo for us, firft; that *his love*, faith the Apoftle, *might conftrain us* 2 *Cor.* 5. 13. by his example fo to fuffer and to dy again, if need be, for him; or alfo for one another. 2 *Cor.* 12. 15. and, that as he died for fin, fo we might dy to it. *Rom.* 6. 6.

§. 4.
2 *In receiving the reward.*

3. Thus our Saviour was made unto us a pattern of fufferings. Next God fent his Son, to be to us in his refurrection from this death, and reception into glory; a pattern of the reward promifed to obedience, life eternal. An example as of performing all the obedience active and paffive, God by him required of us, fo of receiving the reward, God by him

Chap. II.

him promised to us. That so not only the promise of a greater reward then was revealed to the world formerly (at least so expresly) might more encourage us to weldoing ; but also the seeing of that reward bestowed upon the obedient might yet excite us more, then the promise, whilst we being yet in the combate behold another, that used only the same weapons, against the same enemies, in the same infirmities, crowned with victory; and look unto one, who running the same race, for the joy also that was set before him, enduring the Cross, and despising the shame, now for it is set down at the right hand of the Throne of God ; whilst, *considering him that endured such contradiction, &c.* now for it exalted above all gainsaying, *we may not be wearied nor faint in our minds* Heb. 12. 1, 2, 3. Therefore it was necessary that the Prophet that taught a resurrection should dy to shew us an example of deliverance from death; And it was necessary that God should raise again this just person from the dead, and cause him to reign to assure us by this example that whoever *suffers with*, i. e. like, *Him, shall also reign together with him,* Rom. 8. 17. and that we professing to be *dead* with him *to sin*, should now likewise *walk* with him *in newness of life* Rom. 4. 6. For Christs exaltation also was bestowed on him for his obedience. See Heb. 2. 9. Phil. 1. 8, 9. Heb. 1. 9. Rev. 3. 21. -5. 12.

And as the natural Son came thus to be a pattern to us, so must all the adopted Sons of God be a transcript and copy of him. As if we obey and suffer as he, we shall reign as he; so if we will reign as he, we must suffer and obey as he; tho not so much as he, yet in such manner as he. For also neither shall we reign in such eminence as He. It

is

is very well if *the Servant be as his Lord Matt. 10. 25.* [not above Him.] And he that abideth in Chrift *ought himfelf alfo to walk even as he alfo walked.* 1 *Jo.* 2. 6. And that none may juftly pretend inability fo to walk, I mean to fome meafure of perfection, tho not to an equal with his (for neither hath any had an equal meafure of the Spirit to his) he hath purchafed from his Father the Derivation of the fame Spirit on us which inabled himfelf. Which holy Spirit is conferred, and from time to time renewed and increafed by the Sacraments (i. e. *non ponentibus obicem,*to the not wilfully and obftinatly unworthy receivers thereof) and which Spirit alwaies abideth in us (unlefs by great fins, fuch as we are perpetually inabled to avoid, it happen to be expelled) and who fo obeyeth the natural motions thereof, muft as neceffarily operate the work of Chrift, the fecond *Adam* as he that abides ftill in the former ftate of the flefh muft needs do the works of the firft. For as *what is born of Flefh is Flefh*, fo *what is born of Spirit is Spirit:* and the fame Spirit in the man *Jefus* and us, guided that man no otherwife than us; and now doth guide us, as then Him.

CHAP. III.

Jesus Christ *the Mediator of the New Covenant.*

§. 1. *Christ Mediator of the new Covenant.*

GODS former Covenant of works with mankind made at the Creation and called the Law of Nature, and again solemnized at Mount *Sinai* to that Nation, to which he had confined his Church at the delivery of the law of *Moses*, who was then the Mediator that passed between God and man, see *Exod.*14. mentioned *Heb.* 8. 9. being *found unprofitable Heb.* 8. 7, 13. Man not continuing in the promised observance of it; for indeed the promulgation of the law was effectual to make him more conscious of his sin, but not to make him more observant of his duty, see *Rom.* 7. 6. yet served it well to other Gods purposes intended by it. *Gal.* 19, 24. and accordingly God not regarding the promised protection of him; As is plainliest expressed *Heb.* 8. 9. And thus the two parties standing at the greatest enmity, Man being *alienated* faith the Apostle, and *an enemy in his mind by wicked works Col.* 1. 21. and God again thus provoked, giving him up. *Rom.* 1. 28. as a child of wrath to be a slave to sin, to death, to Sathan. *Heb.* 2. 14, 25. Yet so infinite in his mercy was God; *so loved he the world Jo.* 3. 16. *whilst it was yet without strength*; *Rom.* 5. 6. *yet enemy* vers. 10. *yet sinner* vers. 8. being *not willing* that his creature *should thus perish* 2 *Pet.* 3. 9. That he was pleased once more to reconcile it to himself; and to enter into a new, and the last, covenant with man;

man; and so growing still upon the world were his mercies, that this covenant should be so far better then the former, that in comparison thereof the other is stiled faulty, and not good, &c. *Heb. 8.* Now no covenant can be made between Him and mankind *without a Mediator,* a person to go betwixt *1 Tim. 2. 5. Jo. 14. 6.* to declare Gods gracious pleasure unto us: and to procure and receive from us, and offer our submission unto God *2 Cor. 5. 20.* See the manner of this; *Exod. 24.* As therefore *Moses* was of the old *Gal. 3. 19.* so *Jesus Christ* was sent the Mediator of the new. The substance of which Covenant you may read *Heb. 8. 10.* relating to *Jer. 31. 32.* and see the same *Ezek. 36. 25.* and every where in the Gospels and in the Acts. [*Repent and be baptized for the remission of Sins, and bring forth fruits worthy of repentance*] where there is remission covenanted on Gods part, and future obedience on ours.

§. 2. And it was first on Gods part that he would give a free remission of all sins past. [*Their sins and their iniquities will I remember no more, Heb. 8. 12. 2 Cor. 5. 19.*] and for the future by giving them plentifully of his Spirit *Jo. 1. 17. Act. 2. 17. Jo. 14. 26.* would *write his laws* not in tables of Stone, or of the conscience only as formerly, but *in their hearts*; so that *every one should now know the Lord,* vers. 10, 11. and be also enabled by the Spirit to serve him; and that not out of fear but love; His Laws too now (I mean after the Covenant of grace compleated upon our Saviors Incarnation. For else the same Covenant was under the time of the Law and before them from the beginning;) only such as are Spiritual, not Carnal: so called *Heb. 7. 16. -9. 10.* natural and grounded on reason and primitive honesty

(not

CHAP. III.

(not arbitrary and typical Laws) purged from legal Ceremony *Col.* 2. 14, 17. Lastly ; that he would be their gracious God *Heb.* 8. 10. and they should be a peculiar treasure to him above all other people, as the same thing is expressed *Exod.* 19. 5. And this Covenant now he would enlarge from *Abra-* *Enlarged* *hams* seed, to all mankind: Christ by his Mediatorship making peace as between God and man, so between the Jew and the Gentile, pulling down the wall which before parted their Courts in the Temple, the outer being for the Gentiles. See *Eph.* 2. 14, 15. *Eph.* 1. 10. and would establish it likewise *Established* on better promises. *He is the Mediator of a better* *on better pro-* *Covenant which was established on better promises Heb.* *mises.* 8. 6. The heavenly country and reward of eternal life, being not so clearly at least proposed before our Saviors coming, as the typical felicities of the earthly *Canaan*.

But that he required also on mans counter part; That hating and forsaking our former courses we should hereafter (being so much enabled by grace ; so much to be rewarded by eternal glory ; freed from the unsupportable burden of Ceremonials) yeild obedience to his Laws, as explained by his Son, in a more strict manner then had been performed by former ages: Lastly, that as he would be our gracious God, so we should be his obedient people. *Heb.* 8. 10. Else that there were prepared *pares præmio pœnæ*. And as his exceeding favors were now revealed to obedience, even life eternal ; so his exceeding wrath against all impiety, even fire unquenchable *Matt.* 3. 7, 10, 12. This I say is required on mans part. For in this new Covenant (which is done in their baptism by Sponsors, and afterward ratified in Confirmation by themselves.)

Men

The benefits of our Saviour.

Men engage something as well as God, according to the manner of that former *Exod.* 24. 3. where the people engaged with one voice; All the words, &c. will we do. Now *Jesus* it was that brought this Gospel this blessed tidings from his Father, that was the Sponsor; the undertaker, the Surety from God *of a better Testament. Heb.* 7. 22. He the person whom the Lord appointed to preach this good tidings unto the meek, *to bind up the broken hearted, to proclaim liberty,* to open prisons, to comfort all that mourn, to *proclaim the acceptable year of the Lord;* (but also the day of vengeance to the wicked. *Esai.* 6. 1.) He by whom *God commended his love toward us, whilst we were yet sinners Rom.* 5. *by whom we have now received the attonement* with God vers. 11. *Rom.* 5. 1. *by whom it pleased the Father to reconcile all things unto Himself Col.* 1. 20. 2 *Cor.* 5. 18. *Eph.* 1. 10. -3. 12. And as he came offering Reconciliation from Him, so beseeching us to be reconciled also to him 2 *Cor.* 5. 20.

§. 4.   And upon his necessary departure from hence, he left others to do the same office and to beseech men the same thing from generation to generation in his stead. Vers. 10. And by baptism washing away their sins past, to take every ones promise of obedience and fidelity, and so admit them into this Covenant. Baptism being the Sacrament which now answers to Circumcision, (which was the Sacrament to the beleevers under the Law, not of the first Covenant of works (as the Jews misconceived it) but of the second of Righteousness by Faith, which came by Christ *Rom.* 4. 11. *Gal.* 3. 17. In which every single person by Sponsors at the Font (if baptized in Infancy) afterward in Confirmation by himself gives his particular assent to
the

C H A P. III.

the Covenant: and by this is made partaker of the new promises in it: therefore faith the Apostle *Act.* 1.33. *Repent and be baptized, &c. for the promise is to you and to your children*; and therefore a good conscience (in obeying Gods commands) answering our Covenant made in Baptism to do so, called ἐπερώτημα in the vulgar, *Interrogatio*, (because then interrogatories are proposed about it, and engaged for by the baptizand) is said to save us. 1 *Pet.* 3.21.

Christ then being the Mediator of a Covenant; and no solemn Covenant being made without shedding of blood, *Zech.* 9. 11. see *Pf.* 50. 5. *Those that have made a Covenant with me by Sacrifice.* See *Exod.* 24. *Gen.* 15. *Heb.* 9. 15, 18. &c. This blood laying a solemn engagement and obligation on both the parties for performance of promises. (Therefore *Gen.* 15. 10, in Gods covenanting with *Abraham*, were the Beasts divided into two halfs, God passing between them: and *Exod.* 24. In Gods covenanting with *Israel*, the blood divided and half sprinkled on the Altar on Gods part, and half on the people:) beside that in a Covenant of this kind especially between a just Lord and rebellious Subjects, where one part had so highly offended, this blood sprinkled upon them signified a remission (which is never done without blood *Heb.* 9. 22.) Hence no hearty agreement and reconciliation between two formerly differing parties being possible without remission of all former offences; and again no remission of former offences from the just God being without sacrifice or satisfaction; neither was therefore any Covenant without sacrifice. And the eating of such a sacrifice given to God (being as it were an admittance unto Gods Table, and Viands; and to have Communion with him,

§ 5.
The blood of this Covenant.

see

see *Exod.* 24. 5, 11. 1 *Cor.* 10. 16. & c. 21. signified a reentrance into his favor: Thus; sacrifice, shedding and sprinkling of blood I say, being required at the solemnity of a Covenant (which Ancient ceremonies were all only foreadumbrations and types of this we now speak of; and not it fashioned according to what the former were, but they according to what it should be.) It pleased God to give and to confirm likewise and ratifie this last Covenant unto us in the blood of his Son: *Rom.* 5. 10. with whose blood we were sprinkled; this being the infinitely highest expression of his renewed love to mankind; for what greater signification had *Abraham* of his love to God, his Friend, then to offer his only Son? and the same we see God now requited to the children of *Abraham*; tho these his enemies here giving really, what he would not of *Abraham* really accept; making this blood a perpetual witness and assurance of his remitting all those transgressions now, which still remained under the former covenant *Heb.* 9. 15. and an everlasting obligation of him to performance of his promises.

§. 6.
The Death ratifying this Testament.

But yet further this being not only a Covenant but a Testament: both because it was Gods last will, that he hath enjoyned unto man to observe, *Heb.* 8. 8, 10. none other being to come after it; and being in this last will also, a legacying and conveyance to us, from the Son, of that heavenly inheritance which from his Father by birthright from all eternity was his; and no such Testament standing in force, but from the death (first) of the Testator; whom living, perhaps it might be changed, but after death never can. *Heb.* 9. 17. Hence, to make all sure to us every way; our Savior the Testator

CHAP. III.

Testator suffered death. And for these reasons is the Gospel called so often *the new Testament in his blood* Luk. 22. 20. and his blood stiled the *blood of the Covenant* Heb. 10. 29. Zech. 9. 11. That we are said now to be come from Mount *Sinai* and to *Jesus the Mediator of the new Covenant*: and *to the blood of sprinkling that speaketh better things then Abels*; for that spoke revenge, but this remission; and his blood said to witness the remission of our sins, &c. 1 Jo. 5. 8. Heb. 12. 13. Hence we are called *Elect* thro *the sprinkling* upon us *of the blood of Jesus Christ*. 1 Pet. 1. 2. Hence is he said to have *made peace thro the blood of his Cross* Col. 1. 20. And *to have reconciled us in the body of his flesh thro death*. Col. 1. 21, 22. that he suffered, &c. that he might sanctifie the people with his own blood. See *Exod.* 19. 10. -29. 21. Therefore those also who afterward break this Covenant are said *to have troden under foot the Son of God, and to have counted the blood of the Covenant wherewith they were sanctified an unholy thing, &c.* Heb. 10. 29. And lastly, hence as they did eat of their peace-offerings before the Lord *Exod.* 24. 5, 11. in token of their readmittance into his Friendship: so were we likewise in this Covenant to be made partakers of the Lords Table, in eating of this Sacrifice of our Savior, offered for the establishing of the new Covenant; and therefore this his flesh he hath given us to eat and his blood to drink *Jo.* 6. 53. &c.

And God again raised this Mediator (who by his own blood sealed this our peace *Col.* 1. 20, 21, 22.) from the dead, that he might shew that he accepted of this his mediation; and that all things by him transacted in it were according to his Fathers good pleasure; And that God might give also into his own hands the management of all those gracious promises

§ 7. *Performance of the promises put into his hands revived.*

promises made by him in this new Covenant; that he might be the Captain of our Salvation; have power himself of the remiſſion of ſin, and of pouring forth the ſpirit upon all fleſh, ſee *Act.* 3. 26. -5. 31. and of giving eternal life, &c. which were promiſed in it. *Thus it became that God of peace to bring again from the dead our Lord Jeſus, that great Shepheard of the Sheep, thro this blood of the everlaſting Covenant.* Heb. 13. 20. That he might ever live to ſee to the performance of conditions.

CHAP. IV.

Jesus Christ *the Sacrifice Expiatory; Euchariſtical; &c. for remiſſion of ſin; Procurement of Bleſſings, &c.*

§. 1. *Chriſt the Sacrifice.*

GOD would never give any bleſſing; nor forgive any fault abſolutely gratis: but that he would in ſome offering returned, be acknowledged Lord of all, for the one *Mal.* 1. 6, 8, 10. and with ſome offering ſlain, be appeaſed for the other. That he might to the world more ſolemnly appear, by the firſt offerings, a liberal Father to his Creature, and the fountain of all good; and by the ſecond a juſt Judge to the ſinner, and the hater *Pſ.* 5.5. and puniſher of all evil. And hence the firſt worſhip of him, that we find in the very infancy of the world, is *Sacrifice, Gen.* 4. 3, 4. *Sacrifice Euchariſtical; and Expiatory:* offerings of acknowledgment, and thankſgiving for his benefits. (And thoſe of the Firſtlings *Gen.* 4. 4.) And of *expiation* and attonement for our ſin, and that by the death of the Sacrifice; for death being the irreverſible puniſhment of ſin, without it might be no remiſſion. *Heb.* 9. 22. Beſides which two we find alſo another ſort of Sacrifice alwaies tendred unto him; a Sacrifice of a more general devotion and dedication of the Officer to his ſervice; an *Holocauſt* or burnt-offering, wholly conſumed on the Altar, and of the moſt ſweet ſmelling ſavour unto the Lord. *Levit.* 1. 9. *Exod.* 29. 41. Being given freely not out of neceſſity for an offence, as the sin-offering; and given all, not any part shared by the Doner, as in the peace or thank-offering: Of which burnt-offerings one, a Lamb *Jo.* 1. 29. (in which respect our Savior was called the Lamb of God rather then any other offering, because this was the daily sacrifice) was offered every morning, and evening, and was to lie upon the Altar continually, and upon this were all other Eucharistical Sacrifices to be offered. *Lev.* 13. 5.-6. 12.

§. 2. Now as the irreversible doom from Gods eternal justice, of sin, without which undergone it could not be blotted out, was death; so it was also to be the death either of the sinner himself; or of as worthy, or a more noble person in his stead, that should take the guilt of the others sin upon him; God out of his infinite wisdom, and mercy to man leaving this outlet of commutation of the person, that so observing his former decrees by the death of his Son, he might save his creature from destruction. Therefore the sacrifice and blood of Beasts became useless, (and much more that of one guilty person for another, for his death could onely answer for his own sin) *Heb.* 10. 4. *It was not possible for the blood of Bulls and Goats to take away sin,* neither did God *in them take any pleasure. Ps* 50. But only appointed them as types and antifigures of that alsufficient acceptable sacrifice, which in the fulness of times dispensed by God, was to be offered up *Heb.* 10. 14. for us: In presignification of which transferring of mans guilt and sin upon another person that should suffer for him, The sinner was to lay his hand upon the legal sacrifice that was to be accepted for him *Levit.* 5. 5. -44, 15, 26. the like to which tho not with the same purpose, man did also upon his Savior, and that, both the
Gentile,

CHAP. IV.

Gentile (for the *Roman* Soldiers had a part) and the Jew joyntly, making an oblation of him, tho they knew not what they did.

And this was the Son of God, who first, that he might be a sacrifice, was Incarnate and became mortal flesh. *Rom.* 8.3. Secondly, without all sin 2 *Cor.* 5.21. for his own person, and so owed no death to God for himself. In type of which the legal Sacrifices were required to be perfect and without blemish, nor blind, nor broken, nor maimed, nor scabbed *Lev.* 22. 22. and so the fruits to be the very best of them. *Numb.* 18. 12, 29, 30. Thirdly, in voluntarily presenting himself a devoted thing *Jo.* 17. 19. and a curse *Gal.* 3. 13. for others, (For which reason he not only took human nature, but it by descent, from those who had sinned, and from those who were restrained under a Law. See *Gal.* 4. 4, 5. *Heb.* 2. 10, 11, 14. was a reasonable sacrifice in every thing like to those for whom he suffered, bearing our guilt, and Gods wrath that pursued it, after the same manner that our selves should have born it; The torments of which guilt we may a little guess at from those we sometimes have suffered in our own consciences. Imagine him then in every thing assuming the place of a sinner; so lamenting all offences as if he had done them. Imagine him perfectly knowing and weighing (which the sinner never could) the number, the hainousness, the odiousness, the malice of them toward his Father, so holy and so good ; and then proportioning his grief unto it. Consider again that zeal and sense and tenderness he had to his Fathers glory and honour thus violated ; then that knowledge-passing love *Eph.* 3. 19. and compassion to men his Brethren who had thus misbehaved themselves; that whilst all

§. 3.

all other creatures ferved God and obeyed the law he had fet them *Pf.* 148. 6. He *repented himfelf that he had made man upon the earth.* Gen. 5. 6, Next imagine him forefeeing alfo all the fins to come, mine and thine, and among the reft the malice of his own people, the rejection of them and deftruction of their City and his Fathers houfe, which thing even in his triumph had drawn tears from him *Luk.* 19. 41. and this for fhedding his blood the purpofe of which fhedding was to have faved them; that thro their final obftinacy turned that to their ruin; which was of fuch infinite merit: and in this paffion, hear him faying again for them and all impenitent finners. How fain, *how oft would I have gathered, &c.* and *Daughters of Ifrael weep not for me, but &c.* Imagine then the forrows he now underwent, for thefe mens offences that they might, and for thofe, becaufe they could not, be forgiven; and then tell me *if ever forrow was like unto his forrow.* And read his fad complaints *Pf.* 38. and *Pf.* 40. 12. penn'd for our Savior, fee *Heb.* 10. 5. *Rom.* 7. 22. From whence proceeded that deadly fadnefs *Matt.* 26. 37, 38. and fear *Heb.* 5. 7. and amazement and faintings, and bloody fweat, which things never any facrifice fuffered before him, nor any after him of thofe many holy Martyrs; (nay they were in their paffion fuftained by him, but he in his (if I may ufe his own Phrafe) forfaken, nay fmitten *Efai.* 53. 4. by his God, by his Father whom he had never difpleafed) tho enduring perhaps more bodily torment, yet even had a foul fo overcharged, fo anguifhed and afflicted which was fufficiently difcerned, as by thofe ftrange fweats, ftrong crying and tears and paffionate prayers to have put by that bitter cup: fo by that loud exclamation

CHAP. IV.

mation upon the Cross when the spirit left that sacred Temple of the body: forsaken, and yet not forsaking; but committing it self into the hands of his Father. See *Matt. 27. 46. Luk. 23. 46. Heb. 5. 7.* This anguish of Soul *Mark. 14.* is translated by the vulgar *pavor & tædium*, by us *amazedness* and *heaviness*, of which the Prophet *Lam. 1. 12. was there ever sorrow*, and the Psalmist *Ps 69. 20. I looked for some to take pitty but there was none*; except only an Angel to strengthen him to endure his grief: and a fellow to help him to carry his Cross, not to remove them when he fainted under both. For the weight of all the sins of all lay upon this innocent Lamb, even the betraying and murther of those too that betrayed, that murdered him, as if he himself had committed the misdemeanors; he suffered (towards whom mean while he burnt with such an ardent love that upon the Cross he begg'd for them) and he assumed all the sufferings nature was capable of to make abundant satisfaction for them (Which he that will see at length, let him read the 22. 69. 35. Psalms penn'd for him as appears by *Matt. 27. 34, 46, 48. Jo. 2. 17. Jo. 15. 25.*) whilst that all Gods vindicative anger against us was poured out upon him: upon him a Sacrifice reasonable, and so in an human manner sensible of the Divine indignation: which Agonies of the Soul were followed with all the inhumanities and cruelties of his executioners that could be offered to the body; both in the pains, and reproach of his death. But the slaughter of this Lamb is too long a Tragedy to be here set down. And God pittied *Abrahams* Son being a preludium to the death of his own, so much as that he would permit him to suffer no more, then to carry the wood only, the in-

G   strument

strument whereon he was to suffer, and to have his arms tyed. But this sacrifice was not only offered up, but the Altar much changed from that of the sacrifices under the Law. That he might undergo a more accursed, and painful, and publick, and long mactation. Hang'd in a common place of execution full of skulls, *Matt.* 27. 33. by the Highway side : ver. 39. between two thieves, stript naked, and (surely which never happened to any besides) whilst he was suffering those acute pains, whilst the Serpent, and death were thrusting their stings into him, instead of pitty (which is then but humanity) all the world deriding him : (*Pf.* 69. 20. *He looked for some to take pitty but there was none*) mocked, reviled by the chief Priests, Scribes, Elders, verf. 41. by the Soldiers with their bitter gall verf. 34. *Luk.* 23. 35. by the passengers verf. 39. and that nothing might be a wanting, by those miserable creatures too, that were executed with him : whilst *his acquaintance stood a far off.* See *Pfal.* 88. 7, 8. &c.

§. 4. Thus therefore he, as the Lamb of God slain from the beginning in the types of other Sacrifices, bestowed Himself on us, and was offered unto his Father by us, and for us: a Lamb without spot and without blemish, the only sacrifice acceptable unto God, of a *sweet smelling savour Eph.* 5. 2. being an oblation devoted and consecrated to the Lord, not only in his death but in all his life *Rom.* 12. 1. which said of us, is much more true of him. Nor only in his sufferings, see *Esai.* 53. 5. *by his stripes we are healed,* but in all his obedience and service; *not pleasing himself Rom.* 15. 3. or doing his own will in any thing, but his Fathers. Therefore saith he *sacrifice thou wouldst not have :* Then said I *lo I come to do thy will Pf.* 40. 9. And this to fulfil not only one,

CHAP. IV.

one, but all those ends for which those spiritual sacrifices under the Law were ordained, and which they only obumbrated, the *body* being of *Christ*. *Col.* 2. 17. Thro which sacrifice now we do not only receive remission of his sins, pardonable only thro him; but present all our Devotions, praises, thanksgivings, acceptable only through him, and obtain readmission into amity and fellowship with God, and receive all deliverances and blessings temporal and eternal from God, only derivable unto us through Him, To whom be glory for ever. Amen.

§. 5. *Expiatory.* 1 *Sin-offering for remission of guilt.*

1. Then; He was the real Expiatory sacrifice for the *sins of the world Matt.* 26. 28. 1 *Jo.* 3. 1. answering to, and fulfilling the type, of the Legal sin-offerings; both of that slain and burnt without the Camp, (according to which *he* also *suffered without the gate Heb.* 13. 11, 12.) the blood of which was carried and sprinkled before the Lord into the innermost Sanctuary, upon the solemn day of Expiation once a year *Levit.* 16. *cap.* and into the outer Sanctuary at all other times *Levit.* 4. and 5. *cap.* (according to which His also is now presented in the Heavenly Sanctuary *Heb.* 10. 19. -9. 12. -8. 2. of which the other place was but a shaddow and type *Heb.* 8. 5.) And of that other scape-sacrifice *Levit.* 16. 21, 22. which, after the Priest had laid his hands upon its Head, and confessed over it all the iniquities of himself, and of the people, was let go into the wilderness (the like to which was also done, in purifying of bodily uncleanness, in a scape-bird *Lev.* 14. 7.) according to which He also is said to be the Lamb of God, that *took* and carried away *the sins of the world,* after *God had laid on him the iniquities of us all. Esai.* 53. 6. who died so as that he also was delivered from death; and as he was resembled

G 2 by

by the one sin-offering in his being slain; so by the other in his being raised again. In which respect also, leaven, and honey, (which hath the same nature with it) suddenly fermenting, altering, and corrupting things were forbidden, and contrarily salt preserving things, commanded, to be used in all Sacrifices, being types doubtless of that which is said of, and was fulfilled in the true sacrifice *Ps.* 16. 10. *Thou wilt not leave my soul, &c.* which resurrection to life was a sign of Gods accepting this offering made for us; as the Angel ascending to Heaven in the flame of the Altar was unto *Manoah* (*Judg.* 13.20,23.) of the acceptation of his.

§. 6.
2 For purifying uncleannesses.

2. Again he was the *Real*, answering to the *typical* sacrifice under the Law, the purifying of corporal uncleanness. See *Lev.* 14. and 15. *cap. As the blood of Bulls, and the ashes of an Heifer sanctified to the purifying of the flesh; so the sprinkling of his blood offered without spot to God, purging the conscience from dead works, &c. Heb.* 9. 13, 14. see *Heb.* 9. 21, 23. comp. with *Eph.* 1. 10. *Col.* 1. 20. with which blood also as with that other cleansing composition, there was running down from the Cross, a mixture of water, *Jo.* 19. 34. He not suffering the ordinary punishment of other Malefactors: but as on one side *a bone of him* was *not broken* (which was usual) to represent the paschal Lamb; so on the other side his pericardium, and his very heart was pierced (contrary to custome,) that blood and water, the compound of our purification, might be drawn out of his sacred side; one for the expiation of us from the guilt of punishment, for our justification in respect of sins past; and the other for washing out of us the stain of sin, for our sanctification from living in sin for the time to come. Blood signifying our

redemption

CHAP. IV.

redemption by the effusion of his life: and water signifying our regeneration by his effusion of the Holy Spirit *Act.* 2. 33. *Jo.* 7. 39. *Matt.* 3. 11. Therefore this was he, faith the Apostle 1 *Jo.* 5. 6. that came by water and blood, not by water only, but by water and blood: and he that saw them bare record *Jo.* 19. 35. And these also bear record; the two Sacraments of the new Testament; water in Baptism; and blood in the Lords supper; by which Sacraments in vertue of his passion, our sins are now also remitted and cleansed. See *Act.* 2. 38. *Matt.* 26. 28. And these two together with the operations of the Spirit joyned with them shall bear witness on earth, and seal the effects of this Sacrifice unto us, to the end of the world. 1 *Joh.* 5. 8. see *Eph.* 5. 26, 27.

3. He was the Real *Holocaust* fulfilling the type of the legal burnt-offering: *In burnt-offerings and sacrifice for sin thou hadst no pleasure; then said I, Lo I come* Heb. 10. 4, 5. His only sacrifice being of a sweet smelling Savor unto God, *Eph.* 5. 2. comp. with *Lev.* 19. *Exod.* 29. 41. which the sin-offering alone was not; *Lev.* 5. 11. *Numb.* 5. 15. and therefore might have no Frankincense nor Oil upon it. *Lev.* 5. 11. *Numb.* 5. 15. In which only the Father was well pleased; *Matt.* 3. 17. -12. 18. For as he, in our stead, was made sin and an accursed thing; and an offering that calling sin to remembrance, suffered the extreme wrath of the Almighty due to sin; so in himself (and this for our sake too) he was not only in his death, being a voluntary and a free will-offering see *Jo.* 10. 15, 17, 18. comp. with *Jo.* 19. 30, 33. the other living longer: *for this my Father loveth me, &c.* and so also loveth us for whom it is offered, for his sake *Eph.* 1. 6. but all his life

§. 7.
3 *Holocaust.*

The benefits of our Savior.

an *Holocaust*, consumed with the fire of love towards man, and zeal of the glory of his Father, in a perfect devotement and resignation of his whole self to the will of God, and in his perfect obedience and fulfilling of all his Commandements. And then, when he had done working *Jo.* 17. 4. finishing this *Holocaust* in suffering for the divine glory, for the truth; suffering till he was all spent, and consumed with the zeal of his Fathers honor, laid upon which whole burnt-offering, all our imperfect sacrifices of obedience and resignation, of sufferings and martyrdom, of spending and being spent 2 *Cor.* 12. 15. *Phil.* 2. 17. 2 *Tim.* 2. 10. whereby *God is* made *all in all,* (and we, nothing in our selves, and so one with him,) do partake also of the sweet savor of this sacrifice, and all our praiers and petitions for our selves, or intercessions for others, are accepted of God, and the descent of all good things spiritual and temporal from him are procured. *Gen.* 8. 21. *Jo.* 14. 13. *Phil.* 1. 12.

§. 8.
4 *Eucharistical; Peace or thank-offering.*

4. He was the grand *Eucharistical* sacrifice, and peace-offering, answering to those typical ones under the Law. In which respect the memorial which we now celebrate of his passion is called the Eucharist; and in which relation we are made partakers in the Communion, and admitted to eat of this sacrifice, see 1 *Cor.* 10. 16, 20. of which as a burnt or sin-offering (tho these it is also) *Heb.* 13. 11, 12. we might not eat, for none might eat of his own sin-offering. Now the peace-offerings had many several uses; in all which the sacrifice of our Savior fulfilled them.

§. 9.
1. They were a kind of *federal oblation,* after remission of offences, procured by the sin-offering; which was still offered before, not after, the Peace-offerings

CHAP. IV.

offerings, by which the sinner was *(as it were)* readmitted into Gods favour; and (whereas he might not eat of the sin-offering) by eating part of which sacrifice, being Gods bread *Lev.* 21. 6. -22. 25. and partaking of these holy things, he was entertained at the table and accepted into the fellowship of God, &c. Only *none that was unclean or any stranger* upon peril of death *might eat thereof*. See *Lev.*22.

Secondly, they were offerings of thanksgiving for all the Creatures, all the blessings and good things first received from God : *Gen.* 1. 29. -9. 3. *Psf.* 50. 10, 11, 12. and continued by his word *Gen.* 1.22. *Deut.* 8. 3. *Matt.* 4. 4. of which therefore, (both of men and beasts and fruits) the choicest and first were offered and sanctified unto the Lord as his portion and tribute : *Sanctifie unto me all the first born, both of Man, and of Beast* (and so also it was for the first Fruits.) *It is mine Exod.* 13. 15, 2. And these accordingly they offered : (these or their price), both to shew their gratitude and acknowledgment of Gods right as to these, so to all the rest; *Deut.* 8. 18. -28. 4, 5, 8, 11, 12. -26. 2, 10. *Lev.* 25. 23. -19.24. and also to receive his benediction through what was offered to him, upon all the rest. *Ezech*: 44. 30. *Lev.* 23. 11, 14. *Rom.* 11. 16.

§. 9.

Now according to this type Christ, the substance, in whom all things are fulfilled and accepted (for what careth God for Oxen or other Firstlings, or first fruits) not only the first born of his Mother but *of every Creature*, and likewise the first fruits *Col.* 1. 15, 18. *Rom.* 8. 29. 1 *Cor.* 15. 20, 23. was not redeemed but offered in his own person; offered unto God; first, by whom all others were redeemed from the like : And secondly by, and through which offering only, all our praises and thanksgivings are accepted

cepted for all things: *Eph. 1.6. - 3. 21. Col. 3. 17. Heb. 13. 15. Phil. 1. 11.* and the right to, and lawful use of, them procured unto us only by this offering. *Rom. 14. 14. Eph. 1. 3. -4. 1. 1 Pet. 2. 5. Rom. 8. 32.* And again by it as a federal oblation is the Covenant of grace and our peace ratified; To the eating and partaking of which Sacrifice also, (in the myftical Sacrament of his Body and blood) we are admitted to the worlds end:

§. 10.
By eating of which we have Communion 1. with God.

And 1. By the eating of which (as the Jews, and also Idolaters were to the eating of theirs,) we are accepted in partaking of this Table, to the unity, Communion and fellowfhip with God, fee 1 *Cor.* 10. 14. &c. to the 22. Only concerning which it is alfo provided that no unclean perfon, or ftranger unadmitted by Baptifm, may approach to eat thereof 1 *Cor.* 11. 28,29. Secondly, by eating and partaking of which facrifice excelling the other under the law, in as much as it is the Body and blood of the Son of

2 With his Son, and all that is his.

God, we are admitted to Communion with the Son, and myftically incorporated into him; made members of his body, flefh of his flefh, &c. And that not in a Metaphor, but in a great myftery faith the Apoftle *Eph. 5. 32.* And then from being partakers of the body, become alfo partakers of the Spirit of Chrift *1 Cor. 6. 17.* And from partaking of his nature, the body and the fpirit of the Son of God, become alfo Sons of God, and heirs of eternal life 1 *Cor. 12. 13. -6. 13, 15, 17.* &c. *Eph. 5. 29. Jo. 17.2,23.*

§. 11.
3 With the Saints, and all that is theirs.

By eating and partaking of one and the fame nourifhment of this one Sacrifice, of this one bread 1 *Cor.* 10. 17. we alfo become one Bread; and have Communion with all the Saints of God as well thofe in Heaven, as thofe upon earth, partaking of all their glory, praiers, &c. *Heb. 12. 23. Eph. 3. 15. Eph. 2. 19. Col.*

CHAP. IV.

Col. i. 20. 1 *Jo.* 5. 16. *Job.* 42.8. *Gen.* 20.7, 17. 2 *Cor.* i. ii.

5. And hence with reference to this Sacrifice, as also to the tree of life in Paradife; and to the Manna, and water flowing out of the Rock in the Wildernefs, which were types of Chrift 1 *Cor.* 10. 2, 3, 4. -12.13. *Jo.* 6. 32, 35, 49. Our Saviour is faid to be the *bread of life*, preferving him that eats the flefh of this Sacrifice fo, that he shall live for ever. And he that eateth him shall live by him *Jo.* 6. 57.

§. 12. *And are preferved in both foul and body unto life eternal.*

6. Laftly he was the true *Pafsover. Chrift our Pafsover is Sacrificed for us* 1 *Cor.* 5.7. He the true paschal Lamb fulfilling that typical one of the Jews; In relation to which alfo when this Lamb was flain, it was taken care that *a bone of him fhould not be broken*; tho theirs that fuffered with him were. That the Scripture might be in all things fulfilled in him. And by the eating and the fprinkling of the blood of this, as of that (fee *Exod.* 12.) Lamb, it is (but we muft do it with our ftaves in our hands, and our loins girt, as then; i. e. prepared for another country) that we obtain the true and everlafting redemption (of which that other was but a type) from Satan, the deftroying Angel; and from all the plagues which are to fall upon the Spiritual Egypt of the reprobate world, even upon all thofe who have no fhare in this Lamb; who is worthy to receive power, and riches, &c. becaufe he was thus flain, and hath redeemed us with his blood *Rev.* 5. 9, 12.

§. 13. + *The Pafsover.*

H   CHAP.

CHAP. V.
Jesus Christ *the Redeemer from Sin, the Law, Death, Satan.*

§ 1. *Mans debt to, and bondage under, 1 Sin.*

1. MAN made upright but under a Law, not only disposed by the integrity of nature, but enabled by supernatural grace to keep it, upon his fall presently (Gods justice substracting his violated grace) first, became a subject, and slave ever since, to the dominion of *carnal concupiscence* and of *sin*, stiled also frequently the *flesh*; *The old man*; to obey it in all the lusts thereof, and to bring forth perpetual fruits of unrighteousness. See this tyranny of sin and slavery of man *Rom.* 7. 7. expressed so far as that he is said even to be, not only *captiv'd*, but *slain* by it. Ver. 11. so *Eph.* 2. 1. *Dead in trespasses, &c.* and *Rom.* 8. 10. *the body dead because of sin*; *and sin reviv'd and I dyed Rom.* 7. 9. see *Jo.* 8. 34. comp. 32, 35, 36, 44. Man did not abide in the house and family of God, but lost his inheritance; because of a Son of God *Luk.* 3. 38. he became a Servant to sin and a Son of the Devil.

§. 2 *2 The law*

2. Upon this he presently incurred a second miserable servitude and bondage unto the law keeping him under as a strict Schoolmaster, and still exacting its task of him; *Debtor to the whole law Gal.* 4. 3. -5. 3; and no way able now (as before by supernatural grace) to perform it; and he not performing it, It presently wrought *wrath* against him *Rom.* 4. 15. pronouncing its *curse* upon him, *Gal.* 3. 10. and so committing him a *child of wrath Eph.* 2. 3. into the hands of Gods justice.

3. Now

CHAP. V.

3. Now the penalty of this law not obferved was death; and fo man became alfo *fubject unto bondage all the reſt of his life, thro fear of death* Heb. 2. 15. *The wages of his ſin* Rom. 6. 23. which alfo *reigned* over him Rom. 5. 14. the enemy of mankind, and of all of them the laſt ſubdued 1 Cor. 15. 26.

§. 3.
3 *Death.*

4. Of this death Satan was to be the Executioner. As the firſt creature that was the object, fo ever ſince (and that not unwillingly) made the inſtrument, of Gods vengeance toward any other creature; both comforting his own pains as it were with the fociety of their mifery; and ſatisfying his hate againſt God in any mifchief upon his image; And fo upon fin we were prefently feized upon by this Jaylor; his Captives, and prifoners; referved for deſtruction: upon whom he inflicts alſo for the prefent, all other miferies here ſuffered for fin. See 1 Cor. 5. 5. 1 Tim. 1. 20. Pſ. 78. 49. Exod. 12. 23. Rev. 9. 11. 1 Cor. 10. 10. 1 Chron. 21. 1. compared with 2 Sam. 24. 1. Luk. 13. 15, 16. And therefore all venemous and noxious creatures to us, are called his *inſtruments* Luk. 10. 19. But fecondly, we are not fubject to him only as an Executioner and an inflicter of puniſhment, but as the *Prince*, the *God* 2 Cor. 4. 4. *of this lower world*, that upon the departure of the *good ſpirit* prefently poſſeſſed us as his beſt houſe, and lodging here below *Matt.* 12. 44: *Col.* 1. 13. *the ſpirit that worketh mightily* (faith the Apoſtle) *in the children of difobedience Eph.* 2. 2. and we are become of Gods, his children *Act.* 13. 10. *Jo.* 8. 44. And the *luſts* of him our Father now we do; fo that as in innocency we did no good but by the aſſiſtance of the *good ſpirit*; fo ſince the fall we hardly do any evil, but by the ſuggeſtion of the ill *ſpirit*. See *Act.* 5. 3. 1 Cor. 7. 5. 1 Chron. 21. 1. 1 King.

§ 4.
4 *Satan.*

1 *As the executioner of Gods juſtice.*

2 *As Prince of this world.*

22. 22. 1 *Tim.* 5. 15. 2 *Cor.* 2. 11. &c. So that as he hath power as Gods Sergeant to inflict death at laſt; ſo he hath power, as Gods enemy in this his *Kingdom* of the *Air,* of *Darkneſs, of* this *world,* to make us ſerve him while we live; power both regal, and paternal over us: yet without either the protection of a Prince, or affection of a Father; making us do that only, for which afterward he may puniſh us. God indeed having put *enmity between him and man from the beginning. Gen. 3.* He being told that at laſt he ſhould be deſtroyed by the *womans ſeed,* and therefore rejoycing in nothing ſo much as to *deſtroy her ſeed, Rev.* 12. And into the hands of this his enemy was now man faln; And him a very powerful and dreadful enemy *Eph.* 6. 12. For note 1. That as man hath not by his fall, ſo neither the Devil by his, loſt all the priviledges of his nature; and being permitted ſtill his being, is allowed alſo all the operations belonging to it: retaining *power and ſubtilty* 2 *Cor.* 2. 11. *Eph.* 6. 11. according to the meaſure of the ſpiritual ſtrength and knowledg of other Angels. 2. That tho as man ſinning was ejected out of Paradiſe; ſo he out of the bleſſed place of his *firſt habitation Jude.* 6. unto theſe lower and darker regions of the world; called Prince of them becauſe they are the place of his abode; yet here hath he not received the final reſtraint and judgment for his ſin; which ſhall be paſſed upon him when upon others i. e. at the general day of doom as well for Angels, as men ſee *Rev.* 20. 10. 1 *Cor.* 6. 3. 2 *Pet.* 2. 4. 3. That mean while in this dejection, As God hath not taken away their natural power of hurting and ſeducing from wicked men, ſo neither from the wicked ſpirits: which power the Devil exerciſeth

as

CHAP. V.

as a tempter toward the good, and as a Prince, over the wicked in this his kingdom of the air. Only as God restrains the power of wicked, by the opposition of good, men: so of the wicked, by the opposition of good, Angels, of the Holy Spirit, of Christ himself, King over all: and both evil men and angels by the secret limitations of his providence *Job* 1. 10. and restrains those so much more, who are less resistable; and this more in respect of some then of others: the children of God being more protected from his seducements, (by *a greater power of the Holy Spirit residing in them, &c.* 1 *Jo.* 4. 4. *Luk.* 22. 31.) *the children of disobedience* more abandoned to his will and commands. 2 *Tim.* 2. 26. *Eph.* 2. 3.

§. 5. Thus, man being in his lapsed condition; the Apostle makes (as it were) four persons; *sin*, the *law*, and *death*, and *Satan* tyrannizing over him; and keeping him in an irremediable subjection, possessed instead of the free loving good spirit of God, with the *spirit of bondage Rom.* 8. 15. *and of fear, and of this world.* See *sin*, (which is called also *the flesh, and the old man*), described as a person *Rom.* 7. 9, 11. *Jam.* 1. 14, 15. *Gen.* 4. 7.   2. *The law. Rom.* 7. 3, 4. *Gal.* 3. 23, 24.   3. *Death.* 1 *Cor.* 15. 26, 51. *Rom.* 5. 14. And they assault him in this order. Sin slayes him by the dart of the law; for *the strength of sin is the law*: and death slayes him by the sting of sin; for *the sting of death is sin* 1 *Cor.* 15. 56. and Satan slayes him by the hand of death. As he who hath the *power of death* from Gods justice. *Heb.* 2. 14. Lastly (Satan having no power but from God,) the justice of God committeth us into the hands of this officer, till we shall pay the debt of sin, by the first Covenant due unto him.

The benefits of our Saviour.

§. 6
Chriſt our Redeemer.

Man being in this deplorable condition; the Son of God in great pitty to his creature, came to redeem him out of the hands of all theſe that hated him *Eſai.* 61. 1. *Luk.* 4. 18. *Col.* 1. 13. and to make him a freeman again. *Joh. 8.* 34. comp. 32, 36. *Gal.*

1 By paying a ranſom freeing us from debt.

4. 23. &c. *Gal.* 5. 1. And that meanwhile juſtice might be ſatisfied, and every one of the reſt alſo have his due; he put himſelf (in our ſtead) into their hands; and paid the full *ranſom* and *price* that was required, not *ſilver* nor *gold Pſ.* 49. 6, 7, 8, 9. 1 *Tim.* 2. 6. 1 *Pet.* 1. 18, 19, 20. but *life for life Matt.* 20. 28.   1. To deſtroy *ſin in the fleſh, he came in the likeneſs of ſinful fleſh Rom.* 8. 3. and after he had endured with the ſame weak nature all its aſſaults, *Heb.* 2. 18. *Matt.* 4. 1.-16. 23. tho he did not ſin, yet *was he made ſin for us,* i. e. liable to undergo the ill conſequents of ſin, as if he had ſinned. 2 *Cor.* 5. 21. 2. To ſatisfie the law, he was made *under the law* alſo, both the moral: and the ceremonial, in particular reference to the *Jew that he might redeem them that were under the law Gal.* 4. 5. moſt exactly keeping it in Circumciſion and obſervation of the Sabbath (tho they falſly accuſed him of the breach thereof) and all other ordinances. Yet after all this we being under its curſe, he alſo, (tho obedient in every thing to the law) for he became a *curſe,* or *accurſed Gal.* 3.13.   3. Death requiring poſſeſſion where ſin had given it a juſt title, and 4. Satan being not a-wanting to uſe his licenſed power in inflicting it. *Luk.* 22. 53. He therefore being firſt made ſin and a curſe alſo underwent the aſſaults of theſe two laſt for us; underwent and taſted of death for every ſinful man *Heb.* 2. 9. 1 *Cor.* 8. 11. even the death of the croſs.

§. 7.   And his going thus far, perchance might have
ſerved

Chap. V.

served for the discharge of a debt, had we been, saving some trespasses past, in a perfect and entire condition for the future: but besides the fruit already brought forth unto death, for which we owed it, we were also subjected to the dominion of these enemies, to bring forth more still for the future. In respect of which no compleat redemption of us could be without a conquest of them as well as a payment. And had our Redeemer not made a conquest of them; had he been either pierced by sin; or broken any point of the Law; how then indeed could he have paid that death, a ransom for us, which had been due for himself? Again not breaking these, had he yet been any way held by death and Satan; since, tho the ransom was paid for sins past, yet their dominion would have remained still in us for producing more; How could he deliver us from this dominion, from which he could not save himself? In which terms the Devil once began to insult over him on the Cross: *thou that savest others, &c.* How could he rescue us from death, being himself detained in it; how by his spirit in us destroy sin, if that spirit could not raise him from the punishment of sin; for all our spirit and life is only from and in him. In whose death all our hopes were also dead. 1 *Cor.* 15. 14. Therefore saith the Apostle 1 *Cor.* 15. 14, 17. *If Christ be not risen* from death, *ye are yet in your sins.* See *Rom.* 4. 25. 1 *Tim.* 3. 16. Indeed we were not only prisoners for debt to Satan, as an Officer of Gods justice *Matt.* 5. 25, 26; but captives to him as Prince of this world: and therefore our Savior was our Redeemer also in two senses: from *debt*; and from *slavery*: by paying a *ransom*; and by making a *conquest*: which he throughly did. For sin could not enter

2 By making a conquest freeing us from slavery.

The benefits of our Saviour.

enter into him; nor the law could not accuse him in any point: nor could *death*, tho it had him in its arms, hold him *Act.* 2. 24. and so Satan also that had the power of death, yet in his reviving from death was overcome *Heb.* 2. 14. by the power of the holy spirit raising him again from it. See *Rom.* 1.4. 1 *Tim.* 3. 16. *Heb.* 9. 14. *Gal.* 1. 4. And that he might be a pattern unto us in the way and of the victory of sufferings; the manner he chose to conquer these enemies was by subjecting himself unto them, and by making himself capable of their assaults, and by suffering from them, *By comming in the likeness of sinful flesh he destroyed sin in the flesh*: by dying killed and *triumphed over death*. (In which *Sampson* slaying his enemies by his own being slain, and *Eliah* raising the dead child by imitating the same postures were types of him.) Destroyed the Devils tempting, by being tempted by him, and in the likeness of the Serpent *Numb.* 21. 9. *Jo.* 3. 14. being also made a curse like him cured the bitings of the Serpent, by submitting to and most exactly keeping the law annulled it. Thus he for his *obedience* being made Lord of the *law Matt.* 12. 8. and changing the *ordinances* delivered by *Moses Jo.* 4.21. *Col.* 2. 13, 14. *Rom.* 7. 24, 25. *Jo.* 12. 31. *Col,* 1. 13, 14. and translating us out of the kingdom of *darkness*, into *his kingdom. Tit.* 2. 14. *Redeemed us from iniquity, for good works.* 2 *Tim.* 1. 10. *abolished death* 1 *Theff.* 1. 10. *Delivered us out of the hands of justice. Act.* 13. 39. *Eph.* 2. 15. out of the hands of *Moses*'s law. And he triumphing first himself over them all, thus set us also at liberty. *At liberty from them* 2 *Cor.* 3. 17. *Jo.* 8. 32, 36. yet not for our selves, to be now our own Masters, but redeemed us for his service for ever hereafter. See 1 *Cor.* 6. 19, 20. *Rom.* 14. 4, 7.

CHAP. V.

14. 4, 7. &c. *Rev.* 5. 9. 2 *Cor.* 5. 15. That we might be now espoused, and appropriated, to him; and not yield our selves to any other; whom he bought out of their hands with so dear a price; for whom he paid to Gods justice so rich a Dowry (as it was the ancient custome for the husband to pay, not to receive, a Dowry see *Gen.* 34. 12. *Exod.* 22. 16.) even himself *Eph.* 5. 25. *Tit.* 2. 14. *that henceforth we should glorifie him in our bodies and in our spirits,* which are his. Tho indeed this our service of him is our perfect freedom.

Again at liberty from them, yet hitherto not absolutely *Rom.* 23. as neither is our Saviors conquest over them as yet perfect in respect of his members: tho it be for himself. See *Luk.* 21. 28. *Eph.* 4. 30. 1 *Cor.* 1. 30. *Rom.* 16. 20. Why is it not? Because so it seemed good to his wisdom, *by, and for, and to, whom are all things,* as he made not perfect the world all at once, but successively; nor sent this Author of redemption before the latter end thereof, so neither to make perfect our redemption all at once.

§. 8.

Our Redemption not yet fully perfected.

For indeed had sin, and consequently the law, and death, and Satan upon our Saviors resurrection been utterly destroyed, why should not all the Faithful that were before his coming, as well as we since, have enjoyed the same priviledg? Again thus the world must have ended at our Saviors first coming. 1 *Cor.* 15. 26. But the compleating of our redemption is reserved to his second, *Luk.* 21. 28. *Eph.* 4. 30. *Eph.* 1. 14. and *we see not yet all things put under* our Savior in this manner: For it pleased God to make our Savior only the Captain, and we also (but this wholly thro the strength of him, who is the *Author and finisher of our Salvation*) partners in this conquest; giving us arms and strength

§. 9.
And why.

The benefits of our Saviour.

to fight them, but not victory without our fighting too after the same manner, as did our Savior. It pleased him, that we should yet a while longer suffer the assaults of sin, but repel them; overcome the *Devil*, but not without being *tempted*; and *death* but not without *suffering* it; and the *law*, but not without *obedience* to it; Lastly, that in these things we should suffer in some sort for our Savior, i. e. for his honor, as he did for us, i. e. for our wickedness; that herein all virtues might more be exercised; and Gods glory thro opposition more exalted.

§. 10.
How much already performed.
1 *In respect of sin.*

It remains then we enquire next, How much of our redemption is performed already by this our Saviour? First, tho some sin is hitherto still inherent in us, yet we are restored to the spirit of God lost by *Adam* Rom. 8. 23. and 1. by it commanding now within us, freed from the dominion of sin for the future. In which respect we are said to be *dead to sin*. Rom. 6. 11. And 2. by the price that was paid upon the Cross, freed from the guilt and imputation of sins past in the time of sins former raign in us.

§. 11.
2 *Of the law.*

2. 1 Tho we are still tyed to the obedience of the law moral, yet we are freed from the law Ceremonial, it being only typical of the things which were fulfilled in Christ. At his death when he cried *consummatum est* (tho before he both observed it himself, and commanded it also to others, see *Luk*. 2. 21. *Matt.* 10. 5. -15. 24.-8. 4) he freed us perfectly from this. 2. Again, freed from the condemnation of the law Moral: both 1. By having our former debts to it discharged by him; and so this bond, that was kept against us, cancelled and nayled thro upon the Cross *Eph.* 2. 15. *Col.* 2. 14. 2. And freed by grace given us from that inability we had heretofore to perform it, by being now enabled to

observe

CHAP. V.

observe it in all the parts thereof (tho not without some defects). And there is now no sort of sin, how natural, how customary soever (uncleanness, intemperance, revenge, &c.) but we have sufficient ability thro Christ to master, conquer, triumph over it, so as never to commit any one more (*consummate*) act thereof, if we will but use those weapons the spirit affords us, *prayer*, &c. Insomuch, as that we shall admire, upon tryal, the strange transformings of our selves, and the great goodness and power of Christ. 3. And in those deficiencies by being delivered also from the curse of it thro Christ by repentance and faith in him *Act.* 13. 38, 39. Nay yet further; freed not only from the condemning power, but from the commanding and directing power, of the law Mosaick; not that we now are without law, *1 Cor. 9. 21.* but that we have it, much fuller, then it was before in the Tables, written in our hearts; by which we walking in the spirit, and being filled with love, do all things commanded in the law by the demonstration and power of the Spirit: see those places much to be noted *Gal. 5. 13. 1 Tim, 1. 5, 9. Gal. 3. 19. Rom. 8. 15.* And thus we are said to be *dead to the law*, or it to us *Rom. 7. 4. Gal. 2. 19.* Dead to the former delivery of it, by the giving of which we were not able to perform it, as now we are when it is given us by the spirit: for the law is given twice, at the first by *Moses* written in Tables of Stone, so *a killing letter*; afterward by the spirit written on the heart, and so 'tis *a quickening spirit*, that now doth the work of the law, which law abides for ever. *Matt. 5. 18. 2 Cor. 3. 6.* see *Heb. 10. 11. 2 Cor. 3. 7, 8.* the difference of the ministration of the spirit and the ministration of *Moses. Rom. 8. 2.*

I 2   3. Tho

§. 12.
Of Death.

3. Tho we are still subject to death, yet we are freed already from the most considerable death, from that eternal; and from the fear of the temporal; yea we are now inviting and desiring it, as an entrance into our Saviors presence, and eternal bliss. (Nay further taking pride to conquer it the same way our Lord did, and turning all the preparatives thereof, diseases, infirmities, &c. by willing, patient, cheerful suffering thereof, into matter of advantage and reward; so that we had been less happy in a greater present conquest.) *Phil.* 21, 23. Again freed (as our Savior was *Heb.* 5. 7.) tho not from suffering it; yet, that we shall not perish in it, but after a while be recovered from it. Therefore harmless now it hath changed its name in the new Testament Scriptures, and is called *a sleep* 1 *Cor.* 11. 30. In which respect we are said already to be *passed from death to life. Jo.* 5. 24.

§. 13.
Of Satan.

4. Tho we are still subject to the temptations of Satan, yet are we freed from his former power in and over us *Act.* 26. 18. by the more powerful spirit of God, which is now *greater in us then he that is in the world.* 1 *Jo.* 4. 4. And the strong man now cast out by a stronger then he *Jo.* 12. 31. - 16. 11. 1 *Jo.* 3. 8. *Luk.* 10. 18, 19. *Matt.* 12. 21. Accordingly since our Saviors coming wee see the Devils former gross religions and delusions, (except in some out-skirts of the world *America* and *China*, &c.) utterly ruined, and him abridged most what of all his former inspirations, (for many of the lying Prophets were possessed and deceived (themselves) by an evil spirit see *Micah* 2. 11. 1 *King.* 22. 20.) possessions, enthusiasms, apparitions, dictating Oracles, by which he, being very frequent in these, was taken to be the great power of God. See *Act.* 8. 10. - 16. 16. comp.

Chap. V.

comp. 17. 1 *Sam.* 18. 10. 2 *King.* 1. 2. 1 *Cor.* 12. 10. -14. 29, 32. 1 *Jo.* 4. 1, and sustained by his frequent inanimations of them, that gross worship of idols which are since grown contemptible according to the prophecies. *Zech.* 13. 1, 2. *Esai.* 46. 1. comp. *Esa* 45. 13, 16. *Esai.* 2. 18, 20. *Hos.* 2. 17. So that now he is glad to use more fine and subtle arts (for he is not yet utterly to be chained up.) And the cheif religion abhors idols, and worships the true God that made Heaven and Earth; but only opposeth the Savior thereof, and him too not altogether rejecteth, but diminisheth in comparison of the Divels Prophet, *Mahomet*. And tho he is not yet quite chained up from seducing the Nations, nor tempting also the servants of Christ, yet in respect of every one, as he is weaker or stronger in grace, so by him that sits now at the right hand of God, are his temptations moderated and proportioned, none suffering above what they are able to repel. 1 *Cor.* 10. 13. And the weaker, as they loose the glory of a conquest, so have they the security of not being assaulted : whereas tis much to be observed that (for their greater reward) our Savior permits Satan more liberty as it were to try Masteries with those that are stronger (even sometimes to visible apparitions, as he assaulted first their Lord, and there want not examples of this done to many more, when eminent in holiness) as he did to Holy *Job*, to the Apostles : who by this discovered more of Satans wiles, and more easily discern'd the spiritual powers, that war against Christians, and gave readier directions for the fight. See *Luk.* 22. 31. 2 *Cor.* 12. 7. 2 *Cor.* 2. 11. *Eph.* 6. 12, 16. *Jam.* 4. 7. 1 *Pet.* 5. 8, 9. *Eph.* 4. 27.

But when our Redemption is compleated, which § 14. must not be before our Saviors *appearing and his Kingdom*

The benefits of our Savior.

Kingdom 2 Tim. 4. 1. then shall we have, by vertue of this our Redeemers ransom, and conquest already performed, and the full effects of which are already enjoied, in his own person; all freedom from them, that can be imagined. First, Concerning sin: That quite effaced, and we Glorious, Holy, and without blemish, not having spot, or wrinkle, or any such thing, but perfectly sanctified and cleansed, and so *as a pure virgin* presented and espoused unto the Son of God. *Eph.* 5. 26, 27. 2 *Cor.* 11. 2. 2. Concerning the law: love perfected, and we necessitated to good in such a manner, that our actions there shall no more be capable of reward or punishment; and consequently that there shall be no more place for a law. 3. As for *death* it shall be *(swallowed up in victory*, and cast into Hell *Rev.* 20. 14. 1 *Cor.* 15. 26. *Rev.* 22. 2, 3. 4. Satan also who now goeth abroad to *deceive the Nations,* shall then be *cast into the lake of fire and brimstone*: and the Accuser of the Saints shall then be judged by them; and condemned to those *everlasting torments, which are prepared for* him, *and his Angels from the beginning. Rev.* 20. 10. 1 *Cor.*6.3. *Matt.*25.41.

CHAP. VI.

Jesus Christ *the second* Adam, *Author to Man-* *The life.* *kind of life, as the First of Death.*

§. 1.
Christ the second Adam.

BY Gods good will and pleasure; as *Adam* the first man from the Earth, was made a common person; by whose disobedience and fall all dyed. So there was to be a second *Adam* from Heaven, 1 *Cor.* 15. 47. made also a Common person, by whose obedience and merits mankind should be repaired, and have life. *1 Cor.* 15. 22. And this was the Son of God of whose supreme dignity and equality with the Father, (as having the same essence and perfection of nature, and consequently the same glory, power, and all other divine attributes) see *Phil.* 2. 6. *Jo.* 5. 18, 23. -10. 29, 30. -17. 5. *Rev.* 1. 4. -4. 8. comp. with *Rev.* 4. 2. 5. which means the Father, and *Rev.* 1. 8, 17. this the Son. And 'tis not to be passed by; that whereas there have been several apparitions of the first and second person of the Trinity; they are both described much-what alike, see *Esai.* 6. *Rev.* 1. 13. of the Son *Jo.* 12. 31. comp. *Rev.* 4. 2. &c. of the Father as appears *Rev.* 5. 7. and *Dan.* 7. 9. comp. 13. according to which attributes no person is before or after another. And *omnia opera Trinitatis essentialia, & ad extra* i. e. (such as have some influence into the creature, and where there is no relating of one person to another) must needs be *indivisa* i. e. if of one person, of all. Because all are but one and the same God: yet in respect of acts and

Dependent on God the Father.

agency

Before his In- agency perfonal even before the Incarnation; whe-
carnation. ther it be by vertue of eternal generation : (*Ordo fine
subordinatione, cum una tantum sit essentia divina.
Missio in divinis non jussionem, non imperium, sed pro-
cessionem unius personæ ab alia, cum novi effectus con-
notatione, significat.* Bell. Judic. de lib. Concordiæ.)
So *Pater dicitur major filio ratione principii, non ratione naturæ. Notatur enim quædam authoritas in eo,
quod pater est principium filii & non contra. Ita* Bafi-
lius, Nazianz. Hilar. *& multi veteres, &c.* Bell. de
Chrifto l. 1. c. 6. *Cur necesse est si dignitate & ordine
secundus est filius, tertius spiritus, natura quoque ipsos
secundum & tertium esse* Bafil. fee Bell. de Chrifto l. 2.
c. 25. In which fenfe *Qui communicat essentiam &
naturam, communicat potestatem, scientiam, &c.* (as
Aquin.) *& recognitione authoritatis paternæ & do-
nantis,* (as Hilary); or whether it be by the particular economy, and difpenfation of the Divine wif-
dom in order to the Creation and the Redemption of the World ; *even before the Incarnation,* I fay,
as the Father doth nothing without, but all by, the
Son, both in the Church and in the world ; and in
thefe both in the creating, and in the ordering ;
and fuftaining thereof, fee *Jo.* 5. 17, 22. *Heb.* 1. 2, 3.
Jo. 3. 35. *Col.* 1. 16, 17. (Therefore is the Son diftin-
ctively from the Father called *the Lord*, becaufe of
his immediate Dominion over all things *Phil.* 2. 11.
1 *Cor.* 8. 6. *Act.* 2. 36. 1 *Cor.* 15. 24. *Rom.* 1. 7. *Eph.*
4. 5, 6.) So the Son every where acknowledgeth, all
he hath (life, knowledge, power) to the gift and
Communication, and all he doth to the command
and appointment and exemplar, of the Father ;
Himfelf *to live by* him ; *to have life in himfelf as the
Father hath*, but from his gift : to *be fent by him* ;
not only the man Chrift Jefus to be fent to us, in the
flefh

CHAP. VI.

flesh and human nature, but the second Person in the Trinity, then the only begotten Son of God the Father; see *1 Jo. 4. 9.* comp. *Jo. 3. 13, 17. Jo. 6. 38, 39.-17. 5. Heb. 1. 2, 3.* to be first also sent into the flesh, and to take human nature upon him; for he that was sent, descended from Heaven, and was made flesh, see *1 Jo. 4. 2. Jo. 16. 28. Heb. 2. 14, 16. 1 Tim. 3. 16. Jo. 6. 38.* Again to judge, do as he hears from him, as he is taught by him. *Jo. 8. 28.* as he hath seen him do; *the works he shews him*; operating, as it were, after his pattern, see *Jo. 5. 6. 7. 8.* chapters. *Jo. 14. 28. -17. 3. 1 Cor. 15. 27. Jo. 10. 18. -5. 30. -8. 15. -10. 32. Matt. 20. 23.* Many of which places (if not all) cannot be understood of his human nature; Neither are these expressions incongruent to the second person of the Trinity, since the like are granted to be used of the third, the Holy Ghost. See *Jo. 15. 26. -16. 13, 14, 15.*

§. 2. *Much more after it.*

2. But secondly (which is more to our purpose) in the mystery of the Incarnation; here God the Father only represents the whole Deity in its Glory and Majesty; and God the Son then divested, stripped, and emptied Himself of that form of God, in which he was; and (in respect of the use and exercise of it, further then as the Father pleased to dispense it unto him) of all the Majesty and power of his Divinity; In which thing our blessed Lord was fore-typified by *Sampson*: for thus was he for the love of an Harlot (we were no better) willing to part with, and to lay aside all his strength; to be bound by his own Nation, and delivered up to his enemies, *Judg. 15.11.* to be blinded and made sport with, and to be put to death: but by his death (as *Sampson*) destroying his enemies, and getting the victory. See *Judg. 16.*

K   Thus

The benefits of our Savior.

§. 3.
Assuming the infirmities of human nature.

Thus he became in fashion only as a man; *Luk.* 12. 50. undertaking all the imperfections (that are without sin) of human nature, such as others have; and receiving all the perfections of it from the gift of God the Father, so as others do, &c. Suffering the imperfection, and infirmities not only of the body; but those innocent ones of the Soul too; and these not only in the sensitive and appetitive faculties, as fear, sorrow, *Mark.* 14. 34. horror of death, &c. In so much that he was capable of being strengthened by one of those Angels whom he had made *Luk.* 22. 43. (not to name that treating with him by Ambassadors from Heaven *Luk.* 9. 31. one from the law, and another from the Prophets, about his sufferings.) Besides those natural inclinations and velleities (if I may so say), that appeared in him of the lower faculties; solliciting for things convenient to them; tho alwaies ordered (by reason and the Spirit) to conformity with the will of God : see *Jo.* 6. 38. *Rom.* 15. 3. *Matt.* 26. 39. [Where we discover natural propensions diverse from those of the Spirit, tho these proposing their own desires, not opposing the others resolves.] But some think, in the Intellectual part also : either 1. The absence of some knowledge (supernatural to man *& non debita inesse*) for some time by the suspension of the light of his Divinity from it; as it is clear the Beatifical vision was suspended from it in the time of his sad and dolorous passion. Which knowledg increased in him according to the dispensation of the Father. See *Luk.* 1. 80. -2. 52. where Christ is said *to increase in wisdom and spirit, &c.* not in appearance only, but *with God* as well as *men* : see *Mark.* 13. 32. comp. with *Rev.* 1. 1. and this with *Rev.* 5. 5, 6. &c. where the *Lamb is* said to be *worthy*

CHAP. VI.   75

thy to, &c. to have prevailed, to open the book. (Of all future events) and to look thereon, &c. and v. 12. *To receive wisdom* (this being signified verf. 6. by the 7 eyes; as power by the 7 horns,) *for that he was slain, &c.* and *Mark. 6. 6. Matt. 8. 10.* where he is said to wonder, as if some thing happened unexpected. Or; 2. The absence of that experimental knowledg which he afterward acquired by sufferings, see *Heb. 5. 8. -2. 17, 18.* Or, 3. at least see *Jo. 16. 30. -21. 17.* some restraint of the effects, and external manifestations of his knowledge; till the time the Father had appointed for them to be opened. See *Act. 17.* comp. with *Rev. 1. 1.* and *Mark. 13. 32. Matt. 20. 23.* Therefore he is said in his youth to have heard the Doctors of the Law, and conferred with them: (tho by this doubtless he learned not from, but imparted wisdom to, them. *Luk. 2. 46, 47.*) Nor did he offer to teach till the age allowed for Doctors to profess. And not then, till after he had as it were prepared himself for it, in six Weeks solitude, silence, watching, fasting, prayer. (For he who prayed whole nights, when all the day wearied with emploiments, certainly omitted it not in that long vacation.) And so for the external operations of the Spirit it self; tho he was by the Holy Ghost conceived; and had it *not* stinted, and *given by measure* as others *Jo. 3. 34. Col. 1. 19.* (who yet are said also to *be filled with the Holy Ghost* as the blessed Virgin and St *Stephen*, and some even *from the womb*, as St *John Baptist.* See *Luk. 1. 15. Act. 7. 55.*) yet the more publick functions of it were restrained till 30 years of age that he was baptized;& that it, at the solemnity, visibly descended on him; and then he began in the strength of it, to preach, do Miracles,&c. *Luk. 4. 1. Jo. 2. 11. -4. 54.* And so

K 2   his

his power, tho alwaies as God equal to the Fathers, *Jo.* 3. 35. yet for the actual exercise and execution of it as man, succeſſively given him according to the fore-appointments of the Father. In which reſpect he ſaith more emphatically and with ſignification of ſome enlargement of it (I mean as Man) *All power is given me, &c. Matt.* 28. 28. *Jo.* 5. 20. *Jo.* 14. 12.-17. 12.-16. 7. *Matt.* 11. 25. *Eph.* 4. 10. *Rev.* 1. 18. And it ſhall be yet more fully ſaid by him at his ſecond coming; till when his fulneſs and his Kingdom in reſpect of his members is not perfected. See 1 *Cor.* 15. 28. *Eph.* 1. 23.

§ 4.
Receiving the perfections of it from God his Father.

2. Again receiving all perfections of this human nature not from the donation of the Word, the ſecond perſon united to it; but from the Donation of the Father. For tho (as 'tis ſhewed before) he hath all dependence on the Father even in thoſe perfections, wherein he is equal to the Father, by reaſon of his eternal generation, as the Son; yet now he hath another dependence alſo in this emptied condition, as his creature; in which reſpect he became ſo much his inferior. It was the Spirit (called alſo the power, the glory, of the Father *Rom.* 6. 4. 2 *Cor.* 13. 4. *Luk.* 1. 35.) that *overſhadowed* the Virgin at his conception; that *anointed* and ſanctified *Jo.* 10. 36. him at his Baptiſm *Luk.* 4. 18. *Act.* 10. 38. (for he did not anoint or glorifie himſelf *Heb.* 5. 4, 5.) that *ſealed* him *Jo.* 6. 27. comp. *Eph.* 1. 13. that *carried him into the Wilderneſs*, *Matt.* 4. 1. *Luk.* 4. 14. by which he faſted ſo long, and did ſo many Miracles, *Act.* 2. 22. *Matt.* 12. 28. by which *he* was ſaid to be *in the Father, and the Father in him,* (as he prayeth his Diſciples alſo might be) *Jo.* 17. 21, 23.-8. 29. and theſe only by the Spirit could be ſo. By which he had *power to lay down and take up his life*

when

Chap. VI.

when he pleafed in refpect of mens power *Jo.* 10.18. -2.19. and to *give* and to Communicate *life to whom he pleafed, &c.* (for he received both this life, and this Commandement to lay it down from the Father *Jo.* 10. 18. -2. 19. -5. 26.) By which *he offered up himfelf. Heb.* 9. 14. This is it that raifed him from the dead *Rom.* 1. 4. -6. 4. 2 *Cor.* 13. 4. 1 *Pet.* 3. 18. *Heb.* 5. 5. and that *juftified* him, that he was all that he pretended to be. 1 *Tim. 3. 16.* (And the final juftification of all the Saints alfo, and declaration of them to be accepted by God, will be by the fame Spirit at their Refurrection glorifying them); at laft that *exalted him* to Heaven: For from the Father it was, that he received his glory and his Kingdom *Act. 2. 23. Phil.* 2. 8, 9. *Heb.* 1. 9. -2.9. and the adminiftration thereof he fhall one day alfo again give up unto the Father. 1 *Cor.* 15. 28. So God is faid to be *his head,* as he ours, 1 *Cor.* 3. 23. -11. 3. and dying into his hands he *refigned his Spirit. Luk.* 23. 46. As *Stephen* afterward his into our Saviors.

§. 5. Thus he received all things from the Father; And from him, after the ordinary way of Prayers. Which he very often ufed, and thofe very long ones *Luk.* 6. 12. as before the election of the Apoftles *Matt.* 14. 23, 25. after difmiffing his Auditors *Luk.* 9. 1. and likely for the fame purpofe he ufually retired out of the City at night to Mount Oliver, fee *Luk.* 21. 37. *Mark.* 11. 17. which cuftome of his was obferved by *Judas.* Prayer both for himfelf and for others fee *Jo.* 17. 15. where he praies that his Father would *deliver them from the evil, &c. Luk.* 22. 32. That Satan might not overthrow *Peters* faith : and *Matt.* 16. 17. where he imputed *Peters* confeffion to the Revelation of his Father. He praied to the Father for all things when wanted: and returned thanks

The benefits of our Saviour.

thanks for them when received (*Jo.* 11.41. where his giving thanks that he was heard, implies he praied the Father about raising of *Lazarus*, tho this not set down) *Matt.* 11. 25. see *Matt.* 26. 30.. In which praiers too tho the Father heard him alwaies *Jo. 11. 42.* for all things he asked with a deliberate and plenary will *1 Jo. 5. 14.* which was alwaies conformed to the Divine, yet not for all the velleities of his sense and Humanity, looking on things simply according to the bare inclinations of nature; As in the request of the Cup passing from him.: And some think in that petition of exemplary charity. *Luk.* 22. 34.

§. 6. Thus much of our Savior, the eternal Son of God the Father, his ungoding himself as it were, and professing man (which the Apostles sometimes speak so Emphatically *1 Tim. 2. 5. Act. 2. 22..* and call the Father *his God* as he is ours. See *Eph.* 1. 17. *Ps.* 45. 7. *Jo.* 20. 17. And sometimes distinguish him from God; i. e. either as he is man; or as God the Father is the fountain, as it were, of the blessed Trinity. See *1 Cor. 8. 6. Jo. 17. 3. Eph. 4. 5, 6. -5. 20. Col. 2. 2. Rom. 15.6. 2 Cor. 11.31. Eph.3.21.*) Of which descent of his I may say; that this putting on so great weakness; and then against all assaults of it, so faithfully in all things serving his Father, renders him, if it were possible, more capable of his Fathers love; *for this my Father loveth me because I lay down my life, &c. Jo. 10. 17. Jo. 15. 10. Because I keep his Commandements, not seeking my own will but the will of my Father Jo. 5. 30.* as a Saint obtains more here on Earth, then when he serveth God in Heaven, i. e. procureth a reward by his service on Earth, which yet he cannot increase hereafter by his service in Heaven; or as Mans infirmity is also said,

in

CHAP. VI.

in the glorifying God to have some advantage of the Holy Angels perfection, that it can suffer for him. But however this good use we may make of this exinanition and incarnation, namely, to argue of it as St *James* of *Elias Jam. 5. 17. Jesus a man subject to like passions as we*, so weak, so tempted as we; He assisted by the same spirit of the Father as we; he did, he endured, he received so great things: therefore we should, and may do and suffer by the same spirit the like; and if we do so shall receive the like, 1 *Joh.* 3. 2, 3. such as that man now is, such men may be; if such they now be as he was; who was pleased to be in all things as they are, saving the preeminences he hath from the hypostatical union.

§. 7
A Covenant made with the second Adam as with the first involving his seed.

Having shewed how, and how far, he became man, to pass now from the form, to the virtue, of his manship; and to shew how he was the second man, to repair with advantage all the mischiefs coming to mankind by the first; being made such a common person to them, as none besides him but the first man was; who in all things was a type and *figure of him that was to come. Rom. 5. 14.* And the parallel between them we may read at large *Rom. c. 5.* from the 12. *v.* to the end. And *1 Cor. 15. 20. &c. 45. &c.* to the 50*th*. And such a Covenant as was made with *Adam* of Reward for obedience; Reward, to him, and to his seed; if (being enabled by the same spirit) they should follow his steps; (In whom we may gather all the world should have been blessed had he stood; because all were cursed in his fall, unless Gods justice be larger then his mercies:) The same Covenant, upon the first mans miscarriage, we find enter'd into by the early promised seed of him that fell, Christ; that, *as by one man* to us *came death,* so by another might come life,

life; and that the second might conquer the Serpent, by which the first was stung. *I come*, (saith he) *to do thy will O God* which the First disobeyed: *Thy law is within my heart. Psf.* 40. 8. *Heb.* 8. 10. *Matt.* 6. 17. And accordingly he was made under the law; all the law that might be; both Moral and Ceremonial. And to him thus undertaking on the one part, the promise was made by God on the other: the promise not only for himself, which needs not to be doubted, see *Heb.* 11. 6. but for his seed also. See *Gal.* 3. 16, 19, 22. Namely that all the world should be blessed in him, as in the first they were cursed; Blessed, first in receiving the promise of the spirit, as the earnest and seal of the inheritance, *Gal.* 3. 14. *Act.* 2. 32. and then the inheritance it self, of eternal life; which promises he upon his obedience received first himself, and then traduced to his posterity. Of whom indeed *Abraham* and afterward *David* (for with him also was a Covenant made concerning his seed) were but types; the promise of being Father of the faithful and heir of the world *Rom.* 4. 13 being made to *Abraham* only in this seed, see *Heb.*1.2. *Gal.* 3. 17. and so said to be fulfilled now in his Resurrection or rewardment. *Act.* 13. 32, 33. In which seed the Gentiles, as well as the Jews, were first blessed (according to the promise) *Gal.* 3. 8.

§. 8.
He fulfils it.

And so only he the true Father of all the faithful *Heb.* 2. 13, 14. *Esai.* 9. 6. of whom *Abraham* their Father was also a Son. And this second *Adam* coming to perform this obedience, and to obtain these promises for undone man, that he might destroy the former works both of the Devil, and of man by his instigation 1 *Jo.* 3. 8. and shew that our standing is by humility, as our fall was by pride, was made

in

CHAP. VI.

in a quite contrary way to the first. For as the first *By walking in*
came out of the Earth, of no worth in himself: So *a quite contrary*
he came from Heaven no less then the eternal Son *way to the*
of God. And as the first being from so mean an *first.*
extraction, made Lord of all the world and placed
in a Garden of pleasure, yet hearkning to the Serpent, who represented the Divel whose wiles still
tempt us; and to his wife, who being also his own
flesh, then represented the flesh which now tempts
us; and enticed likewise by the fairness of the forbidden fruit, which represents the pleasures of the
world now tempting us; whilst he thought by tasting of this to attain, I know not what, wisdom and
happiness, in the event lost himself and us by his
ambition and pride; after the similitude of whose
transgression his posterity daily offends by the same
temptations. So this second *Adam* of so noble a descent, by the contrary waies to these conquered
and recovered all the former's losses; (that is) 1 By
annihilating himself, when he was before Lord of
all things, to answer the other's magnifying Himself being nothing, and by assuming also amongst
men a low and afflicted condition: His kindred so
mean the people were much offended at it, that a
Prophet should have such a poor alliance. *Mark.* 6.
3, 4. By becoming *a man of sorrows* and acquainted
with griefs; *without form* or comliness, despised
and rejected of men, abhorred of his own Nation,
of his kindred, laughed to scorn and made mouths
at, see *Esai.* 49. 7. - 53. 2, 3. *Pf.* 22. 7. one of a manual trade, a Carpenter *Mark.* 6. 5. *Jo.* 7. 15. and a
long time an Apprentice at it, for any thing we
know, till 30 years old; so much time passed in obscurity and silence *Luk.* 3. 23. for any thing that
is mentioned of him, except his three daies spent

L   at

The benefits of our Saviour.

at *Jerusalem* when twelve years old about his heavenly Fathers busineſs; In the time of his preaching afterwards by being of ſuch profeſſed poverty, as that he *had not where* at night after his toilſome work *to reſt his head, Matt. 8. 20.* (as he told a Scribe what he was to expect if he follow'd him) but when he had taught all day in the City, went at night and lay on an hill *Luk. 21. 37. Mark. 11. 17.* even depriving himſelf of that ordinary proviſion, which his Father makes for the Beaſts and for the Fowles. And as for his followers their eating green Corn, and that on no faſting day, argued they made many hungry meales. *Matt. 12. 1.* So that to follow him might well be called *taking up a* daily *Croſs, Luk. 9. 23.* therefore, 'tis obſerved, he choſe men hardy, not learned, to endure all labors. Eſpecially when as they were likewiſe to do all their work (preach, cure diſeaſes &c. *gratis (gratis accepiſtis, gratis date,)* and without taking any thing for their labour; tho mens charities (by Gods providence) were not a-wanting unto them *Matt. 10. 8, 9.* Again by being of ſuch profeſſed and wonderful humility, ſo avoiding of all honor or applauſe; that, beſides the living ſo obſcurely, and unknown of this wiſdom and power of God for 30 years, he afterwards reſorted to no Princes Courts at all, was ſeldom amongſt the Rabbins, not often in great Cities; very rarely at *Jeruſalem* except a little before his paſſion; (chid for it by his Friends. *Jo. 7. 4.*) Made no oſtentation of his knowledge, but veiled and covered it in Parables and Proverbs; which was not without ſome prejudice to him, ſee *Jo. 16. 29, 30.* and when they admired it, he told them he ſpake not of himſelf; It was not his own wiſdom but his that ſent Him *Jo. 7. 16.* and this over and over again. No oſtentation

Chap. VI.

ostentation of his works so miraculous, but hid them as much as he could: and when brought once before a King to do some, altogether forbare them. No ostentation of his holiness, but used a common and free conversation;neither strict for his diet, nor his company (for he was not to avoid the encountring of any temptation): called therefore *a Winebibber*, and keeper of ill company; questioned for not fasting; and He and his Disciples disesteemed in comparison of the Baptist and his. Matt. 9. 14. In his riding in triumph into *Jerusalem* at the same time, when other paschal Lambs also destined for the slaughter were solemnly brought in, see *Exod*.12. 3,6. taking only an Asse, nay possibly only a little Colt of an Asse to ride on in this his great time of State: from which the Prophet long before noted his great humility and lowliness. *Zech*. 9. 9. *Learn of Him* for *he* was *meek and lowly*. By coming in the quality of a Servant, a voluntary Servant, to secular Rulers *Esai*. 49. 7. to his servants, even to washing their feet *Matt*. 20. 28. to his Father in all things: see *Esai*. 50. 4, 5, 6. *tho he were a Son*, saith the Apostle, *yet learning obedience by the things which he suffered*. *Heb*. 5. 8. In nothing pleasing Himself, nor seeking his own will *Jo*. 5. 30. but doing alwaies whatever pleased his Father. *Jo*. 8. 29. Obedient when by him commanded death, such a death *Phil*. 2.8. as the other disobedient merited, tho threatned with it. And in his glorifying afterward intending chiefly that of his Father, and making Gods glory the end of his own. See *Jo*. 17. 1, 19. *Phil*. 2. 11. *Jo*. 13. 31, 32. -14. 13. But not hearkning to Satans like ambitious proposals, made to him as to our first Parent, with a purpose to beget in him also some pride.

L 2   See

§. 9. See the *parallel* between them in many things. The Devil tempting both about eating contrary to the good pleasure of God (as may be gathered from our Saviors answer *Matt.* 4. 4.) saying to one *yea hath God said ye shall not eat* : and to the other ; *Command that these Stones be made Bread*, encouraging both to presumption: saying to one, *He hath given his Angels charge over thee*, to the other *ye shall not dy* : and alluring both with fair and false promises, *Eritis sicut Dii*, and *Omnia hæc tibi dabo.* But indeed supposing our Savior in a condition much more liable to the temptation in offering meat, and that usual, not prohibited food as *Adam's* was, to one hungry, not to one satiated with all other delicacies : Honor and wealth to one poor and despised : and suggesting special care of Angels to one that was the Son of God, tho then having voluntarily abbridged himself for his Fathers greater Honor the priviledg thereof. Yet he not hearkening to these wiles so much as to do any thing for his own reputation (tho Satan fail'd not to prompt him who, and how great he was): no not to shew his power in flying down from a pinnacle, or in producing bread by Miracle, tho both in a seeming case of necessity ; but answering, he must *live by the word of God,* in every thing doing as God appointed him ; for that was *his bread to do the will of his Father* ; and accordingly he made not bread for himself who made it for others ; but God sent Angels to minister it unto Him. So that the Prince of this world had no such thing in him, as he had in the first man *Jo.* 14. 30 ; Again, by not being entised here by any false beauty of this world, set before, and presented unto, him *Matt.* 4. 8. nor indulging so much as the innocent inclinations of the

flesh ;

C H A P. VI.

flesh; by whose necessities, sleep, hunger, rest, he was often importuned; but versed in continual mortifications of it; watching, fasting, weeping, and all the inconveniences of poverty and travailing; by denying to himself many useful things permitted, as the other longed after unnecessary things forbidden. By earnestly desiring and so chearfully entertaining all sufferings, and that cruel passion, (tho he shewed, how easily he could have avoided it, when at his speaking but one word to them, his apprehenders went backward, and fell to the ground *Jo.* 18. 6. till by his own leave (like *Sampson*) they took and bound him): also that he had the full sense and reluctance of nature towards it, that we have (without which his sufferings had not been so meritorious) in that passionate deprecation of it in the Garden, where he in his own person described unto his Disciples the battel of Sense to shew them the victory of the Spirit, calling it his baptism, his Eucharist. See *Luk.* 22. 15. -12. 50. *Jo.* 14. 31. *Mark.* 10. 32. where he outwent, and lead towards *Jerusalem* the place of this Tragedy, his Disciples afraid and drooping because of that storm he had told them was coming; led them on, tho he foresaw, and numbred, and foretold so punctually every opprobrious circumstance thereof (of which other Martyrs are happily ignorant) even to the Soldiers spitting upon him, verf. 33. see *Jo.* 18. 4, 8. How he sought to save his Disciples, and, I had almost said, prevented *Judas's* betraying him, for whom he was so much troubled in spirit *Jo.* 13. 21. by meeting the Soldiers, and offering himself, and charging them (astonished) to let the others go; by his soveraign authority securing from harm all but himself, *Jo.* 18. 9. and giving himself for them,

not

not only in his paſſion, but to, it. In which ſufferings, he did not one Miracle before the King to ſave his life, nor ſpoke a word to defend ſo innocent a cauſe; but invited as it were their condemnation with a reſolute ſilence. And when as he had power at any time to have laid down his life; yet by his former avoiding ſtoning and precipitation preſerved he himſelf for a more open ſhame and greater torments. Thus by contraries he undid the works of the Devil in the firſt *Adam*; and conquered and triumphed by humility and afflictions, as the other fell by pride and Paradiſe; leaving this ſpecial leſſon to the world, *Learn of me for I am meek and lowly*. After the ſimilitude of whoſe righteouſneſs alſo all his poſterity ſince do overcome; namely by reſiſtance of temptations, by humility, and by ſufferings. See *Phil. 3. 10. 2 Cor. 4. 10. Gal. 6. 7. Col. 1. 12. Gal. 5. 24. 1 Cor. 4. 11. &c. 2 Cor. 6. 4. &c.* Well might he therefore proclaim *learn of me for I am lowly, &c.* And as it is ſaid of the Saints in glory, *quanto altiores, tanto humiliores*; and as himſelf ſaid: the greateſt muſt be as it were a child. *Matt. 18. 4.* So doubtleſs never was there man thus perfectly humble in all things, as was this the Son of God. The meekneſs of whoſe ſpirit may be clearly ſeen in this, that many, whom the ill nature of his Diſciples repulſed, he continually entertained; never denying any help he could give to any that ſought to him. See *Matt. 19. 13, 14. -15. 23, 24. Mark. 10. 48, 49. -9. 38, 39. Luk. 9. 54, 55. Matt. 14. 15.* comp. *Mark. 8. 2, 3.*

§. 10.
Receives the reward.
For himſelf.

And after this performance of all this humility, and obedience without ſin, He alſo received the reward promiſed (for which he had took this pains, and endured this ſhame *Heb. 12. 2.*) even eternal life

CHAP. VI.

life and glory see *Phil.* 2. 8, 9. *Act.* 8. 33. for his humility, &c. *Luk.* 24. 26. *Pf.* 18. 20. -110. 7. 1 *Pet.* 1. 21.-3. 22. *Heb.* 2. 9. -1. 9. *Rev.* 5. 9, 12. being restored to all that was lost by, or promised to, the first *Adam*; For his having been a servant, now made Lord and Christ *Act.* 2. 36. now made the Son of God (being said to be begotten on the day of his Resurrection *Act.* 13. 33. *Luk.* 1. 32. *Rom.* 1. 4.) and so at his transfiguration, the preludium of his glorification, it was celebrated with a voice from Heaven *this is my beloved Son, Matt.* 17. 5. see 2 *Sam.* 7. 14. comp. *Heb.* 1. 5. and as at his Nativity, so at his resurrection called the *first born, Col.* 1. 18. giving then to the Disciples the appellation of *brethren. Jo.* 20. 17. Of whom death was in labour, as it were, while she had him in her womb, *Act,* 2. 24. and at last by the power of his Spirit was delivered of him. By which *we are* also *begotten again, &c.* 1 *Pet.* 1. 3. He also was stiled, *Heb.* 1. 3. the Image and character of God, as the first *Adam* was before him. *Luk.* 3. 38. 2 *Cor.* 4. 4. *Gen.* 1. 27. And heyr of all things, and having the dominion over them, as *Adam* in innocence had *Pf.* 8. 5. comp. with *Heb.* 2. 6. *Pfal.* 2. 8. which are all resanctified, and, as I may so say, redeemed from their former pollution in him, as they were unhallowed by the other; see *Heb.* 1. 2. 1 *Cor.* 10. 25, 26. *Rom.* 8. 19. &c. -14. 14. Now he readmitted into Paradise *Luk.* 23. 43. and to the Tree of life *Rev.* 2. 7. -3. 21. -22. 14. from which the first was expelled. For tho he was and had all these from all eternity, yet emptying himself as it were of all former rights in becoming man, he thus made a new purchase and acquisition of them; that so these his honors might be transferred to his seed, as *For his seed.* were the first *Adams* misfortunes. Which seed he

now

The benefits of our Saviour.

now began to propagate and to multiply, and replenish the Earth with it. He multiplying it not as the first *Adam* by carnal pleasure, but, as a vegetable seed increaseth, by dying; ('tis our Saviors own allusion *Jo.* 12. 24, 23.-3.14, 15. *Esai.* 53. 10, 11.) And as the spirit in seed upon its burying in the Earth, and dying, begins first to operate and dilate it's self: So did his spirit to the production of a numberless progeny. See *Jo.* 7. 39. For which seed also, as well as for himself upon his exaltation he received the promised spirit; to be given them for the present, *Luk.* 24. 49. *Act.* 2. 33. by which the rebelling flesh should be brought again under its dominion. And the Crown of Immortality to be received shortly; being the two things we lost in the fall of *Adam.* So that look how much the first *Adam* contributed to our destruction; much more hath the second for our Salvation.

t The Spirit.

2 Life.

§. 11.
His perticular benefits.

To number up all whose derived blessings upon mankind more particularly, we are first to take notice: that sin having entred into the world by the first man, and after it death; this second Parent was forced in the first place to undo the works of the former; and to clear the malevolent influence that came from him, before he could impart to us his own; and remove the punishment the first brought on us, before regain the reward, he lost us. Therefore as the first *Adam* sinned, and we bare part of his iniquity, so we sinning the second *Adam* bore all our iniquities: and as we by partaking the first *Adams* flesh became heirs of his sin, so he by partaking ours became (if I may so say) heir of our sins. And that even of the sins of the whole world; as not some few but all mankind were sinners and perished in *Adam*; That the restitution might be

3 As our head, communicates absolution from sin by his death for it.

as

CHAP. VI.

as large as the fall. This man upon the precious Cross offered a price of mans redemption, not only sufficient for all the Sons of *Adam*, and yet limited by him to some few i. e. the saved; but also actually tendered to God his Father indifferently without exception for them all. See 2 *Cor.* 5. 14, 15. where the Apostle argues that all the sons of the first *Adam* were dead in sin, because the second *Adam* died for them all. See *Heb.* 2. 9. 2 *Pet.* 2. 1. *Rom.* 14. 15. 1 *Cor.* 8. 11. 1 *Jo.* 2. 2. *Rom.* 5. 18. 1 *Tim.* 2. 6. So those that perish *Heb.* 10. 29. by apostacy could not be said to have *troden under foot the Son of God, and the blood of the Covenant,* if no way pertaining to them: and so in the Holy Communion if not his body offered also for, and to, the wicked, how could they be guilty of his body and blood? 1 *Cor.* 11. 27. That therefore this blood becomes not effectual and profiting to all (in respect of which that phrase *for many* is used *Matt.* 26. 28.) it is because of the conditions to be performed on every mans part, that it may be beneficial unto him. See *Joh.* 3. 16, 17. Or also (to take the strictest opinion of predestination) because the Father hath so pleased to enable only some of the seed of *Adam* to the performance of such conditions. But the Son in all things obedient and subject to his Father chose or picked out none, no not his twelve Disciples, but took into his diligent protection those, whom ever the Father pleased to give him: and even amongst the twelve in submission to his Fathers will chose one of them, well foreknowing it *Jo.* 6. 70. to shed his blood. See *Jo.* 17. 6, 9, 24. *Jo.* 6. 65. *Act.* 13. 48. -15. 13. *Jo.* 10. 26. *Matt.* 11. 25. *Rom.* 11. 7. and with a Divine patience tolerated him, robbing him of his necessary provisions, before he betrayed his sacred person.

person. See *Jo.* 12. 6. Nothing therefore is there on the account of the univerfality of his pretious facrifice, why every fingle Son of *Adam* may not be faved by the plentiful effufion of that all-meritorious ftream of his blood; which gufhed out from fo many Fountains made in his body; from his head, back, breaft, hands, feet, nay (in that Garden-agony) thro every pore. And thofe,who make themfelves uncapable of the benefit thereof, make, in as much as concerns them, the blood of the Son of God who loved them and gave himfelf for them *Gal.* 2. 20. to be fhed (fo grievous a crime) in vain ; and this (by the Apoftle) is making themfelves guilty of his murther. *Heb.* 6. 6. 1 *Cor.* 11. 27. Thus he by Gods promife becoming the fecond head of the body of mankind 1 *Cor.* 11. 3. whereof we by faith are members, by fuffering and dying for us and in our ftead, (*tafting death for every man,* faith the Apoftle *Heb.* 2. 9.) he thus fatisfied Gods juftice, and appeafed his wrath toward us; as one member in the natural body oft fuffers the punifhment for the fault of fome other. *Sicut Homo* (faith *Aquinas*) *per aliquod opus quod manu exerceret, redimeret fe a peccato quod commififfet cum pedibus.* For by this Communication of head and members *Adam* brought in condemnation and death : and therefore fhall not mercy be enlarged as far as juftice by the fame relation, that alfo they may be removed ? For as, *if one member fuffers* 1 *Cor.* 12. 26. *all the members fuffer with it;* fo all the members are counted to fuffer what any one doth , For *all the members of one body, being many, are one body;* and fo is Chrift 1 *Cor.* 12. 12. [and we]. This is certain, the firft *Adam* hath brought no guilt or mifery on his members, which the fecond hath not, (or fhall not

CHAP. VI.

in due season) take away. Nay, saith the Apostle, he hath taken away far more then the first brought; to wit all our own personal guilt too. For one only sin of the first was enough to undo not only himself but all his posterity, and to bring in death: but many millions of sins, besides that, could not hinder the second, to procure us (notwithstanding them) salvation and eternal life. *Rom.* 5. 16.

Now since all our benefit by him comes from our ingrafting and incorporation into him, that so his sufferings may be accounted for ours, the Sacrament or religious Ceremony instituted to convey unto us this first effect of the second *Adams* dying for us, (and so freeing us from the condemnation, and washing us with his blood from the stains of our former sins) is Baptism. After which, tho the infirmity of concupiscence still remain (for the benefits of the second *Adam* are not fully perfected till this life is ended) yet is both the strength thereof much abated; and the *reatus* or guilt thereof totally removed; i. e. that none shall be condemned for the solicitations and importunings thereof (which will happen till our redemption is compleated) so they be by him (for which he is enabled with sufficient grace) mastered and suppreſt. Therefore are we said in the Scripture *to be baptized into Chriſt*; *to put on Chriſt*. *Gal.* 3. 27. *Rom.* 6. 2. *to be in Chriſt Rom.* 8. 1. *Phil.* 3. 9. *by one ſpirit to be baptized into one body.* 1 *Cor.* 12. 13. *To be baptized into his death, to be co-planted in the likeneſs of his death*; and *to be buried with him in Baptiſm Rom.* 6. 3, 4. &c. 1 *Pet.* 4. 1. by baptiſm *to be ſaved from death and ſin* 1 *Pet.* 3. 20, 21. &c. and therefore as Baptiſm is called *our death*, ſo his death by him is called *a Baptiſm Matt.* 20. 23, *Luk.* 12. 50. What by him

Baptiſm incorporating us into his death.

The Sacrament of pardon.

§ 12.

was really performed, being by us too reprefented, and acted in Baptifm. For our Savior is fuppofed (fee *Rom. 6. chap.*) to reprefent till his death, a fon of *Adam* as we are; and one that had took fin upon him; tho he had none in him; and fo to fuffer the punifhment, and dy to it, as well as for it, that is, no more afterward to be charged with it, *Rom. 6. 10.* and then to rife again a new man; according to which we (true finners) in baptifm are fuppofed to dy with him to fin *Rom. 6. 2.* no more to live in it; and then to be born again of him, to begin a new life, a life to holinefs; called alfo *newnefs of life Rom. 6. 4.* life fpiritual oppofed to the former carnal, fee *Gal. 6.1.1 Cor. 2. 15. Rom. 7.6.* according to which we are faid *to be* already *rifen with Chrift. Col. 3. 1.* That is, from death in fin. Baptifm fignifying 1. both our putting on, (fome think fignified by the expreffion borrowed from the pulling of old clothes and putting on new; a Ceremony ufed at Baptifm in the Apoftles times, and after them in the primitive Church) and being ingrafted into Chrift, fo that we have right to his fufferings, &c. and 2. then, by virtue of his death our being cleanfed from fin, typified by the water wafhing us: and then 3. our putting to death, crucifying, and putting off the old man *Rom. 6.6.* the fon of *Adam,* and fo dying to fin; fignified by the ancient manner of immerfion of the body under water (nothing of it to be feen) and 4. then our *putting on the new man,* and Chrift; our *being born again of water and the fpirit,* and being *made a new creature;* reprefented in the emerfion and elevation again out of the water. See *Col. 2. 12. -3. 10. Jo. 3. 5.* As if you ftood by thofe curing waters of *Bethefda,* new ftirred by an Angel, and faw a fon

of

Chap. VI.

of the first *Adam* consisting all of flesh, diving into those waters, all polluted with sin, and dying in them (which thing one man in every ones stead, did for us) and then springing up a new child out of this old stock; the son of the second *Adam*, consisting of spirit *Jo.* 3. 6. 1 *Cor.* 6. 17. washed clean and pure to live a new life in obedience.

2. After he hath thus Communicated unto us, (as many as are his members) absolution from sin, by his dying to it for us; and our implantation into his death by baptism; the second blessing he derives upon his seed is Righteousness *Rom.* 5. 15, 18. 19. *Luk.* 1. 72, 75. that by this we may attain life eternal; as by deliverance from sin we escaped death. And this righteousness this second *Adam* conveighs unto us in two manners; As *Adam* in like manner did sin to his posterity. 1. For first as we derived both from the example of *Adams* disobedience, and from the propagation of his flesh (a natural soliciter even in mans innocence for its own delights, without regard of their lawfulness *Gen.* 3. 6. but much more after the fall) a pronity to evil, and by loss of the Spirit, inability to good: so from the example of Christs obedience, and the traduction of his spirit, we receive a new ability, inclination, and pronity to good and aversion from evil. See *Eph.* 2. 10. *Tit.* 2. 14. *Jo.* 8. 39, 41, 44. *Rom. Rom.* 13. 14. *Eph.* 4. 23, 24. *Rom.* 11. 16. 2. Again, as his posterity, for *Adams* one sin and disobedience, was made sinner; and judgment and condemnation came upon them, who sinned not after the similitude of his transgression, for not their, but his, disobedience; and that also one onely disobedience of his; *Rom.* 5. 12. &c. to the 20th. The branches being holy or unholy as the root is; See *Rom.*

§. 13.
2 *As our head communicates righteousness or life spiritually by his Resurrection.*

1 *Enabling us to perform righteousness.*

2 Compleating our imperfect righteousness.

Rom. 11. 16, 28. Heb. 7. 9, 10. So the posterity of Christ, both when they yeild obedience, yet for his obedience and righteousness, not theirs, is accepted; theirs, (whether devotions, or good works, at least many of them) being by reason of the remains of the old man (as yet only crucified in part) weak and imperfect, but his compleat and exact; for which therefore all the imperfections of theirs, (by faith) are pardoned. And when they disobey, (their obedience likewise being not constant) their repentance (if it be rightly performed; i. e. by now dying to their new sin since baptism in pennance, and mortifications; and commemorating the Lords passion in the Communion *Matt.* 26. 28. 1 *Jo.* 2. 1, 2. serving to the remission of sin; as they died before to their old ones in Baptism; and then by living afterward according to the spirit) for his sufferings and obedience is also accepted for obedience. So that we are made righteous in Christ, see *Rom.* 8. 1. comp. *Heb.* 7. 9. 10. as well as from Christ, in our selves, by his spirit; as also we were sinners in *Adam Rom.* 5. 12. as well as from *Adam,* in our selves by the flesh derived from Him. See *Rom.* 5. 15, 19. *Phil.* 3. 9. *Rom.* 8. 1. 2 *Cor.* 5. 21. 1 *Cor.* 1. 30. *Eph.* 1. 4, 6. 1 *Pet.* 2. 5. *Eph.* 4. 24. *Col.* 3. 17. 3. Thus Jesus Christ the righteous 1 *Joh.* 2. 1. derives to all his members, righteousness and life spiritual, opposed to carnal. Next He for this righteousness advanced by God to Immortality, Kingdom, Glory,

3 As our head communicates glory, or life eternal, in our resurrection.

&c. derives upon his seed the reward of Righteousness, life eternal; opposed to this natural they yet live; in like manner as from the first *Adam* they were heirs of death eternal. See the parallel between them for life and death, 1 *Cor.* 15. 20. and 45. &c. as for sin and righteousness *Rom.* 5.

And

Chap. VI.

And this life in its due time is to be communicated to all the members of Christ; 1. both because the head and members have all the same spirit, i. e. of the Father; which therefore, if it have raised one, must needs also raise the other: As we see in the living Creatures, and the wheels *Ezech.* 2. 21. *when those went, these went, and when those stood, these stood, for the spirit of the living creatures was in the wheels.* Or, as we may imagine a man, of those large Dimensions, that his head were in Heaven, and his feet on Earth, (and such is Christ and the Church *Col.* 2. 19. and both called by one name of Christ : 1 *Cor.* 12. 12. how easily and instantly such a one by the animal spirits communicated from the Head would move here below, which way he pleased his inferior members. See *Rom.* 8. 11. 1 *Cor.* 6. 14. Therefore those priviledges, which the Apostle applies to Christ *Heb.* 2. 6. the Psalmist saith of man in general. *Pf.* 8. And again 'tis argued negatively from us to Christ ; If no resurrection of us, then is not Christ risen neither. 1 *Cor.* 15. 13. If not possible for the spirit to raise our human nature then not his. And 2. because the head (as Christ is to the Church) naturally gives the sense and motion to the members, Therefore, as 'tis said that the head and members are both raised by the same spirit ; so also, that the Head shall raise and quicken the members. See *Jo.* 6. 39. 1 *Cor.* 15. 45. 2 *Cor.* 4. 14. I speak of resurrection to life ; Else , the wicked also shall be raised by him, by his voice *Jo.* 5. 21. as their Judge to be thrown into endless torments; which is but a Gaol-delivery, and an haling them out of prison to execution; an act of his power as God, not of his merits as a Savior, by their having any union to him, as the second *Adam*.

§. 14.
1 *Effected by the same spirit by which his.*

2 *Effected by him.*

And

The benefits of our Savior.

§. 15.
The Eucharist incorporating us into his life.

The Sacrament of Union.

And the proper Sacrament inſtituted to conveigh this life unto us, by union with Jeſus is the Euchariſt; being the Communion, or Communication unto us of all himſelf; firſt of his body and blood 1 *Cor.* 10. 16. by which we are made, not in a Metaphor, but *in a Myſtery*, and that a great one, *members of his body; of his fleſh and of his bones. Eph.* 5. 30, 32. And 2. not only of his body but of his ſpirit too 1 *Cor.* 12. 13. by which ſoveraign receit and incorporating of him, who hath life in himſelf, *our bodies alſo and ſouls* are (according to the ancient form of the Church in the adminiſtration of theſe myſteries) *preſerved unto everlaſting life*; a promiſe by our Savior annexed ſo often to this myſtical partaking of him *Jo.* 6. 56, 57. &c. therefore the conſecrated elements called *Symbola reſurrectionis*, and formerly never neglected (eſpecially) to be received at the hour of death. For 'tis to be noted that tho both the Sacraments have all the ſame effects; Remiſſion of ſins, *Matt.* 26. 28. comp. with *Act.* 2. 38. Union, 1 *Cor.* 10. 16. comp. with *Gal.* 3. 27, 28. *all one in Chriſt Jeſus*. And *Joh.* 3. 5. comp. with 1 *Cor.* 12. 13. And both Sacraments do intimate obligation to ſuffering to the receivers: ſee *Matt.* 20. 22, 23. where alluſion doubtleſs is made to the two Sacraments as 1 *Cor.* 12. 13. (Tho our baptiſm is not with blood as his; nor our cup ſo bitter:) yet either of them have ſome more eminently then others. Therefore Baptiſm (to which we have more eaſy acceſs upon repentance *Act.* 2. 38. and faith of the truth of the Goſpel *Act.* 8. 37. and the promiſe onely of a new life *Matt.* 3. 6, 8.) is, more principally the Sacrament of remiſſion of former ſins *Act.* 2. 38. and of our profeſſion of our death to ſin; and relinquiſhing the old *Adam*; and now putting on Chriſt.

And

Chap. VI.

And then after this cleansing from sins past by baptism, the Eucharist (to which we are to bring not only faith and repentance, but sanctification and holiness; therefore such examination required, see *Matt.* 22. 12. see 1 *Cor.* 11.28. the end of 27. and 29. comp. with 1 *Cor.* 6.15. converted [*shall I then take the members of an harlot,* and make them the members of Christ?] 1 *Cor.* 5. 11. converted [*No fornicators presume to eat, &c. with the Saints*]) is more specially the Sacrament of our union to Christ, and living by him who is the life, by the incorporating of his body, and blood and spirit into ours. 1 *Cor.* 10. 16, 17. By which incorporation we contract such an identity (as it were) with him; that see what he is we are. Is he a Son of God? so are we. His heir? So are we *Rom.* 8. 17. of the Kingdom, the Glory to come: only all this by and from him; *that in all things he might have the preeminence; and amongst many brethren be the first born.*

But we must know, that, as all these effects of our Savior toward us depend on a second generation and being born again of God by the seed of the spirit *Jo.* 3. 9. 2 *Cor.* 3. 18. *Eph.* 2. 22. -3. 16. which giveth life; as the flesh from the first *Adam* soweth corruption, see *Gal.* 6. 8. 2 *Cor.* 3. 6. *Rom.* 8. 11. *Jo.* 4. 14. *Eph.* 4. 22. and on our thus being made the true children and ofspring of Christ, *Heb.* 2. 13. *Esai.* 53. 10, 11. So, that this our second birth is not compleated all at once: but this image of Christ by little and little, at last is perfectly formed in us. See *Gal.* 4. 19. 2 *Cor.* 11. 2. 1 *Pet.* 2. 2. As also all other works of our Savior are not consummate till his second coming and the resurrection. Else, did we walk by sight and not by faith, how should we be transported with joy upon a vision of that infinite glory

§. 15. *All these Benefits depend on our being made his children.*

The benefits of our Saviour.

glory and nobility the poor Sons of *Adam* receive from this their second father? to whom be all glory for ever. And how should we sigh and groan till we were once possessed of it? See 2 *Cor.* 5. 2, 4. and *Rom.* 8. 23.

§. 17. To consider therefore a little the manner and the progress of our regeneration here in this life. Our Savior, as soon as he had died to sin as a son of *Adam*, and lived again as a Son to God *Rom.* 6. 10. presently received this spirit, (by which he begets us) promised long before, and therefore frequently called the promise from the Father, to communicate to his posterity, see *Luk.* 24. 49. *Act.* 1. 4. -2. 33. *Eph.* 4. 10. *Jo.* 7. 39. by which spirit derived from him to us (thro whom we receive all things that we receive from God as it was from his Father to him) and therefore called also his spirit, of Christ, of Jesus, of the Son ; see *Gal.* 4. 6. *1 Pet.* 1. 11. *Act.* 16. 7. vulg. *Jo.* 16. 7, 14. we come to be his sons. Now this spirit is not given promiscuously to all the sons of the first *Adam* ; nor is all the seed of the first (by God the Father's secret will in the dispensation here and there, of the ministery of the Gospel ; and by the default of some of those that hear it ; therefore our Savior useth those limitations. *Jo.* 6. 44, 65. -17. 9, 11, 12.) the seed also of the second. But there is something on mans part prerequired; (for God having given us before in our first Creation, something we may make use of in our second, and besides this the external ministry of the Gospel, where we are called to grace, tho *creavit te sine te, non salvabit te sine te*) to the receiving of this spirit (I mean here in a more eminent degree of its operations) and of our sanctification and union by it unto Christ our Lord, and our incorporation

Which we are by the derivation to us of his nature. ¹ His Spirit.

on and entrance into this heavenly linage.

§. 18. Given to us upon Faith and Repentance.

And these are Faith, some degree of it; i.e. *gladly receiving the word* Act. 2. 41. called also *obedience to the word*, see Act. 8. 12, 13, 37. comp. v. 16. 17. Eph. 1. 13. Jo. 17. 39. *not rejecting the counsel of God* Luk. 7. 30. believing Gods justification of the ungodly. Rom. 4. 5. and *Repentance for sins past*, intending to live no longer in them, see Heb. 6. 2. 1 Pet. 3. 21. (yet which also, both faith and repentance, are the gift of God, see Eph. 2. 8. 2 Tim. 2. 25. Act. 16. 14. tho the first cometh ordinarily by hearing; where (by Gods mercy) the Gospel is preached Rom. 10. 17. and the second by the first. Jonah 3. 5. Upon which two Christ hath appointed Baptism to be administred by his substitutes; and the holy spirit at the same time by himself conferred, see Jo. 7. 39. Eph. 1. 13. Gal. 3. 2, 13, 22. Act. 2. 38. -19. 2. -5. 32. Luk. 11. 13.

§. 19 Our new birth, at our Baptism.

First then at our Baptism, (upon faith and repentance) Pf. 45. 10. we begin to be *born again of water and of the spirit*; but not so, as presently quite cashiering the image of the former Adam; but as being now a compound of an old man, and a new; or of a body and soul from Adam called the flesh, and of a spirit from Christ; I mean not that contradistinguished to the soul, 1 Thess. 5. 23. where by the *spirit* seems to be meant the rational Intellective part or soul, see 1 Cor. 2. 11. Act. 7. 59. Luk. 23. 46. By soul the affective and sensitive part or soul: which is also used for to signify life, but I mean a spirit superadded to this natural spirit. See 1 Cor. 14. 14, 2. where there is a spirit in us plainly distinguished from the natural faculty of the understanding, which operated when the understanding was quiescent, see v. 12. ζηλωται τ̃ πνευμάτων. See Rev. 1. 10. 1 Cor. 12. 10. &c. the spirit of man being the soul

Not yet perfected.

of

The benefits of our Saviour.

of a natural man: besides which the Apostles had another spirit searching all things, &c. as Christ also is compounded of two natures; the Human and Divine *Act*. 10. 38, yet is the one of these dying in us by degrees, as the other grows; and we are putting off, mortifying, crucifying the one, and putting on and renewing the other day by day. *Rom*. 6. 6. *Col*. 3. 5. *Gal*. 6. 14. 2 *Cor*. 4. 16. *Rom*. 12. 2. *Eph*. 4. 22, 23, 24. whilst there is a perpetual combate between them; The spirit lusting against the flesh; and the flesh against the spirit *Gal*. 5. 17. until we are perfected, which is not attained in this life. Yet here the elder man is serving the younger; provided that we do not wither, and fall away from grace; and dy again to God. And by reason of this double (outward and inward) man that is in us; it is that the Apostles, where they tell us that we are dead to sin, &c. yet exhort us also to dy to sin, see *Rom*. 6. 2. comp. 12. 1 *Pet*. 4. 1. comp. 1 *Pet*. 2. 11. and that the Saints where they give thanks, do also pray for a deliverance.

§. 20.
By this spirit the image of Christ first formed in the soul.

Now in this our renovation made by certain steps and degrees, this spirit derived from Christ operateth and produceth the image of Christ first in our soul; and then afterward in our body. After the same manner as it was in Christ himself; who first had grace in his soul with passibility in his body till he died; after which that also was glorified by the same spirit. Here therefore it begins in this life by its mighty working *Col*. 1. 29. 2 *Cor*. 9. 14, 15. to transform and renew us, *Rom*. 12. 2. *Eph*. 4. 13. *Gal*. 2. 19, 20. *Eph*. 3. 16, 17. *Phil*. 1. 21. residing here (after faith and repentance which are certain preludium's and foregifts also of it, See *Matt*. 16. 17. 1 *Cor*. 12. 3. 1 *Jo*. 4. 2. and are increased in us proportionably

CHAP. VI.

portionably as it is,) bringing all its rich graces with it, mentioned 1 *Cor.* 12. 3, 8. &c.   *1.* Illuminating and inspiring and renewing knowledge in the understanding, in vain (without it) sought by us any other way; therefore called the spirit of truth, see *Jo.* 16. 13. 1 *Cor.* 2. 10. &c. 2 *Pet.* 1. 21. 1 *Jo.* 2. 20, 27. and of prophecy. *Rev.* 9. 10. -12. 17. 1 *Jo.* 5. 10.   *2.* Sanctifying the will and affections; Therefore called the spirit of holiness; first quenching (there) all worldly desires; and satiating the soul instead of them, see *Jo.* 7. 37, 39. -4. 14.   *2.* Begetting an ardent and unsatiable love of God, and fervency of praier and obedience to all his commands (written by it in our hearts) out of love, such as was in Christ. *Matt.* 5. 6. *Pf.* 40. 8. *Rom.* 5. 5. 2 *Tim.* 1. 7. 2 *Cor.* 3. 6, 7. *Rom.* 8. 26, 27.   *3.* Producing greater joy in and desire of sufferings. (In imitation of our Savior,) for his, for Gods, for the truths sake; which truth this spirit seals unto us. 1 *Thess.* 1. 6. *Rom.* 5. 2. *Heb.* 10. 34. *Act.* 5. 41. *Phil.* 1. 29. 2 *Cor.* 12. 10. *Col.* 1. 11. 2 *Cor.* 11. 23. *I more, his Minister*, &c. 2 *Cor.* 5. 14. Lastly, comforting alwaies by begetting a lively hope, by witnessing to us what we are and sealing what we shall be, *Gal.* 5. 5. 1 *Pet.* 1. 3. *Jo.* 16. 17. *Rom.* 8. 16. 2 *Thess.* 2. 16. *Gal.* 4. 6. 1 *Jo.* 3. 24. *Eph.* 1. 13. All which graces now are the image of Christ stamped on the soul, called partaking of his holiness *Heb.* 12. 10. and being created after God in righteousness. *Eph.* 4. 24. But yet this image of, or union with, our Savior in the soul is not perfect neither in this life: therefore called, *first fruits* only *of the spirit,* and *tast of the heavenly gifts, and the powers of the world to come;* an earnest and seal of something to be had more fully hereafter, a *Fountain springing up,* and a sowing

Its mighty working in the soul of the like graces to those in Christ.

His image in the soul not perfected in this life.

The benefits of our Saviour.

to everlasting life, a progress from glory to glory, see *Rom.* 8. 23. *Heb.* 6. 4, 5. 2 *Cor.* 1. 22. -5. 5. *Jo.* 4. 14. *Gal.* 6. 8. *Eph.* 1. 13, 14. According to which those prophecies of the effusions of the spirit, which are fulfilled in part upon our Saviors first coming, yet seem not to have their full accomplishment till his second appearing, which in those texts is joyned with the first. See *Act.* 2. 17, 18. comp. 19, 20. *Joel* 2. 28. &c. comp. *Joel* 3. 2. &c. *Mal.* 3. 1. &c. comp. *Mal.* 4. 1, 5. *Esai* 40. 3, 5, 10. And the plentiful flowing of those waters of life (our Saviors ordinary Metaphor in St *Johns* Gospel for the Spirit) which shall be from the Temple or the Throne of God, and the Lamb, mentioned *Rev.* 22. 1.-21. 6. *Ezec.* 47. 1, 3. &c. *Joel* 3. 18. *Ezec.* 13. 1.-14. 8. *Ps.* 36. 8, 9. (for all these prophecies wonderfully accord; and speak of the state of the new world yet to come; expressing heavenly things by earthly, and the truths of the Gospel veil'd under the Ceremonies of the law) must needs be understood of the fuller Communications of the holy spirit yet to come. Blessed be God for his unspeakable gift!

Umbra in lege: Imago in Evangelio: veritas in cœlo: S. Ambros.

§. 21.
2 *Shall be also in the body hereafter.*

The next operation of this spirit is upon our body, but upon this (as upon our Saviors) not till the blessed Resurrection, when we shall begin to *bear the image of the heavenly* Adam as we *now bear the image of the earthly*, 1 *Cor.* 15. 49. and *this vile body shall be changed, and made like to his glorious body*; like it, I mean not, as it appeared after his rising again, to his Disciples, with a wound to thrust ones hand in, eating and drinking, &c. (where to shew the truth of his resurrection, that it was the same body that was crucified, he was glad to veil the glory of it.) But as it appeared to St. *Paul* in the way to *Damascus*, which glory struck him blind, *Act.* 9. 3. comp. *Act.* 22. 14.

CHAP. VI.

22. 14. or as to St. *Stephen* the reflection of which made his face to shine as an Angels, or as *Moses's* in the Mount: or to his Disciples *Matt.* 17. 2. at his transfiguration: where God to qualifie the sad relation of his sufferings gave them an anticipated sight of that glory, which in the apparitions after his Resurrection was necessary to be eclipsed: upon which moment of Beatifick vision, his transported Disciples quite forgetting all former relations to the world would gladly have set up there their perpetual abode. Or as it appeared to St. *John*, *Rev.* 1. 13, 17. at the sight of whose Majesty that beloved Disciple fell at his Masters feet as dead, &c. And after our body is thus made glorious as his in the resurrection; it shall also have an ascension just like his. Our bodies caught up in the Clouds, &c. 1 *Thess.* 4. 17. as his was. *Act.* 1. 9. And when this perfection is produced in the body as well as the soul, then it is that we are properly called the Sons and children *of God; being the children of the resurrection*, *Luk.* 20. 36. as is also noted of our Savior. And as the Angels from their spirituality like God are called his Sons, *Job.* 1. 6. So, is at that time said to be our adoption. *Rom.* 8. 23. The regeneration; the restitution to the state before sin; the manifestation of the Sons of God, see *Matt.* 19. 28. *Act.* 3. 21. *Rom.* 8. 19. comp. with 1. 4. *Rev.* 21. 7. and mean while our life said to *be in Christ*, to *be hid with Christ in God. Col.* 3. 3, 4. 1 *Jo.* 5. 11. For this state was such a longing of the Apostle to attain once the resurrection; such a waiting of the Saints for the coming of the Lord; such a groaning and being burdened in this earthly Tabernacle, not to be shut of it and have none; but to be clothed upon it with another house from Heaven, see *Phil.* 3. 11. 1 *Cor.* 1. 7. 2 *Pet.* 3. 12. 2 *Cor.* 5. 1.

When we shall more properly be the sons of God.

The benefits of our Saviour.

Its mighty working in the body of the like glory to that in Christ.

5. 1. &c. *Rom.* 8. 23. The same individual this shall be (which our Savior kept his wounds to shew ; and perhaps will do for the honorable marks of his sufferings, see *Rev.* 1. 7. *Rev.* 5. 6. he appearing in glory with them *)* but by the operation of the spirit of the Lord, *2 Cor. 3. 18.* strangely changed. For *we sow not* in the grave *that body that shall be,* 1 *Cor.* 15. 37. no more faith St. *Paul* then the seed we sow in the field is the flower, or plant that comes of it (who can guess at the beautiful colors of a Tulip, by looking on its seed ?) therefore the Apostle speaks of the body raised as a superstructure upon this, *2 Cor. 5. 4.* as the seed is clothed upon by the flower or the tree; sown then in shame, it shall come up glorious ; weak, come up in power : natural, come up spiritual. *1 Cor.* 15. 42. For there are bodies spiritual, and we know not but the Angels are such : so spiritual as that there shall be no more belly, at least as for meats, nor no more meats for it. *1 Cor. 6. 13.* As *Moses* and *Elias* here for the 40 daies they enjoyed Gods presence, needed no food. There shall be no flesh nor blood. *1 Cor.* 15. 50. No heaviness, 1 *Thess.* 4. 17. nor grosness, *Luk.* 24. 31. *Jo.* 20. 19. and so no sensual pleasure suiting to corruptible substances (of which for the most part some foregoing pain is the parent) *Luk.* 20. 36. what then shall we be ? like Angels ; nay like the Son of God the second *Adam*, our Father ; like him when he shall appear in his greatest glory *1 Jo. 3. 2.* but what this likeness shall be we know not yet ; nor how far the spirit shall be united to us, in similitude of that unity which Christs human nature now hath with the deity, but as in some kind we are now *partakers,* so much more then shall we be, *of the divine nature,* 2 *Pet.* 1. 4. *nay filled with all the fulness of God.* *Eph.*

CHAP. VI.

Eph. 3. 19. Glorious in body, *Esai.* 13. 12. and enriched with all knowledg, wisdom, holiness, joy, security in soul, after the similitude of that wisdom, and holiness, and glory, which Christs humanity hath received from the Deity; some beams of that Sun being united to us, the body of which dwells in him. *Col.* 2. 9. *Jo.* 17. 21, 23. To whom be all preeminence and glory for ever by all the partakers of his glory ! *O fælix culpa* (said one) *quæ talem meruit habere redemptionem. Ad aliquid majus humana natura perducta est per peccatum* ! And God permitted that great evil of mans fall to raise him to a far greater honor: finishing all his works in goodness and mercy.

Meanwhile as not we, so neither is our Savior, compleat every way before our resurrection; being without us, a Head glorified without its body. Therefore is the Church called *His fulness,* Eph. 1. 23. and as his glory, so his sufferings, in as much as part of hers are yet behind, are said not to be yet compleat. *Col.* 1. 24. And so he is said now to *love the Church, to nourish* and *cherish her* out of the love he bears to himself; for *none ever hated his own flesh.* *Eph.* 5. 28. Especially the head, in which are placed the senses for the good and defence of the whole body, that is most sensible of any thing that happens unto it, see *Act.* 9. 4. and more watchful in providing for it. Therefore is this his love to her noted to be greater, a more merciful, faithful, compassionate love, from his being the second *Adam*, and undergoing the experience of like infirmity, then the blessed Angels; or as he as God, was (if I may so say,) capable of. See *Heb.* 2. 17, 18. We being now the travail of his soul, *Esai.* 53. 11. for whom he endured the birth-throes of death, *Act.* 2. 24.

§. 21.
Before the resurrection as we, so our Head, not compleat.

O and

The benefits of our Saviour.

and therefore he, as a pained mother, the more loves us according to his fufferings for us.

§. 22.
The diverfe relations of Chrift to us as fecond Adam.

Whofe ftrait and intimate connexion and tye unto us, in refpect of this his fecond *Adam*-fhip, the Holy Ghoft in the Scriptures hath expreffed in all the neareft and deareft relations, that can eafily be fancied, ftyling him and us,

Father, Children.

In a new Creation or Regeneration, (where *Chrift is all in all. Col. 3. 11.* as Adam in the former) *Father and Children,* He being made after the perfect image of God, and we after his. He heir and Lord of all things, and we by him, who having loft our former title to the Creatures by the fall of *Adam,* and upon this the ufe of many of them reftrained, have now a new right eftablifhed thro him. They being fanctified, as it were, now again by a new word of God in this new Creation: as they were in the firft; and both thro Chrift; by which they are all free, all clean upon prayer, thankfgiving, and alms, to all his feed; tho ftill unclean to all the reft; See *Rom. 14. 14. 1 Tim. 4. 3. Tit. 1. 15. Rom. 4. 14. Heb. 2. 5. Luk. 11. 41. 1 Cor. 3. 21, 23.-7. 14.* comp. *Tit. 3. 5.* See *Col. 1. 15. Rev. 3. 14. Heb. 1. 2, 3. Heb. 2. 5. Gal. 6. 15. Rom. 8. 29. 2 Cor. 5. 17. Eph. 2. 10. Eph. 4. 24. Col. 3. 10. Efai. 9. 6.-53. 10, 11. Heb. 2. 13. Jo. 3. 3, 4. Pf. 22. 30.*

Husband, Wife.

Husband and Spoufe. A priviledge and relation to the Son of God which we fhall have beyond the bleffed Angels, a fimilitude of nature being only capable of this. For where are the Angels called the Bride, the Lambs wife? See *Rev. 21. 9. Eph. 5. 25. &c. 1 Cor. 6. 13, 15. &c.* In which relation we are faid to be *members of Chrift,* not only as the Hands or Feet are of the body natural, but as Eve was of Adam, *of his flefh and of his bones*: and to be *one fpirit* with

CHAP. VI.

with Chrift, as Adam and Eve were *one flefh*. Of which efpoufal and union of the Church with Chrift, the inftitution of marriage was but a figure and type. And *Adams* faying to new made *Eve; This is now made bone, &c. Gen. 2. 23.* but a prophecy; And her being made out of *Adams* fide, but an allegory of the Churches fpringing out of Chrifts fide, pierced on the Crofs, (fo much obferved by St. *John. Jo. 19. 34, 35. 1 Jo. 5. 8.* That water and blood, which came from thence firft begetting, *Jo. 3. 5.* and then nourifhing, *Jo. 6. 35.* the Church his Spoufe). And mans being made head of the woman, but an emblem of Chrifts being Head of the man, *1 Cor. 11. 3.* that is, of mankind his fpoufe: whom, according to the ancient cuftome of not receiving a dowry with, but paying one for the Virgin *Gen. 34. 13. Exod. 22.16.* Chrift is faid to have *bought with* a dear *price*, 1 *Cor. 6. 20.* even by giving himfelf for her *Eph. 5.25.* that hereafter fhe fhould be wholly for him. But yet tho fhe is betrothed already by the pledge of the fpirit, yet the marriage is not confummate, nor to be celebrated but in Paradife; where the firft was. This fecond Eve being as yet but in the forming, as it were, out of a crooked Rib by the hand of God; *Gen. 2. 21, 22.* in cleanfing, and purifying, and making white, *forgetting her own people and her Fathers houfe. Pf. 45. 10.* fo reproachful unto her future fplendors, &c. that fhe may be *prefented*, at that day not having *fpot or wrinkle*, or any fuch thing, a chaft Virgin, &c. See *2 Cor. 11. 2. Eph. 5. 27.* in dreffing and putting on her wedding Garments, that fhe *may not be found naked*; as, upon her fall, fhe was in Paradife. See *2 Cor. 5. 3. Rev. 3. 18. Rev. 19. 7, 8. -16. 5. Matt. 22. 11.*

Head and Members. This every where occurring. Head, Members. Root

108   *The benefits of our Saviour.*

Root, Branches. — **Root and Branches.** The new stock into which we are ingrafted and planted by Baptism, see *Jo.* 15. 1. &c. *Rom.* 6. 3, 4, 5. -11. 17. -15. 12.

Foundation, building. — **Foundation and Building**: built up a Temple, to be no more profaned and defiled, 1 *Pet.* 2. 4, 5. 1 *Cor.* 3. 16, 17. 1 *Cant.* 8. 9, 10. *Rev.* 21. 9. 10. *Eph.* 2. 20, 21. and Christ the *Corner stone, in whom* the two side-walls of Jew and Gentile *are joined. Eph.* 2. 14, 15.

Elder, younger brethren. — **Elder and younger Brethren**, in respect of God our common Father. *Jo.* 20. 17. The honor of which we shall the more value, when we consider such a a contemptible Prodigal, upon this relation only, so royally entertained. *Luk.* 15. Called also *the first born* consecrated to God for the rest. *The first fruits*; which under the law represented the whole. *Rom.* 11. 16. 1 *Cor.* 15. 20. *Rom-* 8. 29.

Hence all thing done by him, from these relations we have to him, are said also to be done by us, received by him to be received by us, done to him, to be done to us; and done to us, to him. So we now dead to sin. *Rom.* 6. 1. To the law. *Rom.* 7. 4. *Col.* 2. 20. To the world, the affections to it, *Gal.* 6. 14. Now risen, *Col.* 3. 1. now ascended and sitting in heavenly places. *Eph.* 2. 6. Sons of God, Heirs, *Gal.* 3. 27. See *Matt.* 25. 40, 45. Hence all Gods promises are fulfilled unto him, first in his human nature; and then descend only from and thro him, to us. And all that we return, (blessings ; prayer, &c.) ascend and are acceptable only thro him, and for his sake, to God. *Eph.* 1. 6. -3. 21.

Configuration as wrought by him, so to be advanced likewise by us. — But we must know, in this our new Creation and parentage, that (we being once created,) in all the business of our Salvation ; as God worketh in us, so we work together with God ; that there is a concatenation and conspiring of Gods grace and our will.

Chap. VI.

will. That as this new image of God is formed in us by his spirit, so by our endeavors; and that there is a configuration as effected by him, so required of us. A Configuration to all his vertuous and holy life here (many singular patterns of which are set down before) a Configuration to his sufferings and death, *Phil. 3. 10.* as it is, first in our Baptism, and for sins after Baptism ought to be in the painful fruits of repentance, abstaining from worldly pleasures; using the body hardly, &c. which are therefore called mortifications. A Configuration to his resurrection and life after it; In having our conversation in Heaven, *Phil. 3. 20.* living to God only, no more to affections of this life; ever worshipping, praising, loving, admiring, glorifying, offering up, and dedicating our selves to God. For so Saints live that are dead. See *Rev. 4. 8. &c. -5. 9, 12. &c. -7. 9. &c. Quicquid gestum est in sepultura, resurrectione, &c. ita gestum est ut configuretur vita humana quæ hic geritur.* For our participation of Christs merits is only by being his members (they can be communicated to none else); and our being members necessarily implies conformity, (in actions, suffering, &c.) to the Head. For that one should suffer and not the other is quite contrary to the nature of members, *1 Cor. 12. 26.* and argues schism in the body. Should any member therefore so presume on the obedience or sufferings of the head, as that himself now needs nor suffer nor obey; such a one without bearing its part and proportion therein, *Col. 1. 24.* either never was, or is ceased to be, a true member. Christ did nothing for our salvation, which we are not for it, in some sense, to do also our selves. *Gal. 6. 14. -9. 19, 20.*

CHAP. VII.

Jesus Christ *the Melchizedechical Holy Priest, passed into the Heavens, and making Intercession, &c. for ever for us with God.*

§. 1.
The Holy God not admitting to his service the approach of sinners.

GOD being of infinite Holiness and purity, to shew his hatred against sin, would not admit the approach of sinners into his Sanctuary and presence; nor accept (immediately) of their praiers and service offered to him: which, if any, after Discipline was settled, should have presumed to do, they were no less then to dy for it. See *Lev. 3. 10. 1 Sam. 6. 19. Numb. 4. 15. -16. chap. Job 9. 31. -42. 8.* But yet being of infinite mercy too, not to shut out sinners thus from all commerce with his goodness, he selected (from the beginning) some singular persons, taken from the rest of men [*no man taking this honor to himself but*

But of some chosen and consecrated persons in their behalf.

he that was called of God, Heb. 5. 1, 4.] and being first anointed, consecrated, and sanctified after an extraordinary manner, and cleansed with great Ceremony (after the more express delivering of his pleasure in the promulgation of the law, see *Exod. 29. chap. Lev. 8. 12.*) who should be *ordained for men in things pertaining to God, Heb. 5. 1. -2. 17.* who should have the *administration of holy things*, and nearer access to Gods presence; should bring unto the Lord the peoples gifts and offerings; *Heb. 5. 1. make attonement and reconciliation for their sins* and errors, &c. *Heb. 2. 17. Heb. 5. 2.* Amongst which ministers of the Sanctuary some were kept at a greater

CHAP. VII.

greater distance; as the Levite: who had the charge of the Tabernacle and the vessels thereof, and was to minister to the Priest, but might not come nigh the vessels of the Sanctuary or the Altar: [*that they dy not. Numb. 18. 3.*] Some approached nearer as the Priest; (confined to *Aaron* and his seed) who had *the charge of the Sanctuary and of the Altar*; who were to preserve themselves continually undefiled, *Lev. 21. 1. &c.* and amongst them, all such to be excluded from attendance, as had any corporal blemish, tho but a squint eye, or a flat nose, or a dwarf. *Lev. 21. 18. &c.* (The same perfection being required for the sacrificer that was for the Sacrifice, *Lev. 22. 20.*) to whom only it belonged, to offer the daily morning and even Sacrifice, and all other the peoples offerings upon it, and to make attonements for them; to sound with Trumpets (which none else might use) over the burnt and peace-offerings; [*that they might be for a memorial to the people before the Lord. Numb. 10.10.*] In sin-offerings to carry some of the blood into the outer Sanctuary, and to sprinkle part thereof before the Lord before the Veil, and to put also of it on the horns of the Altar of Incense before the Lord: Morning and Evening at the time of the sacrifice, to burn incense before the Veil upon the Altar of the Sanctuary; to dress the Lamps morning and evening, and every Sabbath to renew the shew-bread before the Lord; to discern between clean and unclean; holy and unholy: At the coming out of the Sanctuary, lifting up their hands towards the people, and putting Gods name upon them solemnly in a set form *Numb. 6. ¶, 24. &c. 2 Chron. 30. 27. Ecclus. 50. 5, 19. &c. 1 Chron. 23. 13.* to give the sacerdotal benediction

Some ministring at a greater distance; the Levite.

Some nearer, The Priest; of Aarons line only.

The benefits of our Savior.

ction; And as solemnly to bless, so also to curse. *Deut.* 27. 14. This for the Priest.

§. 2.
And nearer yet the High Priest.
His Office.

But the High Priest approached yet nearer to the Lord, much distinguished from the rest in his typical garments, who once yearly, on the grand day of Expiation, was to enter within the Veil into the *Sanctum Sanctorum* before the glory of the Lord, appearing between the Cherubims (he first making a cloud of Incense,) and there to present and sprinkle with his finger 7 times upon the mercy-seat it self, and seven times on the floor before it. *Lev.* 16. 14. the blood of the sacrifice made for the Priest and the people before the Lord; and to make attonement with it for the Priests, and for all the people; and not only for them, but also for all the holy things; the Tabernacle, the Holy Sanctuary, the Altar it self; to purge and resanctify, and (as if God was also displeased with these for sin) to reconcile them *Lev.* 16. 20. with blood; *to hallow them* (saith the Lord)*from the uncleannesses and transgressions of the children of Israel in the midst of whom they remained;* Such a contagion is our sin to the whole creation. See *Levit.* 16. 16, 19. and when he went in, he was to bear the names of the children of Israel engraven, and upon his two shoulders, and again engraven like the engraving of a Signet upon the brestplate of judgment upon his heart, [*for a memorial of them before the Lord continually. Exod.* 28. 12, 21, 29.] He was also to have engraven upon the front of his Miter in Gold, *Holiness unto the Lord.* [*And it shall be upon Aarons forehead that he may bear the iniquity of the Holy things of the children of Israel.* See *Numb.* 18. 1. *Lev.* 16. 16. *And it shall be alway upon his forehead, that they may be accepted before the Lord. Exod.* 28. 38.] And besides these *Urim* and

CHAP. VII.

and *Thummim* were likewife to be upon his heart; and in any thing doubtful the people were to repair unto him, and he by *Urim* was to ask counfel for them before the Lord, and according to his word they were to do. Laftly, the benediction of the people was in a fpecial manner conferred by him. See *Lev. 9. 22. Eccluf. 50. 5. &c.* Therefore in this Ceremony twice (viz. after the ending of the Sacrifice, and again after his coming out of the *Sanctum Sanctorum*) He folemnly in Gods name bleffed the people. See *Lev. 9. 22, 23.* Upon *Aarons* firft folemn bleffing them, fire came out from before the Lord to abide on the Altar for ever, verf. 24.

Now what was faid before of the Levitical Sacrifice is here to be faid again of the legal Priefts. They continuing finners as well after, as before, their confecration; and offering for their own faults, as well as for the peoples, *Heb. 5. 3.* (a finner for finners) were in themfelves ineffectual Interceffors before God; and, as it was impoffible for thofe facrifices to take away fins, fo for fuch Priefts (being finners and daily conforting with finners, and free from, only fome, not all defilements) to make any attonement; but only in relation to, and as types of, the other Prieft to come, who only was without blemifh, holy, undefiled, and feparate from finners. *Heb. 7. 26.* Add to this that the fervice they did in this office, was very incompleat; For they were not Interceffors before the Lord for all Nations, but prefented only the names of the twelve Tribes of Ifrael; and for them they knew not every ones diverfe confeffions and requefts; nor were able to make particular recommendation of thefe. Or if to recommend, yet had no ability to help fubnexed to their Interceffion for-them: which (we fhall fhew)

§. 3.
Aarons order of Priefthood imperfect, decaying, and except (typically) unferviceable.

P is

The benefits of our Savior.

is a priviledge of the true *Priesthood*: which is alwaies joined with Royalty and power. They entred into the Divine preſence but once a Year, and preſently came out again, did not abide, and wait, and ſit down there, to be perpetual Advocates with God for the people. And then the place, they went into, was not the true Sanctuary which the Lord pitched *Heb*. 8. 2. who, tho he is every where in his eſſence, yet is he only in Heaven as his dwelling place. *1 King*. 8: 39. *then hear thou in Heaven thy dwelling place.* The place of the appearance of his glory and Majeſty; of his Court and Attendants; of his throne where he gives audience unto all his Creatures, is there. But their ſanctuary *ſerved only unto the example and ſhadow of Heavenly things*. *Heb*. 8. 5. And the glory in it was but a ſhadow of his glory. *2 Cor*.*3*. *10, 11*. Laſtly, the Requeſts, they made in it, were rather about temporal then eternal things, about preſent and corporal, not future and ſpiritual. No new *Canaans* for us, no new *Jeruſalems*; no new eternal places of reſt prepared by them; no conferring alſo on all the people their Brethren, that ſacerdotal Honor to wait for ever on God in his holy Temple, which is the complement of all our felicity. Theſe benefits were reſerved to crown the interceſſions of another High Prieſt, of an higher Order.

§. 4.
This Order Expired. Jeſus Chriſt the true High Prieſt.

In the fulneſs of time therefore came the ſubſtance, of whom theſe were types; 1. As a Sacrifice without ſpot, ſo a ſacrifice without ſin; pure, without all blemiſh, not a bone of him broken, unharmable, undefiled, ſeparate from ſinners; not after a while decaying, but continuing for ever, at this day, at this hour; *The ſame yeſterday and to day and for ever*. *Heb*. 7. 24, 26. -*13*. *8*. 2. Tho thus perfect

CHAP. VII.

fect and perpetual; yet (which is strange) 1. one of our selves: a man as we; raised up from the midst of us; *of our brethren. Deut. 18. 15.* For this was altogether necessary for such an office, in which he was to be the Representative of his brethren. Therefore the legal High Priest appeared before the Lord, not only in his person like unto them; but with all their names engraven upon his breft; and this (faith the Text) *for a memorial of them before the Lord continually, Exod. 28. 12, 21.* and therefore the Apostle puts in the definition of an *High Priest, Heb. 5. 1.* [*Taken from amongst men*]. 2. Again, one he was that was to be *compassed with infirmity,* (for a while at least); that standing before the Lord he might have all compassion in him toward those, for whom he officiated; might be the more earnest; the more constant, and diligent; and know how more tenderly to present to the Holy Majesty the temptations, the miseries himself had experienced; and they also might have more confidence to commend their suits unto him, as being their brother; and once, as they, straitned. *Therefore 'tis a Rule, Heb. 2. 11.* [*He that sanctifieth and those who are sanctified are all of one*] and therefore this Priest, *for as much as the children were partakers of flesh and blood, did also himself likewise take part of the same,* v. 14. *not the nature of Angels but of man,* v. 16. *and was not ashamed to call them Brethren,* ver. 11. *and to be made like unto them in all things,* v. 17. and that for the foresaid ends; that he might be merciful, be faithful, unto them. *Heb. 2. 17, 18. -5. 1, 2. -4. 15.* Besides: Before Gods justice no intercession could be effectual without merit; (therefore mediation of sinners for sinners profits not) nor no merit, but in a condition and nature liable to temptations and sufferings;

Made li e unto His Brethren 1. in nature.

2 In the infirmities thereof.

sufferings; (at least such merit not serviceable in the behalf of men, where his merits are not in the same kind, as their demerits were;) and therefore there is the same reason of the humanity of our Savior, for his being a Priest, as for his being a sacrifice. *Called to this office and anointed by God.* 3. Thus being man, and man clothed with infirmity; fitted for this office; he was not appointed by himself, but *called* (as other Priests were) to this office; and *anointed by God.* Heb. 5. 4, 5. Heb. 3. 2. 2 Pet. 1. 17. Act. 10. 38. But far more glorified and honored in it, then any before him; God now anointing a Priest once, and for all; Heb. 7. 28. and not to the same order, of which the former were; (in many things, as is shewed before) deficient, but to the very best, that of *Melchisedeck*, i. e. *Of the order of Melchisedeck, i.e. Regal and Eternal.* a Priesthood everlasting and royal; and that had power joyned with Intercession; and the honor of sitting down by him, to whom he officiated. For *this man was counted worthy of more glory* then any before, *as being the builder*, and afterward, upon its ruin, rebuilder, *of this house* over which God thus made him Lord. Heb. 3. 3.

§. 5. *This Holy Priest offering the sacrifice, a sin-offering.* Thus made a Priest; now let us view the exact discharge of his office in the several parts thereof; and first the Priests office (for expiation of sin, &c.) being first to offer the sacrifice, and then to carry the blood thereof into the Sanctuary, and there make an attonement and intercession with it for the offenders. He therefore first offered the sacrifice, a sin-offering upon the altar of the Cross, such as never Priest offered before him: neither for the worth of it; being all-sufficient, (never any more sin-offering required after it, nor never any beneficial before it, but only thro it): nor for the nearness and dearness of it to the Sacrificer. *Abraham*, the

CHAP. VII.

the rigidst example we have, only offering to offer his son; But this Priest offered himself, and that voluntarily, and that coming out of the bosom of his Father, from the glory he had with him long before the world; i. e. coming out of the *Sanctum Sanctorum* to do it: (as wanting something when he was there before (notwithstanding those rivers of blood of Bulls and Goats that were shed before) with which to appease his Fathers justice) out of the infinite love he bare to sinners. [*Now once*, saith the Apostle, *in the end of the world he appeared to put away sin by the sacrifice of himself, Heb.* 9. 26.] and that sacrifice of himself by himself offered. See *Heb.* 7. 27. *Eph.* 5. 2. *Jo.* 10. 17, 18.

§. 6. *After this entring into the Sanctum Sanctorum.*

But his high, and that Melchisedechical i.e. eternal, *Priesthood* did not so much consist in this transitory act at the Altar, which any Priest might execute; but in the second carrying and appearing with the blood in the *Sanctum Sanctorum* before the Lord, &c. only performed by the *High Priest*. Therefore the Apostle placeth upon him *Priesthood after Melchisedecks order;* which could not be till he was King as well as Priest; not till after he was first risen from the dead, and made perfect (at which time also he was made King and Lord) when ascended and made higher then the Heavens, he had now no more conversation with sinners; was harmless, i. e. no more to be hurted; undefiled, i. e. that needed not to intermit, for this at any time, his office. See *Heb.* 7. 26. when, as before he had become weak, suffered and dyed for us, so now *he lived for evermore;* and was *set down on the Majesty on high, in the Sanctuary which the Lord had pitched;* and there had received all power, to help, to protect us; all gifts to showre down upon us. *We have such an High Priest.*

The benefits of our Saviour.

Priest (faith he): *Such an High Priest becomes us.* In this was his honor and glory above all Priests before him: and in this the certainty of our Salvation; when he is not only the meritorious cause, but the efficient; nor only the price, but Author of it. See *Heb.* 5. 4, 5. comp. 9. *Heb.* 5. 5. comp. *Act.* 13. 33. and *Pf.* 2. 7. comp. 8. *ask of me, &c. Heb.* 5. 9, 10. *being made perfect, called &c. Heb.* 6. 20. *forerunner, made &c.* See *Heb.*8.1,2,4. and 7.26. *Pf.* 110.4. comp. 1, 2. *Heb.* 8. 6. such a ministry following such a mediatorship.) Our Saviors death perfected his Oblation indeed but not his office; nor, our Salvation. And it is since that, that he daily procures, as we repent and believe, the application of the meritorious sacrifice to us, which he then made for us; and we are said no less to be saved by the sprinkling of his blood, which is done in the sanctuary now continually; then by the shedding of it which was done on the Cross. See *Heb.* 12, 24. *1 Pet.* 1. 2. *Heb.* 9. 19, 23. -13. 12. The price of our redemption was then laid down sufficient to satisfie justice, but not yet carried in and accepted by grace: (for tho the sacrifice was sufficient for all, yet it is effectual only to some [i.e. Believers] ; for whom as it was provided at first by meer grace, so by meer grace the satisfaction thereof (being none of theirs) is to them applied, *Heb.* 2. 9. (from whence Gods free grace, notwithstanding our Saviors merits, is so often put for the cause of our Salvation, see *Rom.* 4. 4,16.) before the throne of which grace he now went to appear with it. But then many things there are, besides the expiation of sins past, also necessary for the compleating of our salvation; which we are said to owe chiefly to our Saviors intercession: therefore, as we find our justification and remission of our sins

Without which his office had been imperfect and ineffectual.

(committed

CHAP. VII.

(committed before our conversion) ordinarily imputed to Chrifts death and refurrection; fo, our falvation; all the ftrengthning of us in our new life; that abundance of grace whereby we now ferve God; our confolation and protection in all afflictions, from all our enemies, in the fervice of him; the remiffion of our fins, when after baptifm and converfion relapfing into any faults, &c. are afcribed to our Saviors living evermore in this office of interceffion, and to his fitting now at Gods right hand with all power. See 1 *Jo*.2.1.*Rom*.5.10.-8, 31.*yea rather that he is now at the right hand, &c. and* who now can feparate? for *he is able to the uttermoft. Heb.* 7. 21. *Jo*. 14. 10. This, that we may not fo look on the paft benefits of our Savior, as not alfo to acknowledge, give thanks, and rejoyce in his prefent fervice for us; (which remainder of fervice to be performed after his paffion he feems to intimate in that fomewhat obfcure fpeech to *Mary Magdalene. Jo*. 20. 17. *Touch me not for I am not yet, &c.* i. e. the time of embraces and your full enjoyment of me is not (as you fuppofe it is) yet come, fee *Rev*. 19. 7. for all my bufinefs is not done,&c.) and may behave our felves as gratefully toward one from whom we have received fo rich favors; fo alfo dutifully towards one, on whom we depend for more.

§. 7. *He entring (thro the heavens) to the true fanctuary. The vail of the other being now rent and it made common.*

Now then to view in order the feveral offices this High Prieft after his facrificing did and doth for us: Firft then (the Holy Prieft entring into the *Sanctum Sanctorum* thro the vail) fo the flefh of the Son of God, being a vail, *Heb*. 10. 20. which contained within it, and hid, his Deity, was then rent, and this Holy Prieft now thro it, *Heb*. 9. 12. reentred into his former Majefty and glory before covered by it. Again upon the renting of this vail, *Matt*. 27. 50, 51.

50, 51. presently that in the Temple, that severed the Holy from the most holy, place, was rent also; by which, (the place within being now laid open and made common) was signified both a voiding of that former service of the Levitical *High-Priesthood*; and that the way was now admitted for this new Priest, having already slain his sacrifice, *Heb.* 9. 8. into another *true Sanctuary*, into a Sanctuary of the Lords own erecting, *not* at all *made with hands*; *Higher then the heavens*; to which sanctuary he passed thro the outer Tabernacle of these (which likewise was not made with hands) see *Heb.* 8. 2. -7. 26. -9. 11, 24. of which superceleftial sanctuary both that which was pitched by *Moses*, and that built by *Solomon* were representations; figures, examples, shadows, *Heb.* 9. 23, 24. -8. 5. both made; one *according to the pattern shewed to Moses in the Mount,* where Moses saw God as in a Sanctuary: See *Pf.* 68. 17. And God is said to descend upon it: *Exod.* 34. 5. -33. 21. as afterward upon the other, in a cloud to speak with *Moses*; the other to *David* 1 *Chron.* 28. 19. in a design. Of which heavenly Sanctuary we may have a divine sight a far-off from the several visions and apparitions of Gods glory: both those in the old Testament, see *Esai.* 6. 1. *Ezech.* 1. 4. -10. 1. &c. and those in the new to St. *John*. For 'tis worth the noting that not only Gods glory on the Mount to Moses, *Pf.* 68. 17. but in the heavens to St. *John,* appeared still as in a Temple, or Sanctuary, see *Rev.* 6. 9. -7. 15. -8. 3. -9. 13. -11. 1, 19. -13. 8. -14. 15, 18. -4. 5, 4. where is mention of the *Court, of the Altar of burnt-offerings. Rev.* 11. 1. and 6. 9. of the *Altar of Incense*; upon which were offered *Incense* together *with the Saints prayers,* see *Luk.* 1. 9, 10. comp. *Rev.* 8. 3. *of the Ark of the Covenant*; upon the

1 The description of this Sanctuary.

CHAP. VII.

the top or covering of which was the *Mercy-Seat*, or propitiatory, or throne of grace. For the *Ark*, *Cherubims*, &c. did alwaies reprefent a Throne or triumphant Charet; which befides the *Cherubims* (winged for flying, and footed in such a manner for running), had wheels alfo, for which fee (befides *Ezek.* 1. *chap*. in whofe vifions were oftentimes removals of this Charet or Throne from place to place, and *Dan.* 7. 9.) 1 *Chron.* 28. 18. where the Ark is called the *Charet of the Cherubims*. The *Cherubims*; the 4 *Beafts* (the fame with Ezekiels and Efaiahs) by whom Gods Throne was fupported, of all Creatures his neareft and moft vigilant *Rev.* 4. 6. *Ezek.* 1. 10. attendants; who gave out Gods orders to the reft of the Angels *Rev.* 15. 7. of the *Candleftick with* 7 *Lamps* of fire *burning before the Throne*; the reprefentation of the *Holy Ghoft* as appears by *Rev.* 1. 4. -5. 6. *Ezek.* 4. 2, 10. comp. with 6. *Act.* 1. 3. And, (which never appeared in the former vifions of the old Teftament) of a *Lamb that was flain* before the Throne; and about the Throne on either fide of it of 24 *Presbyters* in a Semicircle, fitting on feats reprefenting the *Church Triumphant*: and the Seffion of the *Prefident* and the Elders in the Jewifh Synagogue or Confiftory; and afterward of the Bifhop and his Presbyters in the Chriftian Churches: thefe encircled with a guard of millions of Angels *Rev.* 7. 11. *Rev.* 5. 11. Habited all like Priefts as alfo our Savior himfelf was in another vifion, *Rev.* 1. 13. *Exod.* 28. 40. *in linnen garments to the foot, white and refplendent*; and *girt about the paps, Crowns on their heads*. See *Exod.* 28. 40. like thofe of the Priefts for ornament and for glory: *Bearing his name on their foreheads*, *Rev.* 22. 4. (as the High Prieft did *holinefs unto the Lord*) Palms and *Inftruments of Mu-*
fick;

sick; and *Vials full of Incense in their hands*, celebrating divine service in this Temple; praising God, and the Lamb; and offering to him (as the Clergy here do) the praiers of the Saints; Praising the Lamb for the redemption of themselves, and of mankind. *Rev.* 5. 9, 10. comp. with 1. 6. Ready to comfort *John* about the power of the Lamb, *Rev.* 5. 5. and to instruct him concerning his suffering Brethren. *Rev.* 7. 13. see *Rev.* 4. 4. -6. 11. -7. 9. -15. 6.

§. 8.
2 *Of his person entring.*

Having thus made a description of the place, (the heavenly Sanctuary and the propiatory or throne of grace there, over the Ark compassed with 4 Cherubims, &c.) according as the Lord Jesus was pleased to represent it to St. *John*: Here first now let us imagine to enter and present himself this great High Priest soon after his work finisht upon the Altar of the Cross; such as he is described, *Heb.* 7. 26. *Holy, unharmable, undefiled, separate from sinners*, needing no washing first, as the Legal did; arrayed with all the truth and substance of those things, which were typified by the ornaments of the legal High Priest, bearing our names upon his shoulders. *Esai.* 53. 6. -9. 6. *Esai.* 63. 9. and again engraven as a Signet upon his heart, according to *Cantic.* 8. 6. *Hagg.* 2. 23. for a *memorial of us before the Lord continually. Exod.* 28. 12, 21. &c; Having engraven upon his Miter *Holiness* [pure and never stained] *unto the Lord*, that so his holiness may *bear the iniquities of our holy things*, and we in and by it may be accepted before the Lord (he *being made unto us wisdom and righteousness and sanctification and redemption. Numb.* 18. 1. *Exod.* 28. 38. 1 *Cor.* 1. 30. *Rom.* 5. 19.) appearing again a *Priest* with the restord *Urim* and *Thummim Ezra* 2. 63. upon his heart, light and perfection; perfect wisdom and perfect righteousness;

CHAP. VII.

teousness; opening the book of all Gods secrets, and shewing them, as he pleaseth, to his Brethren, *Rev.* 5. 5. -1. 1. *Numb.* 27. 21. by the *Holy Ghost*, *Jo.* 16. 13, 14. as it first hears and receives from him. thus passing thro the outer Sanctuary of the heavens, *Heb.* 9. 11. whilst it is proclaim'd before him, *Behold the Lamb of God, &c. my servant whom I have chosen : my Beloved in whom my soul is well pleased*, Let us imagine him, I say, in such equipage to appear in this *Sanctum Sanctorum* before that *Mercy-Seat*, that throne of grace, and to appear in the presence of God there, *not for himself, but for us*, saith the Apostle, *Heb.* 9. 24. -8. 1. for himself had that *glory* there *with his Father before the world was*, and came down out of his bosom for this purpose (for he that would ascend thus must be such a one that descended first) that he might return thither with these new engagements upon him, with a great many names besides his own, new relations and new kindred, entring in thither now for his poor Brethren.

§. 9
Carrying in the sacrifice.

Thus entred, first into this Sanctuary he carries with him not only the blood, but the whole sacrifice, being restored unto him, (after he had offered it as an entire Holocaust, and poured out all the blood thereof at the foot of the Altar) to offer it here a second time to the acceptation of his Father. See *Heb.* 8. 3. comp. 9. 7. carries it with all the wounds, and piercings made in it as honourable marks of his sufferings, and remembrances thereof to his Father, (which 'tis probable that his glorified body still retains); appearing in his Father sight a Lamb as it had been slain. See *Rev.* 5. 6. as also he appeared before for confirming the faith of his Disciples, *Jo.* 20. 27. to which the Apostle alludes,

Q 2   *Gal.*

Gal. 6. 17. and (likely) shall appear at the last day, to the everlasting reproach of his enemies. See *Rev.* 1. 7. In memory whereof also the very Altar (the Cross) is imagined to be that, which is called *the sign of the son of man, Matt.* 24. 30. and which shall appear in the heavens, and be carried before as his royal Ensign in his procession to the last judgment. Which Sacrifice since he appoints here (in the consecrated elements) to be shewed forth by his Priests in our Sanctuaries before God, in commemoration of him ; how much more in that above is it solemnized for us by himself our High Priest? That as the *bow* was *set in the Cloud*, that God looking upon it might remember his Covenant, and forbear to bring a second deluge upon the earth, *Gen.* 9. 16. and the *blood of the Paschal Lamb* was *stricken on the door posts*, that the Lord seeing it there might pass over them with his plague; So when he beholds these wounds, (given our Savior for our sin) displaid before him, he may forbear to revenge sin any more upon his Brethren. And if *Pilate* shewing that our suffering Savior with an *Ecce Homo* thought the beholding such a pitiful and cruel spectacle was enough to have melted the hardhearted Jews his malicious enemies into some mercy and compassion, so as to prosecute his death no further: How much more will such a pale and wanner sight, as was seen afterward upon the Cross,of an only Son voluntarily undergoing all this for our sin, move a pitiful and merciful father no further to prosecute the vengeance thereof upon his brethren, upon his own members ? A second Action there is sprinkling of his blood upon, and before, the Mercy-Seat, not 7, nor 77 times, but continually : and note that all blood-shed, when it comes before the Lord, hath a loud

And sprinkling the blood before the Lord.

CHAP. VII.

loud cry. See the blood of the Saints, *Rev. 6.10.* And *Abels. Gen. 4. 10.* And the Apostle compares the sprinkling of our Saviors blood, for its speaking and crying, unto the sprinkling of *Abel's,* tho His cried not the same way; for it pleaded for mercy as the other for vengeance. For we receive a true attonement, are sanctified, are purifyed (as many of us as serve the Lord) by *the sprinkling of the blood of Jesus.* See *1 Pet.* 1. 2. *Heb.* 12. 24. -13. 12. [Not that our Savior there really sprinkled his blood for us, let none grosly imagine this, for flesh and blood enter not into heaven, *1 Cor.* 15. but that he now by it (poured out by him on the Cross,) in the heavenly Sanctuary procures all the effects, obumbrated by the former sprinkling of the blood of the legal Sacrifices.] Therefore tis observed that the Apostle faith he *entred by it,* not *with* it. *Heb.* 9. 12, 23. Who is therefore called, for this Celestial ceremony before the propitiatory, or throne of grace, our ἱλασμὸς *propitiation.* 1 *Jo.* 2. 2. and our ἱλαστήριον *propitiatory. Rom.* 3. 25. Thus he sprinkled his blood to make attonement for, and to sanctify, us; but, as we read that the legal High Priest purified also the Sanctuary it self, and reconciled the Holy place (said to be defiled by being in the midst of the peoples uncleanness. See *Lev.* 18. 25, 28.) the Apostle makes this also run parallel for our Savior, *Heb.*9.23. by which, as is signifyed the purifying of all the Creatures and particularly of all our imperfect holy services unto us, so perhaps something more may yet be gathered from, *Col.* 1. 16, 20. -2. 10. *Job.* 15. 15.·-4. 18. -25. 5. 2 *Pet.* 3. 7, 12. *Rom.* 8. 22. well considered: for all Principalities and Thrones, i. e. Angels, were made *by him* at first, and *for him*: and by him they now consist; and of them also he is the head; and by

him

him they are said to be reconciled; thro him they are now confirm'd in grace, and perhaps at the laft day thro him shall be advanced in glory; And perhaps the upper regions of the world may be said in some sense to be contaminated (as the earth) by mans, or the faln Angels sin: to which heavenly things also the vanity, bondage, groaning of the Creatures mentioned *Rom*. 8. may extend; which also are said by *Peter* to be reserved, and that they shall be diffolved, and, as it were, purified by fire. But *abscondita Domino Deo nostro, manifesta nobis*.

§. 10. *Making Intercession*.

3. After this appearing there with this Sacrifice, and sprinkling of his blood, follows his *Intercession* also there for us. *Rom*. 8. 34. *Heb*. 7. 25. *Esai*. 53. 12. -59. 16. another office of the Prieft for the People, whose making attonement was not without praier, since this also is called *making attonement*. *Exod*. 32. 30. and so where we tranflate *making attonement* the vulgar renders it *praying for, &c.* See *Lev*. 16. 7, 34, 17. *Quando Pontifex fanctuarium ingreditur, ut roget pro se & pro universo cætu Ifrael*; see *Job*. 42. 8. *Gen*. 20. 7. which appears also by the continual practife of the Priefts and Prophets praying for the people. *Jer*. 7. 16. -27. 18. *Ezra*. 10. 4. *Joel*. 1. 13, 14.

1 *In presenting his own praiers to the Father for us.*

-2. 17. 2 *Chron*. 30. 27. 1. And this firft in presenting continually his own praiers to the Father for us; in which respect he is called also παράκλητος our *Advocate with the Father*; as well as the *Holy Ghoft* is called παράκλητος the Advocate to the Father here on earth with, or in us: (As the spirit is also ftiled by his title of *Intercessor*, here; as he there, *Rom*. 8. 26, 27.) and therefore what office in prayer, when any one fins or suffers, this *Advocate* doth here on earth refiding with us, 1 *Jo*. 5. 7, 8. see *Rom*. 8. 26. the other *Advocate* doth the same in heaven, refiding

Chap. VII.

ing with the Father and with the same unexpressible zeal. The better to conceive which, imagine *Aaron, Numb.* 16. 47. when wrath was gone out from the Lord, *standing with his Censer in his hand between the living and the dead,* and staying the plague: or *Moses,* that great type of him, *Deut.* 18. 15. *like unto me,* his pathetical intercessions, and deprecations so many times for the sinning Israelites: continuing 40 daies at a time with the Lord in supplication for them and for their Priest, see *Exod.* 32. comp. with *Deut.* 9. 18, 20. *Numb.* 14. 13. &c. and proceeding even to *wishing himself accu sed* in their stead (as also did St. *Paul,* but our Savior only was he that really *became* also *a curse* for others) and then be sure our High Priest now makes the same; nay far greater; as much more concerned in our safety, being Master over the house, in which *Moses,* tho a faithful, yet was but, a servant. The exact matter and manner of whose intercessions above, tho it is not manifested unto us, yet what esteem of it and confidence in it may we not have ? [therefore our Mother the Church thinks fit to finish all her prayers in it] if we consider, first that infinite love wherewith he now loveth us. (How can it be silent !) *Eph.* 3. 19. *from which neither things present, nor things to come, neither heights nor depths,* &c. *can ever separate us. Rom.* 8. 38, 35. comp. with 34. 2. The promises which he made in that last comforting Sermon immediatly before his death and departure from hence; the summ of which is to assure his Disciples, and consequently all believers, see *Jo.* 17. 20. of the great care he would take for them in heaven; where also he particularly promiseth to *pray the Father for them,* who was *greater then he,* [and therefore they might rejoyce they had such a friend with him, see

Jo.

Jo. 14. 16, 28. -16. 7, 26.] tho he assured them of his Fathers great affection to them for his sake, even in case himself should not pray for them. 3. His long (many whole nights) and assiduous practises of prayer here on earth, (doubtless for them and us,) tho importuned with so much other business. S. *Peters* suddain repentance and tears, *Matt.* 26. 75. came from his intercession, *Luk.* 22. 32. 4. If we consider the matter of that (one only long) praier of his, that is set down, *Jo.* 17. after his work was finisht here; and he was to leave his Disciples here on earth to the custody of his Father. Ver. 12, 13. And, some part of his Church now and till the end of the world having the same necessities; Many sheep that were not of that fold, of whom he saith also that he must bring them in, *Jo.* 10. 16. How can he not continue for them the same petitions, till he be made compleat also in the whole Church his body? Neither praied he then *for* his *Apostles alone, but for them also that should believe on him thro their word,* vers. 20. for our sanctification, vers. 17. for our perfecter union with him and the Father in this world, vers, 11. 21. for our glorification with him in heaven, vers. 24. Perfectly knowing every ones infirmities. A particular Advocate as any one of his Servants *Heb.* 5. 9. sinneth, procuring remission, 1 *Jo.* 2. 1. and infinitely pitying every ones condition. An Advocate as any one of his is tempted and afflicted, procuring succour, and watching that their suffering may not be beyond their ability, *Heb.* 2. 18. and perfectly foreseeing all their dangers. An Advocate begging deliverance from future evils; as he did here on earth for *Peter,* when Satan would have sifted him [*but I have praied for thee that thy faith fail not*] *Luk.* 22. 23. and going away; for his

CHAP. VII.

his Disciples left behind: [*Father I desire not to have them quite taken out of the world, but keep thou them in it from the evil*, verf. 15. from their powerful and invisible enemy, and from all those wolves among among whom I leave them. Think we then the Shepheard of Ifrael now sleepeth? But we must not let this pass unnoted; That his *Intercession* who is alwaies heard, (for he asketh according to the will of God, *Rom.* 8. 27.) never asketh such things, as God hath decreed by no praiers to be exorable in; As to be capable of his mercies and favors, there are some dispositions prerequisite in the person. See *Ezek.* 14. 3, 5, 14. For such therefore, as want these, our Savior perfectly knowing his Fathers will can ask nothing absolutely, that is against it. Tho with a velleity (if you will) now, (as when he praied in the Garden for himself, or for his enemies when on the Cross, *Luk.* 23. 34.) he desires or wisheth mercy even for all, even for those who shall never receive any. *Velleity* I say, *qua hoc vellet, si aliud non obsisteret*, but his intercession with an absolute will (which is alwaies conform to his Fathers, and so alwaies fulfilled by his Father) is not general and for all; (so we might think it frustrated) but for those that are, or will be rightly disposed, and are, or are to be, of his Church; (even as the High Priest carried in before the Lord only the names of the twelve Tribes.) *I pray for them*, saith he, *I pray not for the world, Jo.* 17. 9. not for those, who have the devil for their Father, 1 *Jo.* 3. 8. not for the man of sin, and those persecutors of his Church; Against whom we may imagine he now deprecates his Father in behalf of the Church, in that form, *Rev.* 6. 10. *How long Lord*, &c. *Pf.* 44. 9, 17. and *Zech.* 1. 12. *How long*, &c. which Angel was the Son of God: and re-

R   ceives

The benefits of our Saviour.

ceives from him that answer in the Psalmist. *Ps.*110.1. *Sit thou on my right hand, till I make, &c.* whom he will at last utterly destroy at his coming; for *there is a sin we may not*, therefore neither doth he, *pray for. 1 Jo. 5. 16.* And this much more indears his intercessions unto his, since they are not common for all; and let us *take heed least there be in any of us an heart of unbelief, Heb. 3. 12.* either not to enter at all, or to run out of, this fold; either not to be ingrafted into, or to be cut off from, his body; and so be made uncapable and loose our share of such dear intercessions and omnipotent praiers, by virtue of which 'tis not possible for the elect to miscarry. *Matt. 24. 24.*

§. 11.
2 In presenting also our praiers and oblations to the Father.

The sacrifices and oblations of Christians.

2. And as this our High Priest intercedes and offers up his own praiers for us, so he offers up all ours too. For God, under the Gospel, is served with spiritual sacrifice, as under the law he was with carnal; both with *sin-offerings* our Confessions; and *peace-offering*, our giving of thanks, of praise and glory unto him; and *Free-will-offerings*, our restraint of some lawful liberty, when this any way conducing more to his service; and *whole burnt-offerings*, our resignation and dedicating of all we have and are to the promoting of his glory. So our praiers are called *Incense*, and the *morning and evening Sacrifice. Rev. 5. 8. Ps. 141. 2.* Our praise the *calves of our lips.* See *Heb. 13. 15.* comp. with *Hos. 14. 2. Ps. 50. 14, 15.* preferred before all the Herds on the Mountains; all our words and actions, even to our eating and drinking, required to have a special dedication to God. *Col. 3. 17. 1 Cor. 10. 31.* And as all our actions, that are by the soul, so all our passions and sufferings, that are by the body, are sacrifices too, and much more properly such, then the former;

CHAP. VII.

former; so both those mortifications and crucifyings of the flesh by our selves, whether for the wiping away, or for the prevention of sin, and killing of our brutish lusts now instead of slaying of beasts, or our patient and contented undergoing those sent from God for sin, are no mean sacrifices: see *Ps.* 51. 16, 17. *Thou delights not, &c. The sacrifices of God are a broken spirit; a broken and a contrite heart, &c.* And those sufferings in the flesh from others, (for righteousness sake, or for the glory of God, or for the benefit of our Brethren,) when we instead of the blood of Beasts, offer up our own to God; and undergo Martyrdom for his sake, this is the highest sacrifice of all, and so St. *Paul* calls his. 2 *Tim.* 4. 6. *Phil.* 2. 17. 2 *Cor.* 12. 15. And these sufferings also our Savior presents to God, as he doth those of his own body; for we also are his body, and as he offers up himself, so us, to the Father. *Tota congregatio societasque sanctorum, universale sacrificium offertur deo per sacerdotem magnum.* Aug. Civ. Dei l. 10. And as spending of our lives for God and our Brethren; so the spending of our Estates; all our Alms, and charities are Evangelical Gifts, and Oblations, and Sacrifices (therefore many times anciently made by Christians at the Altar.) See *Heb.* 13. 16. *Phil.* 4. 18. [*I have received, &c. the things that were sent from you an odour of a sweet smell, a sacrifice acceptable, &c.*] All our doings, then, and all our sufferings; our souls and our bodies, *Rom.* 12. 1. the spending of our lives and of our estates; all these make up one compleat *Holocaust*, which we owe unto God under the Gospel; (of which those under the Elements of the world were types, and in which they are fulfilled;) after that our Savior had first begun to us; and sacrificed, instead of Beasts, himself.

1 *Pet.* 2. 5. *Col.* 1. 24. Now these the peoples sacrifices under the Gospel, as those under the Law, must of necessity have a Priest to offer them for the reason mentioned: not only because they are so nothing worth, the best we can bring of them; and so unprofitable when we have done all we can; and God so self all-sufficient without them; whose offerings to him whatever are only his gifts to us 1 *Chron.* 29. 14. (all of us but our sins being his;) but because, by contagion of sin in us they are also all unclean (for *who can bring a clean thing out of an unclean? Job.* 14. 4.) and he so pure and so holy; that we are in the same condition as *Uzziah* 2 *Chron.* 26. 18. or *Nadab* and *Abihu,* unless there be one to *bear the iniquity of our holy things,* and thro whose merits towards God, and Gods love unto him, they may be accepted. To whom, methink, God speaks as *Moses. Exod.* 19. *Do thou come up, &c. but let not the people, least I break forth upon them.* And unto us as disguised *Joseph* did to his brethren; *see not my face unless you bring your Brother with you.* Or as God to to the Friends of *Job.* 42. c. 8. v. *Take with you a sacrifice and go to my servant Job, and my servant Job shall pray for you, for him I will accept;* or as to *Abimelech* concerning *Abraham. Gen.* 20. 7. *He is a Prophet and he shall pray for thee, and thou shalt live.* For these intercessors were set down for types of this supreme Mediator.

§. 12. By our Savior therefore all these our Sacrifices must be offered, or by us in his name, which is all one, *Phil.* 1. 11. and that, not only our praiers and petitions, where we need and ask something, that they may be heard thro Jesus Christ our Lord; but our giving of thanks and glory to God; (Alas what glory can we give?) where we present something,
that

CHAP. VII.

that they may be accepted. We then first come to him; and he offers them for us: so we are said *to praise, to give thanks, to give glory to God, by him.* See *Heb. 13. 15. Rom. 1. 8. Col. 3. 17. 1 Pet. 2. 4, 5.* Therefore he stiles himself *the way to the Father. Jo. 14. 6. and the door Jo. 10. 9.* thro which we must pass. *And to God be glory in the Church by Christ. Eph. 3. 21.* The tongue being in the head, that speaks for the body.

3. But thirdly, he not only presents and delivers our petitions for us, &c. but he hath procured for us free admission to the Father, to deliver them our selves; not in a body by presence indeed as yet, but by the spirit; *Eph. 2. 18.* and sent us unto the Father to ask any thing in his name; see *Jo. 16. 23, 24, 26, 27.* (according to which the Church directs her praiers not to him (as he saith vers. 23.) but to the Father) telling us that *the Father himself* for his sake, *loveth us,* vers. *27. Eph. 1. 6. Rom. 8. 39. love of God which is in Christ Jesus our Lord.* In this far outdoing the mediation under the law, where *Moses* indeed went up, but the people were rail'd out, and trembling and quaking stood afar off: which preeminence of us the Apostle often intimates in the Epistles. *Heb. 12. 17.* By him therefore now we also are said to *draw nigh unto God; to have access to the Father; access with boldness;* to *come boldly unto the throne of grace; into the Holiest, Heb. 10. 19, 22.* all our words and works to be accepted, if done in his name, &c. See *Heb. 4. 16. Eph. 5. 20. Heb. 7. 19, 25. Eph. 2. 18. -3. 12. Col. 3. 17.* And for these causes above-said it is, that the Church so often in all Divine service repeats that holy dear name; and St. *Paul* ('tis noted) in his Epistles above 500 times; because to, by, thro, and in Him

§. 13.

3 *In procuring our admission to deliver them our selves unto the Father.*

and

and his name are all things, said and done, and to be done, that are well and acceptably done. Which name be it blessed for ever.

§. 14.
The benefits of his intercession.

4. After these acts of this High Priests intercession, let us now proceed to the fruits and benefits thereof. And first. As the legal High Priest first after he had offered the sacrifice, and again after he had carried in the blood into the Holyest, *blessed and put Gods name upon the people. Lev. 9. 22. &c. Numb. 6. 27.* So our Savior (answerable to the first) before he went into the Sanctuary, *Luk. 24. 50.* and at other times blessed his people; and (answerable to the second) also doth it since his going in (blessing us from it, because, by his everlasting Priesthood needing to make no more offerings, he is not to come out of it, till the consummation of all things; when he will yet in a more transcendent manner give us his blessing:) See *Act. 3. 26.* and what the blessing, that he sent us, was, see *Act. 2. 33.* Upon whose blessing us from above, that fire *Act. 2. 2.* descended upon the Apostles, and consequently upon his Church ever since; of which that material one which came out from before the Lord upon Aarons first blessing was a type, *Lev. 9. 24.* Imagine him then (first) now speaking from Heaven, putting his Fathers name upon us, and pronouncing that form, *Numb. 6. 24.* and then after it, all those spiritual and temporal blessings and deliverances of his Church here, showred down by him; but above all that fire of the Holy Spirit for ever burning upon the Altar of our hearts, and hallowing all our sacrifices, and elevating them unto God; the manifold gifts and graces of which are mentioned elsewhere. Only here take notice, 1. Of the time of their collation; and that was after his being ascended,

Procuring us the Holy Spirit from the Father.

And all blessings spiritual and temporal.

CHAP. VII.

scended, and entred into the Sanctuary and having interceded there. See *Jo.* 7. 39. -16. 7. *Act.* 2. 33. *Eph.* 4. 7, 8. *Jo.* 14. 28, 29. So that we have and do receive far greater advantages by his absence and service there, then we could by his corporal presence here; (Blessed be God by whose wisdom all things serve for our good!) as also appears in his Disciples; far more expert in knowledg; powerful in working, (according to the promise *Jo.* 14. 20.) after his departure. 2. Of the manner of their conveyance (which will much advance our confidence, if we consider our near relation.) For we receive them not by his procurement only from the Father, but even from his own hand. *Every good and perfect gift cometh from the Father, &c. Jam.* 1. 17. but thro, and by immediate donation of the Son; and by the same way as all our praiers and sacrifices ascend, and enter in, blessings come forth of, this Sanctuary. Upon his asking all things are given him, *Psal.* 2. 8. (whom the Father alwaies hears) and at his own pleasure he dispenseth them. *Act.* 2. 33. *Eph.* 1. 3. And this, the having in his own power the gift of all things (from whose hands we may be sure we shall want nothing) belongs peculiarly to the tenure of his Priesthood; being Melchisedechial and joyned with Kingship: *Sacerdotium Regale,* or *Sacerdotale regnum,* i. e. having royalty and power joyned with it; as before the law these two were joyned in the Princes of families, so after the law they are united in Christ, a King over all; but Him, whom, as a Priest, he serves. Therefore we find him sitting at the right hand; and the promise of having his enemies made his footstool so frequently joined with his Priesthood and intercession; for to shew the everlasting power of his Priesthood. See *Heb.*

Himself immediatly conferring them upon us.

From his Kingly Priesthood.

Heb. 8. 1. Rom. 8. 34. Pſ. 110. 1. comp. with 4. *Act. 2. 33. Pſ. 2. 8.* Therefore since *he ever liveth to make interceſſion, he is able to ſave* (faith the Apoſtle) not willing only, *Heb. 7. 25. Able to ſuccour, Heb. 2. 18.* ſee *Jo. 17. 2, 24. Father I will that,* &c. *Jo. 14. 13, 14.* [*If ye ſhall ask any thing in my name* (his asking or our asking in his name is all to one effect, as is ſhewed before) *I will do it*] where he ſhews both his dependance on his Father as a Prieſt, and power over all things elſe as a King.

§. 15.
As High Prieſt interceſſor, anſwering to Aaron.
Beſides this officiating as an Interceſſor ; in Heaven as a Sanctuary, (as he is High Prieſt ;) wherein he is compared to *Aaron ;* Our Savior, (by the ſame Apoſtle in his treatiſe of his Prieſthood) is called *the Captain of our Salvation bringing many ſons of God unto glory. Heb. 2. 10. Lord of the houſhold* of God ; and conducter of them into a promiſed place of reſt, and *forerunner entred before them* into Heaven, as it is the land of promiſe ; and this as he is a
So by his royal Prieſthood Captain of Gods people, anſwering to Moſes.
regal High Prieſt, wherein he is compared to *Moſes,* and *Joſhua* his ſucceſſor, conducters of *Iſrael* towards *Canaan.* See *Heb. 2. 10. -3. 1, 2, 6. -4. 8, 9, 14. -6. 20.* comp. with *Heb. 12. 1, 2, 18, 22, 25. -11. 14, 16.* We being in this world after our deliverance from Egypt, the dominion of Satan and ſin ; and paſſing thro the Red Sea of Baptiſm, 1 *Cor. 10. 2.* yet, as in the Wilderneſs ; a *dry and thirſty land where no water is* (as the Pſalmiſt ſpiritually complains of it, ſee *Pſal. 63. 1. -39. 12. -119. 19.* whoever take it for any thing elſe much miſtake it *)* now under Chriſt (I ſpeak of him according to his manhood) our Conductor ; as they were under *Moſes* and *Joſhua*) and all things that were done there were examples. *1 Cor. 10. 6, 11.* Firſt therefore as *Moſes,* [when the mount of God burnt with fire,
nothing

CHAP. VII.

nothing but *blackness, and darkness, and tempest*; nothing but wrath and judgment towards us, and fear least the fire of the Lord should break forth upon us, having all sinned as Israel had, and none durst draw near to speak for us.] Behold him coming forth out of the midst of us (the true Mediator) and going for us into the Mount; and there like *Moses*, *Exod.* 32. 30. making an attonement for us. And tho there is yet to come another shaking of all things, shaking heaven and earth and all in pieces under this second *Moses*, *Heb.* 12. 26. far more terrible then that under the first; wherein he shall come in judgment to destroy his enemies, from which then there shall be no Mediator to hinder him, as *Exod.* 32. 10, 11. yet then to those that obey him, this Mount Sinai shall be changed into Mount Sion, and *the city of the living God*, &c. see *Heb.* 12. 22. &c. where are such and such glorious company. And thither shall he also carry up his Brethren after the remainder of the 40 daies, or 6 weeks of his abode there are expired. Meanwhile from thence, not from an higher place of the earth, but from the highest heaven into which he is gone up, he continually speaks unto us not with that terror as the Angels from Mount Sinai gave the law, but with the soft voice of his spirit, the ministration of which by him is opposed to that of the law by *Moses*. 2 *Cor.* 3. 8, 9. And wo be to all them, that refuse to hear him far beyond those that refused to hear *Moses*. *Heb.* 12. 25. -10. 29.   2. And then, as resembled by 2 *To Joshua*. *Joshua* or *Jesus*, (called so as a type of him) he is the Conductor also of the people of God into the true land of promise, *Heb.* 4.8. the place of rest; the rest of God. *Heb.* 4. 5. Into which God hath sworn no unbelievers shall enter. And into this our blessed
S   Savior

The benefits of our Savior.

Savior is *entred already before us, and set down* (the posture of resting) *at the right hand of God;* entred not only as a forerunner *Heb. 6. 20.* or leader; to give an example, that we should follow him thither; the Anchor of our hope being already cast within the veil, by the taking possession of this our fore-runner. *Heb. 6. 19, 20.* But also a forerunner or Harbinger (as *Joshua* his type also was) to view that good land as it were, and there to prepare a place for us, *Jo. 14. 2, 3. in* that *house where are many mansions* (the heavens that we see, being but a center to it, from whence God looks down upon them as they upon the earth, *Ps. 113.*) not any therefore, but an honourable, a choice place there; see *Rev. 4. 4.* where the Church-men were sitting on either side of Gods Throne in the midst of all the glorious train of Heaven, and the Angels standing in a circle about them. *Rev. 5. 11. -7. 11.*] *Father I will, that those be with me where I am, to behold my Glory, &c. Jo. 17. 24.*] not in the same region, but in the same place of it where his glorious body is; not in the Country only, but of the Court; *following* and waiting on *the Lamb there where ever he goeth;*] which is named as some special honour, *Rev. 16. 4. -7. 15. -3. 4.* And from thence after this place prepared for us, and us for it, he hath promised to come again and accompany us thither in person. (Thus is he a forerunner to all the faithful, in respect of their bodies entring into that celestial Canaan; he being the first-born from the dead: but again forerunner (according to the opinion of antiquity) of the souls too; entring into the heavenly Sanctuary, in respect of the spirits not only of all Saints dying since him (of this no question,) but of all those that deceased before him from the beginning;

And the forerunner into the place of rest.

CHAP. VII.

beginning; the very firſt into this Sanctuary; as none ever entred (for the cauſe) but by, and in relation to, him; ſo none (for the time) before him; which opinion ſeems to be ſtrengthned from the expreſſions of our Savior concerning *Lazarus*. That *He* i. e. his ſoul. (as *Luk*. 21. 43. this day ſhalt thou i. e. thy ſoul) *was carried by Angels into Abrahams boſom*, as being Father of the faithful; a place of bliſs doubtleſs, [being oppoſed to the other's place of torment,] wherein *Lazarus* received conſolations; but now we are ſaid to be gathered unto Chriſt after this life; we, and *Abraham*, and all into Chriſts boſom ours, and *Abrahams*, Father. See *2 Cor.* 5. 1. *&c. Phil.* 1. 23. *Act.* 7. 59. *Eph.* 1. 10. Again; as 'tis ſaid in general. *Heb.* 9. 8. That *the way into the holieſt was not made manifeſt under the old Teſtament;* ſo in particular of the Saints of it, that they *received not the promiſes before us*. Which may be interpreted not only of the promiſes of the Meſſias; but alſo of thoſe obtained thro him ſpoken of, verſ. 13, 14, 16. that *they without us were not made perfect*, *Heb.* 11. 40. and perhaps in reſpect of this is the ſame term uſed, *Heb.* 12. 23. of *the ſpirits of juſt men* [now] τελειωθῶσι made *perfect* i. e. admitted into the Holieſt by τ*ῇ* ἀ*.*ϟ*ρωμῶσι. and with our Savior; (according to the hymn, *having overcome death thou openedſt the kingdom of heaven to all;*) Therefore none of the old Teſtament Celeſtial viſions have any repreſentation of any Church there; none of the new are without it. See *Rev.* 4. 4. *Heb.* 12. 22, 23. where ſetting down the Court of Heaven he numbers the *ſpirits of juſt men*, and the πρωτότοκ*ο*ι (probably) the ſame with thoſe *primitiæ*. *Rev.* 14. 4. To this purpoſe ſome apply *Zech.* 9. 11, 12. comp. 9. *Jo.* 14. 3. *Matt.* 25. 6, 10. Into which, notwithſtanding the good tidings this *Joshuah* hath told us of it, *many fail to enter in*, partly *thro unbelief* of the glory and riches of that place beyond this Egypt, or Wilderness; like those *Numb.* 14. chap. longing and lusting after denyed Onyons and Garlick, whilst they are fed with Manna: and partly thro cowardliness of not fighting their carnal lusts, and withstanding the pleasures of this present life, the enemies and Gyants which hinder them from possessing this Holy land; which, notwithstanding this *Joshua*, and his faithful Souldiers have in many battails discomfited before them. But, *seeing there remaineth a rest, Heb.* 4. 9. and seeing *we have a great High Priest that is passed*, &c. v. 14. *let us lay aside every weight and run with patience, &c. looking unto Jesus, &c. who is set down there. Heb.* 12. 1, 2. that at the last we may be made partakers of of Christ. *Heb.* 3. 14.

§. 16.
The substitutes of this Priest in his own (necessary) absence here on earth
1 *To present his sacrifice.*

Thus much of our Saviors officiating in this perpetual Office of Priest above. But; 1. As God also still retains Sanctuaries on Earth, there are certain persons substituted by him in the same sacred office, to do that in these earthly, which their Master doth in the Heavenly Church. 1. By whom first the sacrifice of his body and blood is presented here unto God for a remembrance of him unto the Father, in the consecrated elements, for all the same purposes, for which it is presented by our great High Priest there; i. e. for all the purposes for which he offered it first on the Cross. See *Mal.* 1. 11. *Gal.* 3. 1. *Itaque veteres in hoc mystico sacrificio, non tam peractæ semel in cruce oblationis, cujus hic memoria celebratur; quam perpetui sacerdotii & jugis sacrificii, ad quotidie in cœlis sempiternus sacerdos offert, rationem habuerunt, cujus hic imago per solennes Ministrorum preces exprimitur.* Cassand p. 169. 2. By whom

CHAP. VII.

whom is Intercession made: both by presenting their own praiers for the people; and also the peoples prayers to God; thro Christ. For God accepteth no praiers but thro Christ; nor yet all those that are made in Chrifts name; except either they come from persons deputed by him, who is so dearly loved; to which persons God hath made extraordinary promises, as those *(* I conceive *)* are *Matt.* 18. 18, 19. *Jo.* 16. 23. &c. or from those that are holy and like unto him; For sinners God heareth not, till reformed. The emploiment of the Saints in heaven, as we have any notice of it, is praier and praises. For first, since the spirits of Saints departed hence are *in paradise, Luk.* 23. 43. and *with Christ Phil.* 1. 23. are now said to be *made perfect, Heb.* 12. 23. *and clothed with white garments, Rev.* 6. 11. that is advances in charity and purity greater then here; are described in Priests habits, having *in their hands vials of incense (* doubtless to offer it *)* which is interpreted by St. *John* to be *praiers of the Saints, Rev.* 5. 8, -8. 3. have a zeal to Gods glory in mens salvation beyond ours, or their own whilst on earth; and more charity, which grace is not decayed by death, but perfected. 1 *Cor.*13.8. 2. Since their *interpellations* there can prejudice our Saviors no more, then the Priests intercessions here, 1 *Tim.* 2. 1. and if any ask what needs theirs, we may as justly reply, what need these; nay what need any praiers at all; see *Matt.* 6. 8. Tho little concerning this their interpellation is revealed; and those Christians, who have implored it, seeming to have grounds partly on Miracles pretended to be done by them; But *(* probably *)* true ones done and that frequently at their memorials. See *Austin. Civit. Dei lib.* 22. *cap.* 8. and partly on pretended apparitions of

2 *To make intercession for the people.*

The benefits of our Saviour.

of them, after deceased; yet in general it seems piously credible, that as Christs members on earth now suffer, as he did on earth; so his members in heaven intercede for these sufferers(at least in general)as he doth there; and echo unto the King of Heaven the words of their Master, as the Angels do to the Church. *Rev.* 5. 12. comp. with 9. *Rev.* 7. 11, 12. comp. with 9, 10. And that petition, *Rev.* 6. 10. I cannot imagine so circumscribed to themselves, that it did not represent to God also the sad condition of their Brethren on earth mentioned, verf. 11. See *Rev.* 5. 9. where the Presbyters give praise for the salvation of others as well as of themselves, for those of every tongue, kindred, people, and Nation. See *Rev.* 11. 17, 18.

§. 17. *This honor of Priesthood from Him to be communicated to all his Brethren.*

Thus much of our Saviors officiating, in the heavenly Sanctuary, and his Ministers, here: Now this discourse (as the former) must be concluded with the communicating of this honour also unto us; who, look whatever he is, that we also shall be; for we shall be like him, *1 Jo.* 3. 2. We are all therefore one day to take holy orders; to be made Priests and Kings; or Priests Melchisedechical. Indeed we are already Priests not only some of us in respect of the rest; (which I have mentioned before) who officiate for them in the publick assemblies; but even all the people of God in comparison of the rest of the world; the Church being a *chosen generation* out of all the rest; *an holy Nation;* a Kingdom of Priests; *Gods peculiar treasure*, the *Israel of God*, separated and sanctified for to serve him. See *Exod.* 19. 5, 6. *Gal.* 6. 16. 1 *Pet.* 2. 5, 9. *Rev.* 1. 6. Every one of whom, not only by the Priest, (in publique assemblies,) but by themselves also, (in their hearts) may offer sacrifices immediately to God the Father, acceptable thro Jesus Christ

In some sort all they officiating in it here on earth.

CHAP. VII.

Chrift, *Heb.* 7. 19. and hence are we alfo called, not only Priefts by whom, but *Temples* alfo; and that not our fouls only but our bodies (inhabited by Gods fpirit; as that Ancient one was by his Glory,) in whom, fuch facrifice is offered; (as our Saviors body alfo (more eminently) was ftiled *a Temple.* See *Jo.* 2. 21. 1 *Cor.* 3. 16. -6. 19. *Eph.* 2. 22.) But this Temple is yet but in building, as it were; we being here κατοικητήρια, and hereafter more perfectly ναὸς: Here Tabernacles, hereafter Temples: fee *Eph.* 2. 21, 22. But thefe we fhall be made yet much more hereafter. 1. After the day of judgment. For then fhall every place become a *Sanctum Sanctorum*, and every one a Prieft: See *Rev.* 21. 22, 23. *But fhall more compleatly after the day of judgment.* where *the new Jerufalem, that after the final judgment, Rev.* 20. 12. *comes down from heaven* (where perhaps, as God expreffeth elfewhere earthly by heavenly things, fo here heavenly by earthly) *hath no Temple* at all *in it;* For that (which indeed makes a Temple whereever it refides) the glory of God and of the Lamb being now fpread all over it; irradiating and illuminating it throughout; (in which refpect there is faid to be neither Sunfhine nor Night there;) it is, all of it nothing but a Temple, verf. 3. or God being the Temple, verf. 22. all over it. See the fame thing prophecyed, *Efai.* 4. 3, 5. that *every one fhould be called holy;* and *every houfe and affembly in Sion have the fame glory upon it,* (cloud by day and fire by night) that *was on the Tabernacle.* And in this *Sanctum Sanctorum* Gods Servants fhall fee his face, (without a cloud of Incenfe betwixt) and ftand before his glory; with his name [*Holinefs unto the Lord*] in their foreheads, *Rev.* 22. 4. and there *they fhall ferve him,* verf. 3. See *Efai.* 61. 6. -66. 21. *night and day in his Temple, Rev.* 7. 15. *Being all made Kings and Priefts as He. And ferving God for ever in his Temple.*

The benefits of our Savior.

7. 15. before the Throne of Glory: in finging eternal glories and praifes to him, for there fhall be no more confeffion where no fin; nor praier where no more want; not infirmity, nor affliction, *the nations being healed by the tree of life,* R*ev.* 22. 2. no καταναθημα any curfe, or excommunication of any R*ev.* 22. 3. there. And fecondly, As then Priefts and Servants to God the Creator; fo are they alfo Kings or Lords over the Creation: *fit down on thrones* with Chrift, and R*ev.* 3. 21. *and reign for ever and ever,* 22. 5. *reign on the earth,* 5. 10. *over the Nations,* 2. 26, 27. *Judge Angels, Judge the* 12 *Tribes, be rulers over Cities, Luk.* 19. 17. fee *Matt.* 25. 21.-24. 47. *Luk.* 16. 10. which expreffions, fo far as they have reference to Chrifts kingdom after the final day of judgment, and not to that profperous condition of the Church which is promifed before it, are metaphors expreffing the unintelligible things of the next, by the more acquainted things of this, world; which cannot be, no more then thofe, *Ezek.* 43. c. &c. fpeaking of the fame things litterally fulfilled.

2 Priefts alfo in fome fenfe (in the foul) after Death.

2. Priefts alfo after Death before the great judgment day, in the better part of us, the foul; the eftate of which, tho it was Gods pleafure that it fhould not be fully revealed to us, yet we may not neglect to take notice of that which is fo.

§. 18
A glympfe of the afterdeath conditi- on of the fouls of the Bleffed.

It feems plain then: 1. That tho there is no formal judgment, or fentence paffed upon any man at the day of Death, or final reward appointed, or any convention or appearance of the foul before the eternal Judge, for why then have not other fpirits that are void of bodies as yet received that judgment? fee 1 *Cor.* 6. 3. And tho the foul (as well as the body) attain not, (as not extenfively, fo neither intenfively) its full beatitude, reward and crown,

Chap. VII.

crown, nor vision and communication of God, and glory, nor a full satisfying of its desires. *Pf.* 16. 15. or punishment, pain, and torment, until the general day of judgment and retribution (which is true not only of men, 2 *Pet.* 2.9. but devils, more great and more Ancient offenders, then men, *Jude* 6.) as may be gathered; from both our Saviors and the Apostles frequent expressions, commanding us to depend and cast our hope on the expectation of the coming of Christ in glory at the last day; and deferring the receit of our salvation, of the reward, and of the crown of glory, &c. till that time. See *Luk.* 14. 14. 2 *Tim.* 4. 8. - 1. 12, 16, 18. 1 *Pet.* 1. 5, 13. 2 *Pet.* 3. 11, 12. *Act.* 3. 19; 20, 21. *Luk.* 21. 27, 28. *Phil.* 2. 16. -3. 11. 1 *Cor.* 1. 7, 8. -15. 19, 32. 2 *Cor.* 5. 1. &c. 2 *Theff.* 1. 6, 7. *Heb.* 9. 27, 29. *Rev.* 22. 7, 12. *Col.* 3. 3. comp. 4. 1 *Jo.* 3. 2. 2 *Pet.* 2. 9. *Jo.* 14. 3. By which it appears that there is a place not to be entered before Christs second coming, prepared by his Ascension; but before this were many souls in Paradise. And this applied not only to the body, but the spirit. *1 Cor.* 5. 5. From the petition and expectation of these souls. *Rev.* 6. 9, 10, 11. From the just punishments of other spirits much worse, and that stay for no bodies, yet defer'd till that day. See *Jude* 6. *Matt.* 8. 19. -25. 42. 2 *Pet.* 2. 4. *Luk.* 8. 31. comp. *Eph.* 2. 2. Some at least it seems dwelling in the Air, and not yet cast into the Abysse: and likewise in this interval between death and judgment, tho 'tis most probable that some souls attain not so much bliss, and glory, and priviledg as some others. See *Rev.* 20. 4. comp. 5. -14. 4. Nor perhaps so much security (I mean not in respect of damnation) but in respect, of that severe tryal, which shall be at that dreadful day: and of the

T mea-

measure of their salvation, bliss, and reward. For since some sins shall come into judgment and scrutiny at that day, which shall not amount to the condemnation of γέεννα τῦ πυρὸς, (by which our Savior expresseth hell here, *Matt.* 5. 22. as frequently elsewhere. See verf. 29. *Matt.* 25. 33.) see *Matt.* 5. 22. comp. *Matt.* 12. 36. And since of those, who shall be saved in that day: yet this salvation shall be much more difficultly attained by some then others. 1 *Cor.* 3. 15. It cannot be imagined that the state of all the souls of those, who rest in peace, are alike blissful in the interval between death and judgment: or equally comforted, of some of whom such a severe examen is afterwards to be passed. It cannot be, that such a difference of the *salvandi* being to be in judgment, there should be none before it; nor the same soul so much in bliss at one time as some other, see *Rev.* 20. 4. -14. 1. -7. 4, 9, 14, 15. comp. *Rev.* 6. 10, 11. Yet it seems plain, I say, that the soul in general, severed from the body, doth afterwards of it self subsist: That it is still intelligent and hath use of its faculties: That it (because other spirits are) is capable of knowing things corporeal: That it, certain of salvation, passeth, (at least those of the more perfect), carried thither by Angels, *Luk.* 16. 22. comp. *Matt.* 24. 31. *Luk.* 16. 9. comp. *Luk.* 12. 20. into a place of rest, consolation, inchoative bliss; or certain of its damnation; of imprisonment, and inchoated pain, till the resurrection of the body. Secondly, That the souls of the faithful (since his resurrection) are gathered to Christ; and do, tho not all in the same proximity and degrees of consolations, then see and behold him, and the blessed Angels. See 2 *Cor.* 5. 7. comp. with 6. 8. for if St. *Paul* desires this change

because

CHAP. VII.

because here we walk by faith, not by sight; therefore we walk there by sight, not by faith. See 1 *Cor.* 13.12. comp. with 10. and *Heb.* 12.23. So *Calvin*, who spake very warily in this point; *Animæ piorum militiæ labore defunctæ in beatam quietem concedunt, ubi cum felici lætitia fruitionem promissæ gloriæ expectant:* and again: *Christus illis præsens est, & eas recipit in paradisum, ut consolationem percipiant, &c. Reproborum vero animæ* (the furthest removed from God and light) *cruciatus, quales meritæ sunt, patiuntur: & vinctæ catenis* (*ut etiam diaboli Jude 6.*) *tenentur, donec ad supplicium, cui addictæ sunt, trahantur.* It is plain I say from these texts well considered. *Matt.* 10. 28. *Job* 1. 8. 2 *Cor.* 12. 2, 4. *Heb.* 12. 23. *Act.* 7. 59. *Luk.* 23. 43, 46. 1 *Pet.* 3. 19. *Phil.* 1. 23. 2 *Cor.* 5. 1, 2, 3. comp. 6. and 8. *Luk.* 16. 22. -12. 20. *Rev.* 19. 22. comp. 20. 12. In some of which, tho some things are said of the person, yet they must needs be understood only of the soul; (*Animus cujusque est quisque.*) And indeed it were unreasonable to deny to the soul in its state of separation, that converse with God, those favors, revelations, &c. from him; which we must grant to it in an extasy (wherein the body lies as it were dead and unserviceable unto it;) which St. *Paul* experienced in his raptures, 2 *Cor.* 12. 2. and to the Prophets in their dreams. These things granted, to see a little further; whether any thing can be discovered concerning the imployments, &c. of the souls of the Blessed, that are with Christ. First, we find the Court of Heaven (as now it is, since our Saviors Ascension) described by the Apostle, *Heb.* 12. 22. &c. to consist of God, Christ, Angels; a Church or general assembly of the first-born; and spirits of just men made perfect; called by him in other places the *Family in Heaven, Eph, 3.15. The Jerusalem above, our Mother-City. Gal. 4. 26. Heb. 12. 22.* In refpect of which we are faid to have our πολίτευμα in heaven. *Phil. 3. 20.* And perhaps that text, *Eph. 2. 6.* where we are faid to be *fet down with Chriſt,* may be meant of that part of the Church which now refides in Heaven. Again, in all St. *Johns* vifions, we (find befides all the ufual appearances of the old Teſtament) firſt the reprefentation of a Church or Ecclefiaſtical Senate now in heaven (defcribed before, *Heb. 12. 22.*) and thefe there praiſing God *for the Creation. Rev. 4. 10, 11.* then *the Lamb, Rev. 5. 8. for his mercy to the Church,* and *for his judgment* upon its enemies (for all the works of God are one of thefe two:) for the reward they had received, *Redemption* of the whole Church *out of every nation and people* amongſt which ſtill this comes in, that *they were made Prieſts and Kings ;* as we find it every where frequent, fee *Rev. 1. 6.-7.15. -20. 6.* and for that they ſhould receive, *reigning upon earth,* i. e. in the new Jerufalem defcending from Heaven , *Rev. 21. 2.* after the execution of Gods judgments upon their, the Churches, enemies. See *Rev. 5. 9, 10.-11. 16, 17, 18.* which praife in the 4. and 11. chap. the 24. Presbyters ſingly perform: and tho (in the 5th) the Cherubims joyn with them, 'tis in the worſhiping, not in the fong, as drawn in that form ; for elfe the Angels every where glorify God, as fellow Servants, *Rev. 19. 10.-22. 9.* for his mercies to the Church. 2dly. Befides this Senate, we find mention of fouls ; firſt of the primitive Martyrs thofe *ſlain for the witneſs of Jefus* appearing *under the Altar,* (where facrifices were ſlain, and the blood, which is the life or foul, *Lev. 17. 14.* poured out at foot thereof) and here crying out,

How

CHAP. VII.

How long before the time of vengeance! Rev. 6. 10. not that they thirst after Revenge, but their reward; (yet this thirst void of impatience) which it seems was not to be bestowed till the *accomplishment of the rest of their Brethren,* (yet under persecution) and the destruction of their enemies, see Rev. 20. *chap.* as Gods reward and punishments have their solemn and set times; and are not of men single, but of many together; thus it is in the first resurrection, Rev. 20. *4, 5.* after destruction of the Beast, &c. Rev. 19. 20. those sooner and later martyred, crowned at once: and thus in the second Resurrection, Rev. 20. *12.* At the destruction of Satan and death, those long and lately dead raised at once. Meanwhile there are *given them white Robes*, and *rest:* Rev. 6. 11. white robes implying both the righteousness, innocency, holiness of these Saints, which they bring with them from the Earth, see Rev. 19. 8. -7. 4. -3. 4. and the glory, and light, and beauty which is given to this innocency, from God: after this, upon their number accomplished; and judgment ready to be executed upon those who killed them. See Rev. 8. 7. &c. we find these souls (*clothed with white robes and palms in their hands*) standing *before the Throne,* &c. *and praising God* and admitted to *serve him in his Temple,* and *to follow the Lamb,* &c. Rev. 7. *9, 15.* &c. Next we find the souls of those, who living in latter times had gotten the victory over the Beast, first with patience resting, and their good works, i. e. their white linnen, following them, Rev. 14. 12, 13. then *their number* likewise being *accomplished,* and now *judgment going forth against the Beast,* &c. *standing* likewise *upon the sea of glass before the Throne with Harps* (as the service of the Temple was celebrated with Musick,

1 *Chron.*

The benefits of our Saviour.

1 *Chron.* 25. 1.) Harps of God, as 1 *Thess.* 4. 16. and *singing Moses's* triumphal *song* over the Egyptians: see *Rev.* 15. 2, 3. -4. 6. To these two may be added those *primitiæ* of Israel, who first upon earth, upon going forth of judgment, were sealed to be preserved, *Rev.* 7. 3. and then are found *Rev.* 14. 3. praising God on Mount Sion. Lastly, after judgment executed and finisht as well upon the Beast, false prophet, &c. *Rev.* 19. 20. as upon the persecutors of the primitive Martyrs. *Rev.* 8. 7. *&c.* We find the promised reward given to the souls both of those *who were beheaded for the witness of Jesus, Rev.* 6. 10. and those (after) *who had not worshipped the Beast,* (*Rev.* 15. 2. both joined *Rev.* 20. 4.) *in the first resurrection;* being then made *Priests of God* and *of Christ. Rev.* 20. 6. When also Christ himself is said in a more special manner to be admitted to, and possessed of, his Kindom: i. e. after his enemies destroyed (in respect of his members.) See *Rev.* 19. 6. -11. 17. -15. 4. *Dan.* 7. 13, 14, 17. And is yet again to be advanced higher in it; after the day of judgment; and *death destroyed.* For that *giving up the kingdom to the Father,* 1 *Cor.* 15. 24. and *God* being *all in all,* vers. 28. is not an annulling, (except for the manner of it only) but perfecting of our Saviors kingdom. And all this is done before the last general resurrection of bodies, set down. *Rev.* 20.12. Now this first Resurrection is either to be restrained to the Martyrs under the two great persecutions, storied, the first, *Rev.* 6. *chap.* the 2d. *Rev.* 13. *chap.* as *first fruits;* and those, who are *come out of great tribulation, Rev.* 7. 14. -14. 4. and to some others (perhaps) of extraordinary sanctity; whose other zealous service for God hath equalled the Martyrs sufferings; who shall have some extraordinary priviledge

CHAP. VII.

viledge beyond the rest, either in a proper former resurrection of their bodies upon the destruction of the Beast; (as the general resurrection follows that of Satan). Which will not seem so great a Paradox after one hath well considered that such a resurrection of bodies not of a few, but many old Testament Saints hath already been accomplished; namely at our Saviors resurrection, see *Matt.* 27. 52, 53. who accompanied him ascending as the first fruits of the Resurrection of the rest by the same Christ to come. Nor will it be a stranger thing then for some before others to enjoy in their bodies celestial bliss, then now it is that *Enoch* and *Elias* do so. Or in a Metaphorical one of the soul; (*Martyres fruuntur (ut loquuntur veteres) prærogativa resurrectionis : sunt jam nunc* ἐπίγραφοι, *sicut alii futuri sunt post universalem resurrectionem.* Grotius Annot. Cassand. Art. 21. which as it is capable of the expression of a resurrection to grace, *Jo.* 5. 25. *Col.* 3. 1. (according to that of the Schools, *Mors animæ separatio à Deo.* So perhaps, it may be said to have one, and as it were, a new life, when it is advanced to a far greater glory (according as Hereticks, that held no other resurrection, applied this term only to it, 2 *Tim.* 2. 18. 1 *Cor.* 15. 12.) whilst the souls of the wicked, that still lie in prison till the great day, are said not to live again till the day of judgment, and then to be condemned to a second death. See *Matt.* 10. 28. and the souls of other faithful only to be at rest. See 1 *Cor.* 5. 5. Or if the first resurrection be thus understood, namely of souls to greater glory, then may it be applied not only to the Martyrs, (who are named by St. *John* living in times of persecution) κατ' ἐξοχήν only but to the spirits of all the Saints that are deceased before our Saviors 1000 years

The benefits of our Saviour.

years reign. Especially if we consider; first that St. *John* names such infinite numbers of them of all nations, &c. *Rev.* 7. 9. 2. The marriage of the Lamb, which (likely) excludes no Saints mentioned at this time. *Rev.* 19. 9. 3. The same reward of reigning, security, of not being hurt by the second death, &c. *Rev.* 2. 11, 26, 27. promised not only to the Martyrs, but all repenting and doing good works: tho I allow them to the first in a far higher measure. *Rev.* 2. and 3. *chap.* 4. Because he no where makes mention of other Saints, not having the same priviledges; but of other dead. Where, his saying that *blessed* and *holy are they that have part in the first resurrection, for on such the second death hath no power* seems to imply, that the second death should have power over all the formerly deceased that had not part in it. See *Rev.* 2. 11. And thus much of our being admitted first in soul, then also in body by Christ, to the same honor with him of Priesthood, and vision, and attendance, on God in the holyest of all. Blessed be such love to sinners for evermore! For what joy do we imagine would an Israelite have had, to have been introduced within the veil, and to have beheld the glory between the Cherubims, which yet the High Priest might then see only thro a cloud of incense? How passionately did enamoured *Moses* beg for one sight of Gods face, (which only the Gospel admits us to;) and was suffered only to *see his back*? and Elias on the Mount of God, after 40 daies fast, admitted only to *hear his voice*? But we all by this High Priest are advanced in due time even to *see face to face.* 1 *Cor.* 13. 12. And this, it is that holy *David* inflam'd and melted with Divine love every where so much longs and sighs for, to dwell in Gods house for ever;

to

CHAP. VII.

to behold his beauty in his Temple: i. e. to live for ever in his presence: for as a Prince makes the Court, so Gods presence makes a Temple. See *Pf.* 23. 6. -84. 1. &c. *How amiable. My soul thirsteth. Blessed are they that dwell. A day in thy Courts.* Pf. 42. 1. &c. *As the Hart panteth.* And so his chief praier to God *not to turn away his face ; to cause his face to shine*; to *lift up the light of his countenance* upon him; never to be enjoyed but in his holy place; into which this our great High Priest first conducted him. The greatness of which Divine bliss of his, and of all Saints, we may measure (but how infinitely doth the other exceed it,) by the joy we should take in the possession of some earthly thing with which we are desperately in love; and by the mourning we make for the loss, i. e. in the absence of it when despaired. So the soul as soon as it hath once cast its eye on the beauty of God; the Original of all that is called fair, in that Sanctuary, is struck infinitely in love therewith, and enamoured cries out *whom have I in heaven*, &c. *Pf.* 73. 25. the vehement longing after which, ('tis supposed) drew those expressions from the High Priest himself, in this his exile from it. *How am I straitned,* Luk. 12. 50. and *with desire have I desired,* Luk. 22. 15. and from his servant St. *Paul*; *I am in a strait cupiens dissolvi,* &c. *Phil.* 1. 23. And then this love to the Deity of the Temple, will naturally produce the service of it; *In his Temple doth every man speak of his glory,* Pf. 29. 9. eternal singing of praise, and giving of glory unto him; even like those inflamed *Cherubims, that rest not night nor day* nor no more do the Saints, Rev. 7. 15. crying one to another alternately *Sanctus, Sanctus, Sanctus.* Rev. 4. 8. Esai. 6. 3. whose imploiment we envy not, only because we
love

The benefits of our Savior.

love not. God grant that we may not flothfully, or heavily perform that duty here, which muft be our eternal imploiment hereafter; unlefs we be eternally miferable.

§. 19
This High Priefts (at the laft day) return out of the Sanctuary, and reappearance to the people.

To conclude: the laft act of our Savior, as High Prieft, is coming again out of the Sanctuary. For as the people waited without, praying *Luk.* 1. until the Legal High Prieft having made a full attonement came forth again, and bleffed them from the Lord. *Numb. 6. 23. Lev. 9. 22.* So, unto them that look for him, fhall Chrift, who was once offered to bear the fins of many, appear a fecond time here without fin, (i. e. bringing us full remiffion hereof) unto our final falvation. *Heb. 9. 28.* For tho before it was noted, how he (ftaying there) bleffed us from the Sanctuary; yet 'tis not a compleat bleffing, till his return; when coming forth with his face fhineing, like *Mofes*, from the glory of him before whom he ftands, he fhall alfo glorifie us (not only in foul, but in body) like himfelf: and take and carry us in with him into the Sanctuary to fee his glory and his Fathers glory, *Jo. 17. 24.* and to be for ever with them. *1 Theff. 4. 7.* Which coming forth, and glorious appearance of the great God and our Savior therefore all the Saints (as the Ifraelites did of old) are faid by the Apoftle to love, to look for, and patiently to wait for. *1 Cor. 1. 7. 2 Tim. 4. 8. 2 Theff. 3. 5. Tit. 2. 13.* Who yet a little while, and he that fhall come will come and will not tarry. *Heb. 10. 17.* Amen.

CHAP. VIII.

Jesus Christ the Lord and King; governing, protecting the Church.

G OD in the beginning made the world by his Son the second Person of the Trinity. *Jo.* 1. 3. *Heb.* 1. 2. *&c.* (God the Father, working by interior purpose or decree; the Son, in exterior production of the effect; The Holy Ghost, by an internal virtue, residing, as it were, in the thing that is produced), God the Father; in or thro the Son; doth all things by the spirit. The Father resolves; the Son commands, the Holy Ghost works. The first the Agent: the second the wisdom: the third the power. See 1 *Cor.* 12. 4, 5, 6. the three persons. And by him sustained and conserved it into its being, *Heb.* 1. 3. *Col.* 1. 17. And by him governed it in all its motions and changes. The divine eternal relations of the Son to the Father must needs conclude this; since he is *the word, Jo.* 1. 1. *the wisdom,* 1 *Cor.* 1. 24. *of the Father,* without which none will say the world was made or is governed. See *Prov.* 8. 22. But yet in a more special manner by him in all ages governed the Church, of which God the Son was alwaies the Head, *Eph.* 1. 22. and the careful Conductor amongst all its enemies, even from the Creation; as it were in a preludium of its redemption by him. And the Holy Spirit that guided the Prophets (as now, so then) was sent from him, by which he alwaies preached the will of his Father unto men.

§. 1. *Before our Saviors incarnation God the Father by him created, sustained, governed the whole world.*

And more specially the Church.

1 *Pet.*

The benefits of our Savior.

1 *Pet.* 3. 19. and *he was* alwaies *in the world*, tho *the world knew him not*, and alwaies *the light of men, that enlightned every one coming into the world.* See 1 *Pet.* 1. 11. 2 *Pet.* 1. 21. 1 *Pet.* 3. 19. comp. 2 *Pet.* 2. 4, 5. *Jude* 14. 2 *Sam.* 23. 2. *Jo.* 8. 56, 58. where note that St. *John,* every where much vindicating *(* for in his time it received some oppofition *)* the eternal divine nature of our Savior, (whence, in *honorem* he was ftiled *Theologus, John* the Divine) fpeaks frequently of his operations: not only as come in the flefh, but alfo as the eternal Son of God, and as working all things with the Father before incarnate. *Jo.* 12. 41. *1 Cor.* 10. 9. *Heb.* 11. 26. *Exod.* 23. 20, 21. comp. 33. 3, 14. *1 Cor.* 10. 9. By which it appears our Savior was the Conductor of the Church in the wildernefs, refufing afterward upon their fin to go with them himfelf, leaft his holinefs and hatred to wickednefs fhould confume them, &c. *Exod.* 33. 2, 3. and deputing another Angel for this office: but deprecated by *Mofes*, verf. 12, 14. *Deut.* 4. 34. *Efai.* 63. 9. and reaffuming their conduct, &c. fee *Act.* 7. 38, 39. *Eph.* 2. 20. He called the *Corner ftone* and *foundation of the Prophets*, as well as *Apoftles*, *Gen.* 32. 24, 28. and *Hof.* 12. 3, 4. Anciently affuming many times an human fhape, as a fore-perfonating of his Incarnation, See *Jofh.* 5. 13, 14, 15. comp.*Exod.*3. 5.and *Rev.*19. 10. -22. 9. *Head of the Army of God. Judg.* 2. 1, 5. *Exod.* 14. 10. comp. 13. 21. *Judg.* 6. 12, 14. *&c.* And as *by him all things were* thus *made* and governed, &c. fo being the eternal Son of God the Father, he was alwaies *the Heyr of all things*, *Heb.* 1. 2. -3. 3, 4, 6. and *for him they were made, Col.* 1. 16. Thus was our Savior before his Incarnation enthroned in the *bofom of the Father* ; *Jo.* 1. 18. and the moft High in his glory *before the world*

CHAP. VIII.

world was; *Jo.* 17. 5. And all power and government and judgment committed to him from the beginning, and in a particular manner the protection and Headship of the Church. In which office he gave his spirit, as since to the Apostles, so also of old to the Prophets; and when he came into the world, is said to have *come to his own*, and to be born King, &c. *Jo.* 1. 10, 11. Yet this he did first out of an infinite desire of his Fathers greater glory; and to (If I may so say) recover his kingdom, and reduce it into peace; first, by the rebellion of the Angels, and then the revolt and falling away, and enmity to him of man also, by the instigations of the Prince of the air, much troubled as it were, and diminished from what at first it was. (Not that all things forced by his overuling power, do not still yield subjection unto God (*for who hath resisted his will?*) but that he chose rather to found his kingdom over Creatures of reason in another way; i. e. in a voluntary, free, and chosen submission unto him; which might be to them an obedience of more reward; and to their Soveraign of greater honor: (but they straight abused it to his great dishonor and their own shame;) to repair therefore this kingdom of his Father again, in the way God first established it, i. e. in mans free submission to, and elected service of, God.

And out of a zeal to his Fathers greater glory, in procuring him also to be glorified by us his Creatures, as he also glorified him. For his chief end of his now-to-be-acquired Kindom was the glorifying of, his Father not himself; (see *Jo.* 17. 1. -13. 31, 32. -14. 13. 1 *Cor.* 15. 28. comp. 24, 25. where after perfecting of our salvation he resigns his kingdom, and as man, becomes a subject). for what glory could

§. 2.

Our Saviours descent from his eternal throne for mans sake.

could he purchase a new, which he had not before voluntarily quitted? see *Jo.* 17. 5. 2. Next out of the singular honour he destined for man, to carry up our nature, and set it *above al' principalities and powers,* &c. and to give us those near relations to God as no Creature besides is honored with, to be *the Lambs wife; to sit down with him,* and *judge the nation,* nay, *Angels, &c. made lower then the Angels to be crowned* in Him *with majesty and Honor* above them. *Ps.* 8. *Heb.* 2. 3. Again out of compassion to man, (who at the beginning made in Gods image had a kingdom and immortality promised him, and by his folly lost it) to give him a pattern, and shew him the way how he might regain it. 4. Lastly, to exercise his kingdom, (which he alwaies had over the Church) now with more tenderness of love (by contracting new relations unto his subjects, and investing their nature, and making it a dominion fraternal,) and with (if I may so say) more pity and compassion from his experirience, by tasting the same infirmities with them, by which he might also much more strengthen their hope and confidence in him; and so advance their endeavors. For these and many more reasons foreseen by this the wisdom of the Father, He emptied Himself of all his eternal glories; forgat his Creation of all things; laid aside his Crown, his right to any thing;so rich, and having all things, became poor, and having nothing. For which how lively doth he resemble his type *Abraham* in his *leaving his own Country,* and *his Fathers house,* and coming *to sojourn,* as it were, *into a strange land.* That so *he might be made* likewise (for the promise to *Abraham* was chiefly performed to Christ) *Heyr of the world* and Lord of all Nations. Till God should

Chap. VIII.

should rebestow all these upon him as a reward to a Creature, of yielding obedience to his Commands, and exercising all sinless patience in all temptations; according to those promises of a kingdom upon the like patience and obedience made to man.

For God from the beginning had destined man unto a kingdom; *Matt. 25. 34.* comp. *41.* but according, as his eternal wisdom had decreed, mutability and variation in the things here below, and the building by degrees of perfection out of imperfection; and the bringing forth of good out of the womb of evil, this kingdom and this glory was to be attained by man, thro free will, thro temptations of the threefold enemy, and by a conquest over them. Therefore the first man also, to come to this happiness, was first to encounter the world, the flesh, and the devil. A *tree* set afore him *in* the very *midst of the Garden* standing by the tree of life, *Gen. 3. 3. -2. 9. good for food, pleasant for sight,* soveraign for its virtue, being called *the tree of knowledg*, and *desirable* (saith the text, *to make one wise. Gen. 3. 6.* A woman of the same flesh with him, and Satan setting her on, &c. And as he, if standing thro all these, so his posterity ever since, whosoever of them shall pass thro these temptations in all obedience and patience, are to have a kingdom, &c. But so it happened; That the first man created to this hope, yet weakly failed under those assaults; and forsaking Gods word, and believing the divels lyes, sought a kingdom indeed, but not by the way of humility, and obedience, and shutting his eyes, which God had prescribed; but by the ambition of wisdom, and having his eyes open, and knowing good and evil, and being as Gods which the devil suggested; and so both he and his posterity were defeated of it.

§. 2
A kingdom promised to man at the first.

Our

The benefits of our Saviour.

§. 4.
Our Savior became man: and by obedience and sufferings gained it.

Our Savior therefore to repair this loss became man, to win a kingdom upon the same promises; and this second *Adam* conquered, where the first was foiled; and for this victory was afterward crowned. *To this end Christ both died, and rose, and revived, that he might be Lord,* &c. *Rom.* 14. 9. see *Jo.* 5. 27. *Because* or *as he is, Phil.* 2. 6, 7, 8. &c. 1 *Tim.* 3. 16. *Jo.* 13. 3. *Luk.* 1. 32. *Esai.* 9. 6. *Heb.* 2. 9, 10, 14. *Psal.* 45. 7. *Act.* 2. 36. -10. 42. -17. 31. *Matt.* 28. 18. &c. to shew to man the truth and performance of Gods promises; and to be an example of the possibility of attaining them, and being made perfect, to

And so by him all Adams posterity, that follow him.

be a *Joseph* in the Court of heaven, and an Author of salvation unto his Brethren; who animated by his example, assisted by his spirit, and protected by his power, thro the same way of obedience and sufferings, shall attain the same reign and dominion, and kingdom, as the man Christ Jesus hath. See *Luk.* 12. 32. -22. 30. *Rev.* 2. 26, 27. -3. 21. 1 *Cor.* 6. 2, 3. *Rev.* 20. 4. - 5. 10. *Dan.* 7. 22. And this by the everlasting appointment of the Father *Matt.* 25. 34. thro the Son. *Luk.* 22. 29.

§. 5.
The power and extent of Christs kingdom.

And now to view the greatness and extent of this kingdom of the man Christ Jesus, bestowed upon him for his perfect obedience, and willing sufferings, we find it as large as that of God the Father: who is for this universal dominion given him of the Father stiled ordinarily in scripture *the Lord,* as the Father, God. See *Rom.* 1. 7. *Act.* 2. 36. *Phil.* 2. 11.

1 *Over Angels, Good, Evil.*

All power that can be named, *over every name, that can be named, in Heaven, Earth, under earth.* As over the evil Angels; (not only to quel them in all opposition; but also to imploy them in his service, see 1 *Cor.* 5. 4, 5. 1 *Tim.* 1, 20. and to dispose of them in their motions. See *Matt.* 8. 31, 32.) so over all the

CHAP. VIII.

the good, (and that for his humiliations, *Phil.* 2. 9, 10. comp. with 8. *1 Pet.* 3. 22.) whom he imploies as his Ministers and servants in all affairs of *his* government. See *Matt.* 13. 41. *Rev.* 1. 1. called *his* Angels as well as, *of God. Act.* 12. 11. *Jo.* 5. 28. comp. with 2 *Thess.* 4. 16. whom they all adore. *Heb.* 1. 6. And from whom, they not having naturally or originally all knowledg of the various wisdom of God and mysteries of his works; but being successively in the due time increased in it, according to the dispensation of the Almighty, see *Eph.* 3. 10. *1 Pet.* 1. 12. continually receive their greater illumination, and perfection of knowledg: he being the *eternal wisdom of God*; and *light of the* whole *world.* Of whom he is head also, as he is of the Church, therefore called *the elect Angels*, as men *1 Tim.* 5. 21. from whom 'tis conceived (for doubtless they are conserved by, and in all things depend on, him, by whom they were created) they possess their present confirmative grace, and illuminations, *Rev.* 19. 10. and shall hereafter receive at the end of the world a greater glory, see *Eph.* 1. 10. *Col.* 2. 10. -1. 20. As over the Church, so over the adversaries of it. *Luk.* 19. 27. *Rev.* 19. 15. -1. 7. *2 Thess.* 1, 7, 8. As over Christian, so over Heathen, Kingdoms, governing them also with his providence and by his Angels, *Dan.* 10. 13, 20. *Dan.* 11. 1. As over bodies, so over souls and consciences, to know, convince, to send torment and self-condemnation into them. *Rom.* 2. 16. *1 Cor.* 4. 5. -14. 24. *2 Cor.* 10. 2, 3. &c. *Act.* 5. 5. -2. 37. -24. 25. *Jo.* 16. 8. *Tit.* 3. 11. having power over the laws; what shall oblige them, what not. Annulling the former Ceremonials of Moses, *Lord of the Sabbath*, &c. *Col.* 2. 8, 9, 17, 21. *Act.* 15, 10. *Gal.* 5. 1. -4. 3. *Eph.* 2. 14. Power to remit, and to retain

2 *Men, Good, Evil.*

3 *Souls, Bodies.*

4 *Laws to enact, and annul.*

The benefits of our Savior.

5 Sins, to remit, to retain them.
6 Over living, over dead.

retain sins; with the key of *David* opening and shutting as he pleaseth; *Joh. 5. 22. Act. 10. 42. Act. 17. 31.* Power, as over the living, so over the dead; the Author of the raising again of their bodies, 1 *Cor. 15. 45. Jo. 5. 28. all that are in the grave shall hear his voice, &c.* and the disposer of eternal life, or torments, to whom he pleaseth. *Jo. 6. 54. -10. 28. Phil. 3. 21.*

The last Judge.

The final Judge, and this as man, *Act. 17. 31. Rev. 1. 7. Jo. 5. 22. Act. 10. 42.* before whose tribunal all must appear, 2 *Cor. 5. 10.* judging most righteously, being *the wisdom of the Father, the word, the truth.* Most throughly, and those things especially which escape all former judgments of men; *the secrets of men, Rom. 2. 16. the counsels of the heart.* 1 *Cor. 4. 5.* See what a word it is that we have to do with in that day, described *Heb. 4. 12, 13.* Very accurate and punctual in weighing the several worths of every mans works, and putting fire to those that are drossy, even of those whom he saves. See 1 *Cor. 3. 13, 15. Gal. 6. 4, 5.* Judging not only men, but Angels, 1 *Cor. 6. 3.* and these not only the evil to pass their sentence; and deliver them up to torments; *Matt. 8. 29. 2 Pet. 2. 4.* but probably the good also; for their reward *non disquisitione meritorum, sed retributione præmiorum*: for tho from the beginning of the world, they both (in respect of their own demenor in themselves) have had their sentence; and the one, then, confirm'd in grace and goodness, the other having left to them no regress from evil; yet in *quantum actibus hominum communicati; & ratione eorum, quæ circa homines operantur* (as the Schools) the one sort here not doing more necessarily good, then the other, evil; nor the other more rejoycing in our straying from God, then the other in our Conversion; *Luk. 15. 10.* which argues the diligence

1 Of men brought back to life.

2 And also Angels.

The good and the bad.

CHAP. VIII.

diligence of the one for our salvation; as of the other for our destruction. Therefore I say if these have not all their punishment already; (but shall suffer also for deceiving men, *Rev.* 20. 10. and who knows whether this likewise in a just proportion) why should we imagine the other to have all their advancement? Especially since they are not yet freed from many charges and imployments about persons in dignity much inferior unto them: and the perfection of blessedness seems to consist in rest, and the end of motion, which alwaies tends to something yet desired, not attained. But *occulta Domino Deo nostro*. Meanwhile how terrible this to those who *tread the blood of the Covenant under foot*, to have their violated enemy their Judge. 2 *Cor.* 5. 11! How comfortable this to those who obey him, to have their Brother to have Power as over men, so much more over all the other Creatures; Seas, Winds, and Heaven and Earth! who as he made the old, so hereafter shall make a new, world; ending with a Creation of it, as he began; by the same power, by which here He *(to our astonishment)* or another in his name, i. e. by his power *Act.* 3. 16. did create or repair an eye, or leg, or some small piece thereof. He being the grand Liberator of the whole world at last; as well as of the Sons of God, *Rom.* 8. 21. and Heaven and Earth being in his power, as well as all the power therein given him. See *Heb.* 5. 5. 2 *Pet.* 3. 13. *Rev.* 21. 1. That we may know that there is nothing, nor present, nor to come, nor high, nor low from which he cannot defend us, out of which he cannot deliver us, *Rom.* 8. 38, 39. and over which we also are not rulers and conquerors thro him that being flesh of our flesh, loveth us, v. 37.

Appointer of b[i]fs and torments.

7 Over all the Creatures.

A new world to be made by Him.

As men have seen some pieces of it by him repaired.

But

§. 6.

The manner of exercising this hi. Regal power.

But amongst all these, over whom he hath power, yet his care is now more special toward the Church his body. *Eph.* 1. 21. *Heb.* 3. 6. sending abroad Teachers, *Eph.*4.7,11.&c. distributing to several, several gifts of the spirit; *Phil.* 4. 13. communicating a great part of his power to them: whatever they ask, doing it for them, &c. helping them in miseries, afflictions, tho not as yet keeping these from them; delivering them from the mastery, tho not as yet from the assaults, of their enemies. For tho *all power* every where *is given him*; and when any is executed 'tis executed by him; and no part almost of this his universal power, but hath in a specimen, for an essay and testimony of it, been executed by Him already, even to that highest one, of raising the Dead; by him, and by others also by his power; yet this power was not received to be, in every part, executed all at once; but according to the dispensation of the times appointed by the Father, who gave him this power. See *Heb.* 2. 8, 9. 1.*Cor.* 15. 23. &c. *Matt.* 20. 23. He governing all according to his Fathers will, whose will yet is the same with his own. Therefore is he, in respect of some acts of his power, described sitting down at Gods right hand, and resting and expecting *Heb.* 10. 13. till the time comes of doing every thing in that order that the Prophets have foretold it; i. e. that the Father hath fore-ordained it. *Act.* 3. 21. who hath *put the times and seasons* of every thing *in his own power*, as our Savior answered his Disciples, when they were inquisitive about his Kingdom, *Act.* 1. 7. as in other acts, *going forth* already *conquering and to conquer.* Neither are all his enemies to be subdued at once; but one after another; First Antichrist; then Satan; the last death : See *Rev.*19.20.

—20. 10,

CHAP. VIII.

-20.10,14. 1 *Cor.* 15.26. And so are the same enemies also overcome by degrees. They first hindred from conquering his elect (which power over them he received at the very first); then hindred from assaulting. For already by the power of his spirit, neither the flesh, nor Satan are suffered to overcome us, except by our own default: but only permitted for the exercise of our virtues still to assail us; And that meanwhile many by these assaults perish, 'tis not from any defect of the power, or goodness of this king: who is so diligent that of all that his Father gives him, he *calleth* them *all by their names; goeth before them, leadeth them out; fleeth not* from them *when the wolf cometh, looseth not one, Jo.* 10.13,12.-17.12. *Ps.* 23.1. and in heaven, *in the presence of the Angels*, rejoyceth (like the woman that had found her lost piece; and the shepheard that had regain'd his straying sheep) for the recovery of every sinner. See *Luk.* 15.7,10. But from the eternal wisdom and law of the Father, (which law his power must not transgress) not to take away free will from man, (which done all further *demerit* and *reward ceaseth*, and by which left he must still have a possibility to sin) till the consummation of the world. But this only Free-will being continued to man, without which as vice, so all virtue expireth, and *what is there that he could have done for his vineyard that he hath not done?* for there is nothing in or without us, that can oppose him concerning us, if we our selves do not See *Rom.* 11. 23. [When we believe not, when we will not *Matt.* 23. 37. *Mark.* 6. 5. *Rom.* 11. 23. *Jo.* 16. 12.] These are the bounds the Father, not to overthrow the nature of man, hath set to the power of his Son; they arguing no impotency, nor unwillingness in him, but incapa-
bility

bility in us. Elfe all things that can make man happy fhall be accomplifhed by the omnipotent power of this King of Saints in their proper feafon.

§. 7. But to exprefs the manner of this kingdom yet more fully; we are to know; that as God by our Saviors coming into the world, and firft appearance of the kingdom of God, removed away the weak elements and imperfections of the former times; and by this light caufed all thofe fhadows to vanifh; *Which is by certain degrees advancing.* fo he compleats not this kingdom neither all at once, but makes it to grow like Elijah's *cloud* from the *bignefs of a man's hand, till it cover all the earth;* and like thofe *waters, Ezek.* 47. 3. &c. by which doubtlefs are meant the larger and larger effufions of the fpirit till the day of the Lord come. *Act.* 2. 17, 18, comp. 19, 20. *Umbra in Lege, Imago in Evangelio; veritas in Cœlo.* (S. Ambrofe) and advanceth it by gentle degrees to more and more perfection till the end come; therefore compared to *a muftardfeed,* and *a piece of leaven. Luk.* 13. 19, 21. It was the Difciples error *Act.* 1. to think that the *Kingdom of Chrift,* that was but then vagient in its infancy, *fhould prefently appear* in its full ftrength without any intermediate growth: which had it then come to pafs, and fo nothing have been capable of any further perfection, the world muft alfo prefently have concluded: the fulnefs of all perfection being only in the laft fcene of the laft Act thereof. For there is no decreafe or revolution to imperfection, or ftanding at a ftay in the work of God (Man, his image cannot endure this in his petty contrivances,) but increafing alwaies and advancing to that juft height he hath determined for them. A prognoftication of which governing the world he hath left us in the 6 daies work of the

Creation

Chap. VIII.

Creation of it. And so our Saviors kingdom is not yet come to its period of perfection. See *Dan.* 7. 14, 9. *Heb.* 2. 8. *Rev.* 11. 15. -16. 17. -19. 6. *Luk.* 19. 11. &c. 1 *Cor.* 15. 25, 26. *Dan.* 2. 34, 44. *Act.* 3. 21, 23. but in a constant progress toward it, both in respect of the subduing of his enemies; And the more and more enlarging of his dominion; till *all* the *Heathen be his inheritance, and the uttermost parts of the Earth his possession.*

And for the first:*(*To repeat more largely what was briefly said before*)* *tho all power in heaven and earth be* already *given unto Him,* in respect of himself. *Matt.* 28. 18. Tho *God hath made him both Lord and Christ, Act.* 2. 36. and *we see him crowned already with glory and honor, Heb.* 2. 9. yet *all things are not as yet put under him* in reference to his body : tho sitting at the right hand of God in his person, he is suffering still in his members, *Col.* v. 4. *Saul, why persecutest thou me?* At his resurrection long ago *he* then *led captivity,* (i.e. Sin, Satan, and his instruments, Death and its associates,) *captive,* so as to suffer no more at all from them in his own person ; nor to suffer in his body the Church so far, as that it should be conquered by them, *Luk.* 22. 32. *Matt.* 16. 18. he then disarming them of their formerly mortal weapons, but yet not so far, that it should by them be no more assaulted ; nay the stronger assaults are now toward the latter end of the world ; as his members are more by him enabled to bear them. His servants also conquering the same way, as himself, they never so much, as now, since he sits on the Throne, being given up to martyrdom, and overcoming death by death. Christianity is yet only under the conduct of their spiritual *Moses* travailing afresh in the wilderness toward another *Canaan,*

§. 8.

¹ In respect of subduing his Enemies.

The benefits of our Savior.

naan; expecting, not entred into, rest. *Moses* was but a type of Christ; the Israelites of the Church:

1 *Antichrist.* *Egypt*, and *Babylon*, and *Antiochus* of *Antichrist*; that is to be revealed in the last times: against whom Christ comes first with aids of grace;before he comes with the glory of his presence *going forth conquering and to conquer*, but by several degrees, and one enemy after another: first triumphing *over the Beast*, and then *over his image, and the false Prophet*; first by the *constancy, the witness, and blood of the Saints*. *Rev.* 12. 11. Then by the sword of vengeance. *Rev.*

2 *Satan.* 19. 15. Then over Satan, first, so far as to bind him from doing hurt: then casting him into destructi-

3 *Death.* on, *Rev.* 20. 2, 10. and last of all over Death, *the last of all his enemies that shall be destroyed.* vers. 14. And as the subduing of his Enemies, so the enlarging of

2 *In respect of enlarging his dominion.* his dominion, is effected by certain degrees. He brought salvation to all people, but not therefore it tendered to all persons in all times; but only to some generations (according to the good pleasure of the Father to whom his kingdom is subject) in every country, and again to some Countries in every age. *Matt.* 24. 14. How narrow was the sound of the promulgation of his kingdom at first? [*Into any*

1 *To the Jew in part.* *Village of the Samaritans enter ye not.*] How obscure his Sermons? [*And without a parable spake he not unto them.*] How uncapable his Auditors? [*Not able to bear his doctrines*, *Jo.* 16. 12. *Luk.* 24. 21.] Great works were done when he was present here, but greater to be done after his departing hence. *Jo.* 14. 12. His personal presence with his servants,which was a great encouragement to them, being advanced into an assisting them with his presence with God in heaven, and his spiritual presence not with, but in, them; receiving there from the Father and
giving

CHAP. VIII.

giving unto them the Holy Ghost, by which themselves, (ignorant whilst his body was with them) were *enlightned with all truth*; and thousands now at a time converted to the Truth. Therefore was it expedient for the promoting of his kingdom to go hence; His Commission before being only from the Jews; [*I am not sent, &c. Mat. 15. 24.*] but after his ascent, receiving the promise for the Gentiles; [when he *asked of God and had given him the Heathen also for his inheritance. Ps. 2. 8.*] And shedding the gift of all manner of tongues upon his Disciples for instructing them. And ever since hath he enlarged his borders, and advanced to a further perfection towards *his fulnes; which is his body the Church, Eph. 1. 21.* still bringing more sheep into his fold, *Jo. 10. 16.* and gathering up the children of the kingdom, as his Father hath given them him, here, and there; in this or in the next generation; *not loosing one of those he gives him*, and *sending his Laborers* hither and thither according as his harvest is ripe: Now forbidding his Apostles to sow their seed in one place, where he sees the ground is yet too stubborn to receive it [as in *Asia, Act. 16. 6.* and in *Bithynia*, vers. 7. *They assayed to go into Bithynia, but the spirit of Jesus* (as many Copies) *suffered them not* and in Jerusalem, *Act. 22. 18, 21. They in Jerusalem will not receive thy testimony concerning me:* make haft, *depart, I will send thee to the Gentiles,*] Again guiding them, (and that by appearing himself in person) to other places, where he saw he had [by his Father given him] much people: as at Corinth, Antioch, Ephesus. See *Act. 13. 48.-16. 10.-18. 9, 10.-8. 39. Then spake the Lord to Paul, Be not afraid for I have much people in this City*: So, in places where they might do him more service,

2 *To the Gentile.*

The benefits of our Savior.

vice, pricking them forward extraordinarily with the secret instigations of his spirit. See *Act.* 17. 16. -18. 5. -19. 21. driving *Paul* without any rest to *Jerusalem*, that he might convey him thence, by occasion of a false accusation to sow the Gospel at *Rome*. See *Act.* 13. 2. -8. 1, 4. more spreading the Gospel, by a persecution of the professors. [Gods work being not, good without evil; But, Good out of evil.] All this zeal toward the Gentile; after he had, (out of his dear affection to his own nation) first made tender of their ministry to the Jew: where (then refused) yet in the time appointed his standard shall be set up; and they also shall bow unto his Scepter, and unto *Sion shall come the deliverer. Rom.* 11. 26. comp. with *Esai.* 59. 20. and *the light of the Gentiles* shall also be *the glory of Israel*. Thus the Sun of righteousness goeth on and prospereth; and none are hid from the heat thereof; but also, as the Sun, he enlightneth not all this Sphere at once: First, rising upon the Jew; from them shining on the Gentile; amongst these, first visiting the proselytes, and those who were before introducted into the Jew's religion (for such were most of the first Converts. *Act.*16. 14. -17. 4, 12, 17. 18. 7.) but from these by little and little spreading to the rest of the Gentiles, those before abounding in all idolatry: and amongst these to the Eastern and Asiatick people sooner (the light of the Gospel holding the same course with that of the Sun, and night also since having succeeded the day in places where it first shined) then to the European and the West (those whom the Gospel visited later being recompensed in this that they have retained it longer.)

§. 9. But this so, as the light is still increasing; and far more here added to the fold of that great Shepheard,

3 To the Jew Apostatized.

CHAP. VIII.

heard, then have there apoſtatized from it; and ſtill it proceeds, and hath paſſed over the broadeſt Seas, to new diſcovered kingdoms; America; and ſo from them hath made the round to the furtheſt Eaſt; *China* to the poſterity of *Sem*; (For by him was the Eaſt generally peopled, as the North by *Japhet*, and the South by *Cham*) and from them ſhall at laſt return to the poſterity of *Abraham*, the body of the Jewiſh nation from whence it ſet forth; *Rom.* 11. with whom we hope that a remnant of *Cham's* ſeed alſo, out of which hath ſprung that great enemy of Chriſt, ſhall be gathered to the Church, *Pſ.* 72. 10, 11. and then that wicked one, with thoſe that obſtinately follow him, be utterly deſtroyed, and then *Noah's* curſe fully accompliſhed. And 'tis obſervable that, at the ſame time the Goſpel began to decay in ſome parts, it began to be planted in others. When the Eaſtern and African Churches began to be overgrown with Apoſtacy and Hereſy; the Northern nations, *Germany*, *Pole*, *Denmark*, *Sweden*, *Norway*, &c. began to be gathered into the Church. And after that the Weſt (again) had been overrun with the groſſeſt ſuperſtitions, Sects and Diviſions; the Goſpel was haſtily transferred to the Eaſt and Weſt-Indies. From Chriſtian aſſemblies it hath grown to Chriſtian States; and from theſe again (as it has been of a long time generally belived) ſhall encreaſe into a Chriſtian, and the fifth and laſt, Empire: (not that all that live then ſhall be Saints; (or that the world ſhall be under one Monarch; an opinion made to ſerve the ends of ſedition and tyranny), but all or moſt for their religion. Chriſtians,) neither ſhall Antichriſtianiſm be univerſal either for place or time. Of the 10 horns, this Enemy ſhall prevail but over three; *Dan.* 7. 8. and

At laſt perfectly reigning in his members here on earth.

as he shall be toward the end of the world; so shall he not continue unto it; nor have the honor, *mundo secum moriente, mori;* but those Kings at last shall make him desolate, who before gave their strength unto him. And our Saviour shall conquer the world first another way; before, by setting it on fire. His spirit, his word first shall prevail over it; over the hearts and souls of men; and they shall one day, before the last, become subjects, not only to his power, but to his truth: when Satan also himself, before the time that he shall be utterly destroyed, shall first have shackles laid upon him, that he cannot walk about and seduce. After which conquest first over the ministers and the temptations of Satan; he shall also destroy Satan himself; and take his Saints also out of the hands of death: and raise them again by his power given him from the Father, and glorifie them.

§ 10.
The three Ascents of his throne.

His Kingdom, in respect of his members, seeming to have three degrees of its growth; and his throne 3 steps or ascents one much higher then another. The first beginning at his resurrection, a kingdom of grace chiefly, when our Savior first goes forth conquering and to conquer. *Rev.* 6. 2. The second beginning at the fall of Antichrist, and restraint of Satan. *Rev.* 19. 20. -20. 2. The entrance of our Savior into a kingdom of power; a kingdom mixt of grace and of glory too; his kingdom on earth. See *Rev.* 19. 6. -20. 4. The third, which is the consummation of it, and the kingdom of absolute glory, his kingdom in heaven, beginning at the destroying the last enemy Death, and the general resurrection. *Rev.* 20. 12. 2 *Tim.* 4. 1. *Matt.* 25. 31. *Luk.* 19. 12. And then *he shall give up this kingdom unto the Father,* when *God shall become all*

CHAP. VIII.

in all, in him and in us. That is when this Vicegerent in a kingdom now full of opposition, shall have gathered all Gods elect into safety and felicity; destroyed all enemies, and gathered out of it all things that offend, *Matt.* 13. 41. finished his business for which he reigned, i. e. our salvation.

Then shall this General give up his Commission (as we say, there needs no government where nothing can disobey) and return with the Father, and and the Holy Spirit, to govern after a new, and, in respect of the manner of it *(if I may so say,)* after an higher way; i. e. God shall govern immediately without any appropriated service of Christ, or Angels, or men, his substitutes; or use of external means, without the least contradiction or opposition of any thing in his kingdom, whereby his glory now is, as it were, violated and diminished; himself offended and displeased. When God takes again to him, as it were, his great power, see the expression *Rev.*11.17. (for God the Father, by the wickedness of free will, now as it were, admits and undergoes some diminution of his glory) and governs with as entire and pure a glory as we may imagine he did before the world was, and when there was nothing but himself; and perfect and infinite glory reflected only from himself. Our Savior also having this kingdom resign'd, (as he then had it) with him. *Jo.* 17. 5. So now, as then, *above all, and thro all, and in all, Eph.* 4. 6. as all being nothing, but himself all. So that this resignment of our Saviors government (such as now it is,) is only the transition of it into a greater perfection, for *it endures for ever and ever. Luk.* 1. 33. The more things multiplicious are united, and things diverse annihilated into God; the more they also being perfected. Which

§. 11.
The whole work finish't, all his members compleated, enemies conquered, resigning up his kingdom to the Father.

as

The benefits of our Saviour,

as it is true in all other creatures, so also (according to his humanity) may be verified of our Savior, *blessed for evermore!* In respect of which consummation of all things, that is yet to come, all the present things, which are consummations of the types of former times, are but types themselves, and imperfections; as also many of those prophecies that are already fulfilled in these are to have a second fuller accomplishment hereafter. Our Saviors first coming but a type of the second; and the prophecies applyed to this, see *Mal.* 3. 1. *Matt.* 3. 10, 12. much more verified and fulfilled in that. Our Sabbaths but types of the rest to come; the present communion of Christs body and blood, and the present inhabitation of his spirit, but types and earnest-pence of a more intimate incorporation and union to him hereafter. When whatever he is *we shall be like him,* tho we cannot now imagine *what we shall be:* and our present knowledg and conceit of things, seeing them under the law, *thro a veil*; under the Gospel, *thro a glass,* somewhat clearer, but *not yet face to face,* 2 *Cor.* 3. 14, 18. 1 *Cor.* 13. 12. such as *shall* hereafter *vanish away,* 1 *Cor.* 13. 8, 12. but by improvement, as Stars vanish in a greater light. Meanwhile all things under this King of Saints go on apace to their perfection; by whom all that *is imperfect shall* at last *be done away.* And in his Majesty may he *ride on prosperously*; and may his *arrows be sharp in the heart of his enemies*; *and the people be subdued unto him*; and may he remember his poor servants now he is in his kingdom;to whom be glory for ever. Amen.

§ 12. Lastly, to conclude this chapter as the rest, what is said of his Kingdom, is verifyed also of the Saints; By whose merits, after whose example, under

C H A P. IX.

der whose conduct, assisted by his spirit, protected by his power, all those who depend on him *shall also overcome, shall have a kingdom, thrones, reign on Earth, rule over the nations, judge men and Angels,&c.* only saving to him the primogeniture, the preeminence, the right hand, &c. *Rev.* 2. chap. 3.

C H A P. IX.
The Benefits of our Savior common to all Generations ever since the Creation.

LASTLY. As all these benefits come to mankind by and thro Christ; so they came, alwaies, by him; to all generations of men ever since the Creation; And as well these before, as those since, his coming in the flesh attained salvation and were blessed only by, in, and thro, him. God, (perfecting, as all his other works, so that of our redemption by degrees; and still reserving some better thing behind, to superinduce upon the former; that the precedent, without the following, times might not be made perfect; *Heb.* 11. 40.) appointed not the full-manifestation of his Son, for taking away our sin, &c. nor, (after the Son reascended,) the visible and more plenary descension of the Holy Ghost, for enabling our obedience, &c. till the last times indeed: But yet he not only promised them, (I mean to his Church,) from the beginning, [where note; that in what manner the sending of the Messias or the promised seed, so the sending of the spirit, was only promised to former ages. See for this (which is less taken notice of) *Gal.* 3. 14. *Act.* 2. 33, 39. *Esai.* 32. 15. -44. 3. *Jer.* 31. 33. -32. 40. *Ezek.* 11. 19. -36. 27.

§. 1.
The Old world had not only the types, but the benefits, of the promises.

Joel

Joel 2. 29. *Zech.* 12. 10. &c.] and raised a continued expectation and longing for them ; both in men, and Angels ; *Mal.* 3. 1. 1 *Pet.* 1. 12. [and therefore the faithful were, then, called the *children of the promises* ; and the priviledges of the Jews (the then Church of God) said to be great, in that they *had the promises* ; see *Rom.* 9. 4. -3. 3. *Act.* 2. 39.] But he also exhibited them ; and this, not only in types, (the figures and representations of what was to come:) [As all former times were, almost in all things, types of the latter, see 1 *Cor.* 10. 6, 11. *Rom.* 15. 4. *Eccles.* 1. 9. that the whole world might know Gods waies, (in his mercies, judgments, &c.) what they are, and what they will be, by what they alwaies have been ; and so, in both kinds, might hope, and fear, the same things to fall out to them; which have come from God formerly upon others, for their example] but in the virtue and benefit of them. *Thro the grace of our Lord Jesus Christ* (saith St. Peter) *we shall be saved, even as they* : i. e. the Fathers, see *Act.* 15. 11, comp. 10. nor only this ; but in the presence of them : First for the Son ; The government of the Church of God under the old Testament was by this only begotten of God, 1 *Cor.* 10. 9. *Heb.* 11. 26. tho not yet incarnate.

Had, the presence and conduct of the Son of God ; and the presence, and assistance of the Holy Spirit.

§. 2.
The Government of the old world by the Son.

Humanity indeed was not assumed till the appointed time ; nor any of those offices that necessarily depend on it ; no sacrifice, no sufferings for us ; no obedience to the laws, which were enjoyned us ; no intercession as yet as High Priest for men, his Brethren ; as yet a Mediator, in respect of man, to God he was not : being in all things (till he emptied himself) equal to God the Father ; yet the benefits of all these, tho not to be acted till their season were participated and equally communicated

to

CHAP. IX.

to all ages before thro faith in those to come; as to ages since thro faith of these past. And thus the Lamb may be said to be slain from the beginning. But yet it seems plain; that, (by the divine Oeconomy,) from the person of the Son of God (which was alwaies), *The first* as well as *last*, *Alpha and Omega*, *Davids ofspring or branch, and root*, *Rev.* 1. 11, 17. -22. 16. and all things as of the Father so by the Son, 1 *Cor.* 8. 6. *Jo.* 1. 4. As *the first begotten from the dead, Rev.* 1. 5. *Col.* 1. 18. *so the first born of every Creature. Col.* 1. 15. comp. 17. From this person, I say, as it were a Mediator from the Father to us, came in all times the *enlightning* and *teaching*; *Jo.* 1. 9. *Esai.* 60. 1. comp. *Eph.* 5. 14. he was alwaies *the light* the conduct and protection; *Pf.* 80. 1. he was alwaies *the shepheard Esai.* 27. 3, 6. of the Church of God. From this person all blessings derived upon Her; She was ruled with his more extraordinary personal presence and immediate presidence, (and not by subordinate Angels;) and this done with his *great delight*, *Prov.* 8. 30. with great compassion, and affliction for their miseries, *Judg.* 10. 16. *Exod.* 19. 4. *Deut.* 1. 31. *Esai.* 46. 3. -63. 7, 9. and with great patience, grief, and 10-times *provocations* from their sins. *Numb.* 14. 22. *Pf.* 95. 10. He often assuming an human figure, as a preamble to his incarnation, tho not yet a real and natural body: and appearing to, and discoursing with, and seen by, the Saints of old, before his coming in the flesh; as he hath done to others since, after his ascension, many times to one man (*St. Paul*) that are mentioned, *Act.* 9. 4. -18. 9. -22. 18. 2 *Tim.* 4. 17. All the promises of Himself to come were from Himself, and from his spirit; 1 *Pet.* 1. 11. and amongst the rest that gracious designation (made to

Z   his

his Father) of his person to be emptied and to assume flesh [*Lo I come*] the Father again promising, before the world was, all the blessings that should come to mankind there from. See *Tit.* 1. 2. comp. *Gen.* 1. 26. and -3. 22. and -11. 7.

§. 3
All judgments and vengeance.

And as all mercies upon the Church and the Godly; so all judgments upon the wicked and the enemies thereof were executed by the person of the Son, as well before, as since, the incarnation, see *Jo.* 5. 22, 23. All judgments also being a proper effect of the word of God. See *Rev.* 19. 13, 15. *Heb.* 4. 12. All those judgments upon the old world were by him; being forerunning types of the world to be judged by him at that last day. Therefore is he said in the same manner, since his incarnation as before, to come often (still) to execute judgments without any descent of his humanity. See *Rev.* 2. 5. *Matt.* 16. 28. -24. 34, 50. *Rom.* 11. 26. comp. *Isai.* 35. 4. -40. 10.

§. 4.
Executed by the second person of the Trinity.

And from Him all these as the second Person in the Trinity, contradistinguished from the Father. For tho *opera trinitatis sunt indivisa*; and all external works are of the whole Trinity, yet in the operation, the same manner of concurrence cannot be attributed to the 3 persons: we cannot say that as the Father made the world by the Son; so that the Son, by the Father. Nor that as the Son became incarnate; so the Father: Nor because our Saviours praiers were addressed to the Father, therefore they were to the Holy Ghost, or to the Son i. e. himself. Now then to prove this, that we pretend, more fully; and here to pass by that deduction (firm enough) of God the Fathers creating, upholding, governing all things by his eternal Son, therefore governing the Church (his people Elect, whose

Chap. IX.

whose God he more specially calls himself) these, I say, more especially by the same person his Son.

1. This seems to appear from two Lords, several times named in the old Testament: see *Pf.* 110. 1. where the second Lord, whom *David* calls *his Lord,* is expresly by our Saviour expounded to be himself, *Matt.* 22. 44. and Himself, not as he was *Davids Son,* since by his question he implyed that Christ as Davids Son could not be his Lord; but as Gods Son; which the blind Jews imagined not. So of God and God *Pfal.* 45. 6. comp. 7. see *Heb.* 1. 10, and 8. David making many addresses unto God the Son, as appears by the quotations in the new Testament: see *Pfal.* 68. 24. comp. 18. and *Eph.* 4. 8, 9. After this consider *Gen.* 19. 24. which diversity of expression seems to arise from that Lords being yet on earth, that discoursed with Abraham. *Gen.* 18. 1, 3, 21. Add to these *Ezek.* 13. 7. comp. *Matt.* 26. 31. *Esai.* 5. 1.

Mention of two Lords.

§. 5.

2. From those many places; where the same divine person is (promiscuously) called the *Angel of the Lord* (therefore not God the Father) and also is himself named God; *The Lord; The God of Israel;* is delivering his message (if I may so call it) in his own name; receiving worship, dedication of Altars, Sacrifice, as God; and (seeing God and living) with wonder applyed to him by those trembling mortals to whom he appeared; by all which joyned together (tho to some it may seem the phrase of those daies to give any Angel the name of God. See *Judg.* 13. 21, 22. And their opinion that the sight of an Angel was death to a mortal, see *Judg.* 6. 22. it is as evident that he was distinguished from all created Angels. See *Gen* 32. 1, 2. no such ceremonies used. Therefore is this Angel in an especial manner called *the Angel of Gods face* or presence,

Of an Angel having divine Attributes.

The benefits of our Saviour.

prefence, and *Gods name* faid to *be in* Him. *Exod.* 23.21. *Efai.* 63.9. which feems plainly applyed to our Saviour by the whole defcription, and by 1 *Cor.* 10.9. yet the fame is called alfo Gods face, *Exod.* 33.14. and *God himfelf,* verf. 3. who refufing upon their idolatry to conduct them any longer; yet afterward condefcended unto it, upon the interceffion of Mofes: fhewing in the firft the malignity of fin; in the fecond the power of Chrifts interceffion for finners; typified by that of Mofes. See *Exod.* 33. 14.-34.10. Now for the coincidence of thefe two [*God the Lord*] and [*The Angel*] &c. fee *Gen.* 16.7. comp. 10, 13, 14. *Gen.* 22.11. comp. 12.-32.34. comp. 30. and *Hof.* 12.4, 5. *Gen.* 48.16. comp. 15. *Gen.* 31.11. comp. 13. *Exod.* 14.19. comp. 24.-3.2. comp. 3, 4, 6, 7, 14. *Deut.* 33.16. and *Zech.* 3.1, 2. where *Jofhua* appearing before the Angel, as a Judge, is accufed by Satan, fee verf. 4. *Mark.* 12.26. *Act.* 7.38, 35. comp. 53. *Heb.* 12.26. And many more places to this purpofe. Which intereft, agency, and appearance of our Saviour in the old Teftament, thofe other places in the new feem to glance it. *1 Cor.* 10. 9. comp. *Exod.* 17.2. *Numb.* 21.5. *Heb.* 11.26, 1 *Pet.* 3.19.-1.11. *Matt.* 23.37. where *How oft would I,*&c. feems to be meant alfo before his incarnation, by the Prophets, whom he alwaies fent; before, and fince. Neither doth that faying, 1 *Jo.* 4.12. *Jo.* 1. 18. [*No man hath feen God at any time*] 1 *Tim.* 6.16. [*nor can fee him*] (grounded on Gods words in *Exod.* 33.20, 22.) thwart that, which hath been faid; or oppofe the vifions and apparitions of God veil'd in created reprefentations and images; but only thofe vifions of him in his own nature and effence: or that more proper glory, wherein he fhall be feen by us in the next world, 1 *Cor.* 13.12. which devouring fire

and

CHAP. IX.

and unaccessible light nothing mortal can behold without being melted and consumed ; the image of which also is sometimes represented so glorious, as neither is it beholdable, see *Lev.* 16. 13. and most-what so glorious, as not seen without great horror and trembling ; the ordinary symptomes in all apparitions ; even those not only of God, but of Angels. And this invisible glory is called *Gods face,* *Exod.* 33. 20. Not but that Gods face also hath been seen, see *Gen.* 32. 30. *Judg.* 6. 22. &c. But that face was only a vizard (if I may so say) over his own face; and that glory but a shadow of his own glory (therefore *Moses* after a sight of these, *Exod.* 24. 10, 16. *Numb.* 12. 8. still affectionately desired a sight of the other. *Exod.* 33. 18.) Sometimes made more, sometimes less, glorious ; as when in the form of a man he dined with *Abraham*. But yet except when the divine Majesty personated an ordinary man, seldom in any glorious apparition under the times of the law was his figure, or at least his face, seen ; this familiarity being reserved, in the incarnation of God, for the times of the Gospel. *1 Jo.* 1. 1. *Jo.* 1. 14. The appearance to *Abraham* (in a vision or reality it matters not for our purpose) *Gen.* 15. 17. comp. 12. was a blazing flame issuing out of a Fornace environed with darkness. *Exod.* 24. 16. The sight of the glory of the Lord was like a devouring fire to the people , and to the Elders who had more clear vision, verf. 10. there is mention only of (as it were) a Saphire-pavement under his feet : and *remember* (faith Moses) *Deut.* 4. 15. *that ye saw no manner of similitude.* Moses his importunity afterward only saw his shoulders passant, and was entertained chiefly, as also Elijah, and as Adam in Paradise, *Gen.* 3. 8, 10. like some terrible noise in the air indicating

The benefits of our Saviour.

Gods prefence with a voice and a proclamation. This being the time of hearing his word, hereafter of vifion; fee *Exod.* 33. 19. -34. 6. 1 *King.* 19.12. *Ezek.* 1. 26, 27. the appearance of the loines of a man, and flames covering the upper and the lower parts. *Efai.* 6.1. No defcription of his perfon, fave the pofture only fitting on a Throne; only a particularizing of the Cherubims. *Dan.* 7. 9. A defcription of his covering, his veftment, and his hair, but not of his perfon. *Rev.* 4. 3. no defcription of any figure, only the luftre like a Jafper or Sardin-ftone; only *Rev.* 1. 12. In St. *Johns* vifion of our glorified Savior, there we find all the parts of his body punctually defcribed, much refembling *Daniels* of that glorious Angel, c. 10. 5. which fome alfo imagine to have been our Saviour.

§. 6.
Some old Teftament apparitions muft be granted to be of the fecond perfon.

3. This appears in that fome of the apparitions of God in the old Teftament muft be granted to be of the fecond perfon; as that vifion *Efai.* 6. 1. which is interpreted exprefsly of Chrift *Jo.* 12. 41. comp. 40. quoted out of *Efai.* 6. where this vifion is related and this being the Lord, whofe glory refided in the Temple, and fate between the Cherubims. That vifion *Ezek.* 1. 26. muft needs be of the fame Lord too; fee *Pfal.* 68. 24. comp. 18. now the fame Lord refiding in the Temple, and before, in, or upon the Tabernacle; it follows that the Lord conducting the Church in the wildernefs, was alfo the fecond perfon. And from thefe, which muft be granted, many other appearances in reafon cannot be denyed to have been of the fame perfon. Efpecially moft of them being acts of care, and providence, and mercies toward the Church. Amongft which (to name only fome of them) that to *Abraham* feems to be, *Gen.* 18. where 'tis plain, that one of

From thefe granted others in reafon cannot be denyed.

As thofe to Abraham.

the

CHAP. IX.

the 3 celeftial perfons was the Lord; *Abraham* fpeaking in the fingular, and but calling one of them Lord, verf. *13, 17.* And two of them only entring *Sodom;* whilft the third, which was the Lord, ftayed and difcovered the deftruction of the City, verf. *22, 33.* whom fee again, *Gen. 19. 16,17.* talking with *Lot*, and verf. *24.* executing judgment on the wicked, after he had faved the Righteous: coming then with falvation and promifes in one hand for the good; promifes of himfelf to come: and thro him of the inheritance of heaven, typified in *Canaan*; and deliverance from Hell, typified in *Lot;* and with judgments in the other hand upon the impious; judgment of fire and brimftone, and being caft into a bottomlefs lake in hell, typified in *Sodom*. And fince our Saviour faith when the Jews asked him *Jo. 8.* whether he *had feen Abraham*, that *he was before Abraham*, and that *Abraham had feen his day and was glad:* (where it feems plain by verf. *38, 23.* that he was difcourfing of himfelf, as being the eternal Son of God; which the Jews fo much ftumbled at, and St. *Johns* relations every where fo much vindicate. And that the day, he fpeaks of, is that permanent one of eternity, which never ends; and to which all time *is but as one day, 2 Pet. 3. 8.* why may he not exprefsly mean it of thefe vifions of *Abraham?* and the glad tidings he brought him in them of that coming, which the Jews then, yet without rejoycing as *Abraham*, beheld? And might not *Abraham* be faid thus to fee his glory; as well as *Efai* (it muft be granted) did? 2. And next the defcent of the Lord in the times of *Noah*; how like is it to this in *Abraham's* time before the firing of *Sodom?* And his conference with and complaint to *Noah*, fee *Gen. 6. 3, 7, 8, 12, 13. -7. 1, 16.* and his

To Noah.

promifes

promises to him and Covenant with him, and his seed; *Gen. 6. 18. -9. 9.* &c. to those with *Abraham*. And his preserving of *Noah* with his family, and his shutting them up in the Ark, *Gen. 7. 16.* to his delivering of *Lot* and his leading him forth by the hand; And his causing it to rain those miraculous waters by *opening the windows of heaven*, and *springs of the deep, Gen. 7. 4, 11.* to the fiery rain upon *Sodom?* and how well do these agree with that expression. *1 Pet. 3. 19?* So that it seems without doubt these two of the firing of *Sodom*; and of the flood; and that of drowning the Egyptians in the Red sea, with the salvation of *Noah, Lot,* and *Israel* being the 3 grand types to the world of the last great judgment to come, see *2 Pet. 2. 5, 6. Jude 5. 7.* that they were executed by the same hand, see *2 Pet. 2. 5, 6. Luk. 17. 26, 28.* that the other shall be even the Son of God; to whom the Father for ever hath committed all mercy and judgment. 3. The same

To Jacob, &c. person it seems to be, that first wrestled with, (as he doth in afflictions with all the pious) and then blessed, *Jacob: Gen. 32. 24.* That appeared to, and was adored by, *Joshuah. Josh. 5. 13. 14, 15.* comp. *Exod. 3. 5.* To Gideon, *Judg. 6. 22.* To Manoah, *Judg. 13. 15. &c.* all which may be gathered from the arguments forementioned. And I can call to mind in the sacred story only, 2 apparitions or visions which certainly appear to be of God the Father: That of the Ancient of dayes, *Dan. 7. 9.* comp.

That to Moses on Mount Sinai, on the Tabernacle, In the Wilderness, In the Temple, &c. 13. and *Rev. 4. 2.* comp. *c. 5. 5.* 4. Lastly, he was the Angel that *conducted the Church in the wilderness*, as is shewed above; and by consequence that gave them the law in Mount *Sinai:* for tho the law is said to *be given by the disposition* and promulgation *of Angels, Act. 7. 53. Gal. 3. 19. Heb. 2. 2.* multitudes
of

Chap. IX.

of whom appeared in the Mount, *Deut.* 33. 2. *Pſal.* 68. 17. by whom thoſe voices were formed in the Air. *Heb.* 2. 2. In which ſpeaking of the law to the people the Angels were Mediators, as afterward in receiving from the Angel and carrying the law to them, Moſes was, *Gal.* 3. 19. [which is taken notice of ſeveral times in the new Teſtament, to ſhew the preeminence of the Goſpel: ſince the law was delivered to men by the intermediation of Angels and Moſes, Servants and Miniſters; but the Goſpel by the mediation of his only Son, made fleſh that he might familiarly converſe with man, without thoſe terrors that accompanied the law:] yet the ſupreme Legiſlator was God: *Deut.* 33. 2. *Exod.* 20. 1. *Exterior loquela Angelorum, interior Dei per Angelum*; and that the Son, the eternal word, and Vicegerent of the Father; called the Angel *Act.* 7. 38. that ſpoke with Moſes upon the Mount, from whom he received the law written with his finger: the ſame Angel that appeared in the buſh, verſ. 35. that conducted them in the cloud. Which ſoveraign Legiſlator, for the glorifying of his Father and the ſaving of man, humbled himſelf afterward to become Himſelf the Mediator. The type of which mediation of his, Moſes then was; both in delivering the will of God to the people, coming down to them from the Holy place in the Mount; and alſo aſcending and interceding forty daies to God for the people. *Deut.* 9. 18, 25, 26. As he ſince hath both deſcended in fleſh from the boſom of the Father, to declare and reveal all his will to us, *Jo.* 1. 18. who only *ſaw his face*, but *Moſes* only *his back-parts*: and in whoſe face the glory of the Goſpel ſhone, as of the law in Moſes his face, ſee 2 *Cor.* 4. 6. comp. 3. 7. and is aſcended again to the Father to intercede

Moſes then Mediator to, and from, Him; He now, to, and from, the Father.

intercede for us; this Real Moses remembring him, not of our righteousness, &c. but of the promise he made to them of the blessed seed, *Deut.* 9. 27. and of the triumph the spiritual and temporal enemies of God would make over the deserted, tho most worthy to be deserted, Church vers. 28. By whose prayers and intercessions it now standeth, and shall stand for ever. Amen.

§. 7.
The descent of the Holy Ghost under the old Testament.

Thus much, that the Government of the Church of God also under the old Testament was by the Son of God. Next for the Holy Ghost: The operations also of Holiness in men under the old Testament was by the same spirit. By it, then, Regeneration, *Gal.* 4. 29. and our Saviour wondred at a *Doctor in Israel*, *Jo.* 3. 10. that he was ignorant of it. Tho therefore Christ not yet ascended, and this Holy Spirit not then received and poured out in so full a measure upon all flesh; yet as of the Son the Author; so of the Holy Spirit the promise; of the Gospel; there were made some predescents in the old Testament, *Esai.* 63. 10, 11. *Nehem.* 9. 30. *Zech.* 4. 6. some sprinklings and drops of those large effusions which have been poured out in the latter daies; and of almost all those several kinds of its rich graces mentioned, 1 *Cor.* 12. &c. some first-fruits, as it were, and samplars we find in the Ancient Church of God.

Some sprinklines then of all its gifts.

The spirit of wisdom eminent in Solomon. 1 *King.* 3. 12. and *Exod.* 31. 3. The power of miracles eminent in Moses, Elijah, Elishah; and in these a specimen of almost all sorts of them, that are exhibited in the new. *Command over the waters, Exod.* 14. 21. 2 *King.* 2. 8. *fire* 2 *King.* 1. 10. *Dan.* 3. 27. *Air* 1 *King.* 18. 44. *The Heavens, Josh.* 10. 12. *The multiplying of oyl, meal, bread;* like that of our Saviours. 1 *King.* 17. 14. 2 *King.* 4. 6, 43, 44.

The

CHAP. IX.

The Resurrection, 1 *King.* 17. 21. 2 *King.* 4. 34. -8. 5. *The Ascension,* in Enoch and Elijah. Pentecost, in the spirit descending upon his Disciple Elisha from ascending Elijah, the type of Christ. *Gifts of healing,* 2 *King.* 5. 10. -4. 41. -2. 19. *Esai.* 38. 21. *Prophecy,* that called the proper season of the Prophets. *Helps in Government;* see the operations of the spirit upon Joshua; and the Judges of Israel; and the 70 Elders. *Interpretation of tongues;* and hearts too; of dreams, &c. eminent in Joseph and Daniel; see *Dan.* 5. 12, 25. Only one, *the gift of tongues* we find reserved as a property to the Gospel upon the enlarging of the Church from one before, at this time to all nations, and languages. We find this Holy Spirit also represented of old (both in the Tabernacle and the Temple,) in those 7 lamps of the 7 branched candlestick; as also in the first descent upon the Apostles it appeared in a flame or tongue of fire: *Act.* 2. 1. see *Exod.* 25. 40. comp. *Rev.* 4. 5. and 5. 6. and *Zech.* 4. 10, 2. comp. 6. We find it then poured upon Moses, in type of Christ; and from him portions of it derived upon the 70 Elders, *Numb.* 11. 18. &c. whose sudden prophecying upon it became then also, as in the Acts, a wonder to the people, vers. 27. 28. as it was from Christ upon the Apostles; and so many thousands ever since, and shall be on others to the end of the world. *Jo.* 1. 16. *Eph.* 4. 17. We find it then conferred upon the extraordinary Captains of Gods people; exciting them to heroick actions: Joshuah *Numb.* 26. 16, 18. Gideon *Judg.* 6. 34. Jephtah *Judg.* 11. 29. Samson *Judg.* 13. 25. Giving him corporal strength, a type of that spiritual, which it now bestows upon the Saints; as illuminating and sanctifying, so strengthning and giving courage and comfort in afflictions;

Its wonderful operations then in some chosen men.

this

The benefits of our Saviour.

this being a special operation of this divine Agent. Therefore one attribute, *Esai.* 11. 2. is *spirit of might* ; and in the new Testament, *Comforter* : Upon Saul, and David ; presently upon their anointing ; by which they were changed and became new men. 1 *Sam.* 10. 6. -16. 13. see its inspiration of the holy writers ; Moses ; David ; the Prophets : *Matt.* 22. 43. *Heb.* 8. 9. -3. 7. *Mark.* 12. 36. *Act.* 7. 51. *Luk.* 2. 26. *And specially on the sons of the Prophets.* *Act.* 1. 16. 1 *Cor.* 2. 13. Its wonderful operations upon the *sons of the Prophets ;* whereby they were put at certain times into wonderful extasies and raptures, (like those under the Gospel. *Act.* 10. 10. -22. 17. -9. 9. comp. 12. 2 *Cor.* 12. 2, 7.) into strange and unusual actions and agitations of their bodies. 2 *Sam.* 6. 14. *Psal.* 26. 6. 2 *King.* 4. 35. -2. 16. -9. 11. 1 *King.* 18. 12. *Ezra* 3. 12, 14. (see the like. *Matt.* 4. 1. *Act.* 8. 39. -20. 22. -16. 7. -18. 5.) So violent that Saul, (in their society possessed with the same) is said to have *stript himself of his clothes,* i. e. his upper garment, and to have *lain down all night unclothed,* being wearied with ose strange motions,&c. perhaps *Psal.* 149. 3. meant of this. They in these raptures not foretelling things to come,2*King.*2.3,5. but conceiving, and on a sudden, after an unusual manner,dictating,psalms, songs, the praises of God, or explanation of some mystery, or former prophecy. See 1 *Sam.* 18. 10. 1 *King.* 18. 29. 1 *Chron.* 25. 3. comp. 1 *Cor.* 11. 5. And the spirit then as now did more ordinarily inspire persons, first by their profession consecrated to God, *Jo:* 11. 51. prepared by studies and exercises of devotion in Schools for this purpose ; amongst which means was composing the spirits by musick. 1 *Sam.* 10. 5. -16. 16. *Ps.* 43. 4. 2 *King.* 3. 15. Some of the singers Prophets, Asaph, &c. There being many Colledges of them in several

places ;

CHAP. IX.

places; Naioth, Bethel, Hiericho, inhabited by great numbers. See 2 *King.* 2. 3, 5, 7. -4. 38. So the Levites, that were the fingers, were also spiritual composers of holy psalms, 1 *Chron.* 25. 2, 5. 2 *Chron.* 29. 30. And many of the Prophets were Priests or Levites, Samuel, Ezekiel, Jeremy. And now also that the miraculous graces of the spirit are someway both procured and improved by industry, study, prayer, faith, expecting and desiring to receive them seems to appear from. 1 *Cor.* 12. 31. -14. 1. *Rom.* 12. 6. 1 *Tim.* 4. 13, 14. 2 *Tim.* 1. 6. 1 *Pet.* 11. 10, 11, 12. And this may serve to shew that the Ancient world were not unacquainted with the operations of the spirit; and in some measure pretasted this promise of the latter daies; which wrought in all times after the same manner; and came then also from the same Author, the Lord Christ: see 1 *Pet.* 1. 11. -3. 19. 2 *Pet.* 1. 21. 1 *Cor.* 12. 5. Only now its illuminations are greater under the Gospel, *Matt.* 11. 11. *Jo.* 16. 13. and further extended; even to all flesh; amongst whom it continues all its rich gifts; For we must not make the times of Christ inferior to those of the law; nor the times of the making of the promises, to be perfecter then those of their accomplishment. Thus much of the energyes, and actings of the Holy Ghost in men under the old Testament as well as under the new. And accordingly, there hath been alwaies the same Covenant of Grace: the same faith in, and by, the Son and Holy Spirit, *Gal.* 3. 8, 17. &c. and the same Sacraments 1 *Cor.* 10. 2, 3. from the beginning.

§. 8. *The 2 Covenants from the beginning.*

To shew which things somewhat more punctually and particularly. First Gods prescience, seeing mans use of his Free-will and his fall, foreordained our Saviour before the foundation of the world, tho he

manifested

The benefits of our Savior.

manifested him not till *the last times.* 1 *Pet.* 1. 20. And presently after the fall, (out of overflowing mercy) in the very curse, he delivered also the cure of it; and condemned the seducer of man to be destroyed by the (then first promised) seed of the woman, i. e. Christ, who also (immediatly) was the seed of the woman only, whom Satan first seduced; that he might be destroyed also by the same instrument i. e. woman, by which he thought to destroy man. Upon the multiplying of this seed, we find accordingly, because the promise of God did not take effect in all the seed, see *Rom.* 9. 6. &c. *Gal.* 4. 26. &c. we find in that infancy of the world, the same distinction of men, as now, noted indeed by the Apostle more expressly of *Abrahams* double seed, *Gal.* 4.22. but as true of *Adams*, and of all the times since the beginning: as likewise those other remarks that are made upon them, *Gal.* 4. 29. *Rom.* 9. 12. (*that the elder should* first persecute, *at last serve, the younger,*) we find then one generation after the flesh, another after the spirit; one of old *Adam* involved in no covenant but that of works, and by those (being evil) loosing the heavenly inheritance; the other of the promise, and attaining it by faith. And these we find called the sons of God, (which none are but by Christ.) *Gen.* 5. 2. The other *sons of men* or in opposition to the former *sons of the wicked one* the devil. 1 *Jo.* 3. 10, 12. In which respect the wicked Jews seem to be reckoned as the spiritual race or succession of *Cain*; since *Abels* blood is required of them, *Matt.* 23. 35, 36. *Jo.* 8. 44. (God and the Divel being the two spiritual fathers of the progeny of man. *Jo.* 8. 42. &c.) The one *pilgrims on the earth, Heb.* 11.13. The other *men of this world*; noted for their building of Cities as *Cain, Gen.* 4. 17.

Two generations alwaies: One of works, the other of faith.

and

and *Nimrod; Gen.* 10. 8, 9, 10. not so the others. The city and type of the one, *Babylon*, called confusion;and of the other, *Jerusalem*,intimating peace and unity.The one having a confusion of languages amongst them; The other retaining (as proper to them) the first language of paradise; called afterward the Hebrew, from Heber, (in whose time the earth was divided); and afterward, amongst his multiplied posterity, adhering only to *Abrahams* race. And of the former of these there was a Church of God erected from the beginning; which had Gods more special presence in the same land where paradise was. *Gen.* 4. 16. Which Church seems (from *Matt.* 19. 4, 8. comp. *Gen.* 6. 1, 2. and 4. 19. and *Mal.* 2. 15.) to have been then restrained both from polygamy, and marrying with the unbelievers; which matching with them afterwards was cursed with a gigantick, (and consequently tyrannous) ofspring, like that of *Cain's*, the wicked generation, *Gen.* 6. 4. -4. 23, 24. and of which matching after the flood *Abraham* and the Patriachs had much abhorrence: doubtless because the worship and fear of the true God was not among them. See *Gen.* 20. 11. -24. 3. -27. 24. From which wicked *Cain* was excommunicated and banished, whose murthering of his brother may be guessed [by *the way of Cain*] being joyned with [*the gainsaying of Core*] *Jude* 11. to have been, not only out of envy to him; because his sacrifice was more accepted, but out of emulation; for his being some way or other more specially preferred in the ministration also of the divine worship: and his race proved like him, full of violence, murders, many wives, &c. *Gen.* 4. 23, 24. -6. 11. see *Gen.* 4. 3, 12, 14, 16.

Amongst these sons of God *Abel* was the first, recorded

§. 9. *Such Abel.*

corded in the *Heb.* c. 11. declared there to be *righteous*; or juftifyed and accepted of God by faith: and that faith was; that God *was a rewarder of all thofe that diligently feek him,* verf. 6. which is a faith in Gods promifes: and *a faith of things not feen,* verf. 1. a faith therefore of promifes not yet attained; and indeed why elfe *his blood cry* after death? verf. 4. how elfe did he and the reft dy in faith? verf. 13. if not fomething hoped for after death? viz. the reftoring of that paradife which was loft; fee verf. 16, 26, 39. and the reftoring of life again to the innocent; as well as future vengeance on the oppreffor. Righteous *Abel* flain by him that was born after the flefh; that God might fhew in the firft Saint the lot of his Church here on earth; Seth is given in his ftead the Father of the holy race; faid to be *begotten in Adams image,* as *Adam* was *in the likenefs of God;* Gen. 5. 1, 2, 3. which is not faid of the former iffue, it may be, with reference to reftoring of man in Chrift, to the image in which God created *Adam.* Col. 3. 10. Eph. 2. 10. And born after long expectation firft, (as *Abrah·m's* fon of promife was) *Adam* being 130 years old before he had this feed, that was appointed by God inftead of *Abel.* Gen. 5. 3. -4. 25. After him *Enos,* who comparing Gen. 4. 26. with 2 *Pet.* 2. 5. was the firft more publick *preacher of righteoufnefs;* as *Noah was the eighth.* The fifth after him, Enoch; a Prophet; *Jude* 14. and after a fingular manner pious; who ferved God out of *faith* that *he was a rewarder of the diligent feekers of him*; and accordingly *received that reward* in an anticipated tranflation: that the times before the law might in him have a type of the advancement of the promifed feed, and an example of the promifed reward to all beleevers thro him;

as

Seth: the firft Father of the Holy Race.

Enos.

Enoch.

CHAP. IX.

as those under the law had in Elias; and those under the Gospel saw in the seed it self. See *Heb.* 11. 5, 6. The *eighth preacher of righteousness was Noah;* And here (in the tenth generation from *Adam*) the world that then was, was to be (as this second also shall be) for its wickedness destroyed, but, after first the preaching to them by Christ, *1 Pet.* 3. *19.* i. e. by the spirit of Christ, *1 Pet. 1. 11.* the same Gospel which is preached to us, viz. that as Christ was (in the appointed time) *put to death in the flesh,* but *quickned in the spirit;* so they might be judged and be put to death or become dead in the flesh, according to the former will and lusts of men; and be quickned in the spirit according to the will of God. See *1 Pet.* 4. *6.* comp. verf. 1, 2. and *1 Pet. 3. 18, 19. 2 Pet. 8. 9.*

Noah.

At which time (the world after this preaching of the Gospel unto them and the long-suffering of God *1 Pet. 3. 20.* for an 120 years, *Gen.* 6. 3. still continuing disobedient), and being to be destroyed by water (the type of the end of it to come by fire) we find the first express mention of a *Covenant; established with Noah and his seed, Gen.* 6. *18.* (where [my] not [a] seems to me to imply the continuation, not the beginning of a Covenant) in which God makes a promise to save him in this ark of the Covenant, and to bless the earth unto him; which was cursed for sin; and then should have been destroyed. *Gen.* 6. *13.* Which also his Father at his birth prophecyed of him, *Gen.* 5. *29.* and to regive to him and his seed the dominion of the world; which after the flood he gives him the possession of: see *Gen. 9. 1.* &c. And this promise we find made to *Noah* almost in the same terms, (that we need not doubt of the same thing intended by it) as it was

§. 9.
Of the Covenant of Grace made, or rather renewed with him.

after-

afterward to Abraham (*that he alfo fhould be the heir of the world,* Rom. 14. 13. *&c.*) fo alfo, of *Noah* as of *Abraham,* 'tis faid, that *he became heir of the righteoufnefs which is by faith,* Heb. 11. 7. that is heir of the benefits thereof, promifed unto him. And the promife was one and the fame from the beginning, firft of the coming into the world of the promifed feed, which is already fulfilled: and then of the reftoring of man, (firft *in,* and then *by* the promifed feed) to the inheritance which he forfeited by *Adams* fall; which inheritance was, 1. a right both to the earth and the creatures therein, (which fince *Adams* fall none have right to before God, but only thro Chrift.) 2. And more fpecially to the heavenly country and city, Heb. 11. 16. called alfo *entring into Gods reft,* Heb. 4. 6. *&c.* that *yet to come,* verf. 7, 8, 9. In the prefignification of which reft to come the Sabbath was appointed from the beginning to be obferved with reft, &c. fee Heb. 4. 3, 9, 10. after the 6 daies labour of this world, and after our deliverance from the perfecutions of Egypt, that is, all (whatever) the Churches enemies. For becaufe both thefe are the fame in the fubftance, therefore was it inftituted as a fymbole of both, fee *Exod.* 31. 17. (Gods work in the creation, after which he is faid to be refrefhed, being a type of his work in the redemption of the world, and in the Elect) from which alfo being perfected he fhall reft at the day of judgment: which city thefe holy men alfo looked after. Heb. 11. 10, 13, 39. comp. with Heb. 8. 2. -9. 11. And we alfo yet expect till the fecond coming of our Saviour. Of which promife that of the earth was a type to *Noah;* as that of *Canaan* to *Abraham.* Which promife is already made good to the feed; and fhall be by him to *Noah;* and to *Abraham;*

and

CHAP. IX.

and to all those who are of the Covenant, and of faith; who shall be blessed with faithful Abraham, *Gal.* 3. 9. thro the seed of Abraham; to whom the promise is (in the first place) made, *Gal.* 3. 16. being heir of all things, *Heb.* 1. 2. and in whom the Covenant is conformed to Abraham and the rest, *Gal.* 3. 17. to be fulfilled in its due time; As they were looking at the promise of the seed to come afar off, and not made perfect in that without us, who have already seen it fulfilled; so we also yet looking afar off at the promise of our inheritance (by the seed) yet to come; and neither they nor we made perfect in this till the end come. When the wicked shall be finally destroyed, and the righteous delivered and saved: of which eternal salvation the preserving of Noah and his family in the general deluge was an eminent type, see 2 *Pet.* 2. 5. comp. with 9. as also the saving of Lot and his family in the second fiery judgment of Sodom; and the saving of the Israelites, (i.e. the Church of God, *Act.* 7. 38.) in the third great day of judgment, in the slaying the first-born, and drowning of the Egyptians. Of which Israelites afterward not believing, only two, (in the consuming of all the rest in the wilderness) entred *Canaan*. Where the saving also so few in comparison of the world that perished (because men loved evil more then righteousness) is a type of the paucity of the saved at the last day. See *Rom.* 9. 27. And the manner of Noah's being saved was also a type; His being saved by or upon the water was a figure of *Baptism, by which we are now saved*, 1 *Pet.* 3. 21. as also was the passing of the Israelites to their preservation thro the Red sea. 1 *Cor.* 10. 2. And if we may say the same of the Rainbow the seal of the Covenant with Noah, as of the

Receiving the type of Baptism.

Bb 2   cloud

cloud that conducted the Ifraelites; this alfo was the figure of Baptifm, 1 *Cor*. 10. 2. which is the feal now current of the Covenant of grace. And if they had then the feals, they had alfo the Covenant to which they belonged. Now for the other Sacrament of the Eucharift; the Euchariftical facrifices (which were from the beginning) of the flefh of which the offerers did partake, were ever the types thereof. Nor may I pafs over, (in fhewing the Gofpel of Noah) the Covenant then that was made not only with Noah but alfo the Creatures, *Gen*. 9. 10, 12. which, as they (the earth, &c.) were curfed for finning Adams fake, *Gen*. 3. 17. -4. 12. *Rom*. 8. 20. and with man were to be deftroyed, *Gen*. 6. 7, 12, 13. fo in the Covenant of grace, by the promifed feed they alfo fhall be freed from the bondage of corruption into the glorious liberty of the Sons of God, *Rom*. 8. 20, 21. &c. of which, their deliverance with Noah was a preludium, *Gen*. 5. 29.

§. 11.
Shem,

After Noah Shem for his filial Duty, *Gen*. 9. 24. was the heir of the Covenant of grace, and Father of the holy feed; imagined by fome to be Melchifedeck, but the Father of Heber and the Hebrew's he was, *Gen*. 10. 21. and as God vouchfafed afterwards to be called the God of Abraham, fo before him he was called the God of Shem; *Gen*.9.26. And then alfo Noah prophecyed of the pofterity of Japhet, the Gentiles, their being united alfo to the Church defcended from Shem; which prediction was fulfilled upon the coming of the promifed feed. *Gen*. 9. 26, 27. And 'tis noted, as of Noah, that he lived to fee the 9th generation, even till the 58th year of Abraham; fo of Shem, and Salah, and Heber, that they all outliv'd Abraham: which long life

The Lord called the God of Shem.

Of the Eucharift.

CHAP. IX.

life of these holy men was surely a great advantage for catechizing their children in the true service of God. Yet many of *Shem's* race in time fell away to idolatry. See *Josh.* 24. 2, 14, 15. *Gen.* 3. 53.

And therefore God 17 years after *Noah's* death and 367 years after the flood called *Abraham* out of the house and country of his idolatrous Fathers, and opens the same way of salvation, (i. e. the Gospel) more clearly yet to him (therefore he called *the Father of the faithful*) *God promising him, that he should be heir of the world,* (*Rom.* 4. 13. (that is) in his seed: and *that seed, Christ Gal.* 3. 16, 17. Christ, the promise that was made both to him and to all the Fathers. See *Act.* 13. 32, 33. 2 *Cor.* 1. 20. *Heb.* 11. 13. comp. 39. And they possest of their inheritance first in his resurrection, *Act.* 13. 33. and not only that he *Rom.* 4. 23, 24. but that in all Nations those who were the children of the faith of *Abraham Rom.* 4. 16. *Luk.* 19. 9. should be coheirs of the promise made to *Abraham*. And this the Apostle calls *the Gospel that was preached to Abraham, Gal.* 3. 8. and *the Covenant made with him in Christ,* vers. 17. *Luk.* 1. 72. comp. 68. And *the adoption. Rom.* 9. 4. *From which commonwealth of* Abraham or *Israel* the Gentiles being *aliens,* and having no title to the Fathers, *Rom.* 9. 5. are there said to have been formerly in the times of the old Testament *without Christ, strangers from the Covenants of promise; having no hope,* &c. *Eph.* 2. 12. Of which covenant of Grace and the Gospel and not of that of works (for at the giving of the law there was no such ceremony required or practised, *Josh.* 5. 2, 7. tho mistaken perhaps to be so by the children of works, see *Rom.* 9. 32. *Gal.* 5. 3. or at least it being a part of the antiquated ceremonies, (the same reason that (they conceived) bound

§. 11.
Abraham.

Of the Covenant of Grace renewed with and the Gospel preached to him.

And of the Sacraments belonging to it.

bound them to the observing of it, binding them to the observance also of all the rest) was *circumcision* then a *seal.* See *Rom.* 4. 11, 13. *Act.* 2. 38, 39. and the Antitype of our baptism. God beginning now more ceremoniously and solemnly to own his Church; setting a corporeal mark upon it, whereby his people might be more signally separated and distinguished from the rest of men; as afterward (they multiplying into a nation,) in *Moses's* time, he distinguished them by peculiar laws. Fourteen generations after *Abraham* was the Gospel yet more evidently preached to *David* (that his seed, his son should rule over all the whole world, &c.) which seed promised to *David* also was Christ, see *Act.* 13. 23. and this covenant again established with him. See *Ps.* 89. 3. *1 Chron.* 17. 11. *Act.* 13. 23, 24. and *Ps.* 72. and 89. The subject of whose songs is almost nothing else but Christ; as we see from the expositions of them in the new Testament. And because the promises were made more fully to *Abraham* and to *David*; therefore hath our Saviour more chiefly the title, of [*the seed of Abraham, and of the Son of David*] then of others. See *Matt.* 1. 1. And *David* was followed by the *goodly fellowship of the Prophets*, whose *light shined brighter and brighter*, 2 *Pet.* 1. 19. in those former darker ages (so that some of them are called rather Evangelists then Prophets) till the *open day* of the Gospel at last ascended upon the Earth in its full lustre and perfection.

And let this be observed to the glory of the mercies of God everlasting, certain, never-failing, (neither by Satans polices, nor by mens sin); how at a certain distance of time, God alway mindful of his covenant with his elect. (For though *God is no accepter of persons, Act.* 10. 34. *Gal.* 2. 6.) for any external

David.

The same Covenant renewed to him.

The Prophets. Of Gods frequent renewing of the covenant of grace to his people by them.

§. 12.

Chap. IX.

external confiderations of nation, &c. nor internal of properties and parts (for the reafon why any have thefe better then others is purely becaufe he gave them); yet he is an admitter or receiver of one mans perfon, not anothers; of one nation, not another; they being in all things equal (or moftwhat he whom he receives fome way inferior); to gratuital favors for his own to us unknown pleafure, no way grounded upon any thing in the perfon. He preaccepteth none in point of juftice, fo as to do wrong to any; or deny to any their merit and due, tho due only upon his promife, by which he hath tyed himfelf to reward induftry, and our right ufe of his former gifts; *Matt.* 25. 29. fee *Matt.* 20. 13, 14, 15. But in point of liberality he doth, fo as to do more good to fome then others, without any caufe at all that is in the perfon: *Rom.* 9. 11. -3. 3. -11. 29. *Efai.* 41. 2, 4. Nor is this faid, as if he did not ordinarily give more with refpect to fome former gifts of his (either thofe of nature, or thofe of grace; thofe acquifit by mans induftry, or infufed by Gods mercy) that are in fuch or fuch a perfon, fee *Matt.*25.15,29.but that he hath not tyed himfelf to give only where are former gifts;and many times doth otherwife out of refpect of the fuperabundance and overflowings of his mercies, and of his Church upon earth: which his everlafting purpofe had determined (notwithftanding mens frequent Apoftacies) to maintain from the beginning to the end of the world, *Rom.* 3. 3, 4. -11. 29, 36. even then when he had moft reafon of all to defert it; after it had begun to decline to idolatry, Atheifm, &c. fent new preachers of this Covenant, and renewed the true Religion by them. And how not in the beft of times, for a reward of obedience; but in the worft, ever

And by extraordinary Teachers conftantly reforming the Church at certain times, when much declining from his true worfhip, and leaft deferving it.

ever out of a necessity of repair; not in the growth but the decadency of former piety; his eternal pitty still visited the world with new light and new *As by Enoch* Ambassadors. Some 600 years after the Creation, the world then full of ungodly sinners both in words and deeds, *Jude 14.* Enoch was sent a Prophet; who walked with God; and in whom was shewed to the world the reward of righteousness; and who denounced the last judgment day against the then *Noah.* wicked. Again at a certain distance from *Enoch*, before the flood; when now not only the rest of the world, but also the holy race was corrupt with oppression and violence from Gigantick people, *Gen. 4. 23, 24.* and illegal conjunctions upon multiplication of women. *Gen. 6. 2.* comp. *1, 4, 13. Mal. 2. 15.* God sent *Noah*, who *walked* also *with God*, and was a Preacher of righteousness 367 years after the flood. Idolatry also now growing rife, and *Shems* holy race fallen away into it. *Josh. 24. 2, 14. Gen. 31. 30, 53.* *Abraham.* God called *Abraham*; who *commanded his children to keep the way of the Lord, Gen.* 18. 19. &c. 430 years after this, *Gal. 3. 17.* when the children of Israel were full of the Idols, whoredoms and abominations of Egypt; sacrificing unto Devils, &c. see *Josh.* 24. 14. -5. 9. *Lev.* 17. 7. *Ezek.* 20. 7, 8, 9, 14. -23 .3. (The reason why they were so prone to it at *Sinai*: and upon every occasion so ready to start from the Lord) God sent *Moses*, but not for any merit of theirs at all: therefore are they every where so frequently told of it. See *Deut.* 9. 4, 5, 6. &c. [*Not for thy righteousness, nor for the uprightness of thine heart, for thou* wert, &c. but *to perform the word which the Lord sware.*] And *Ezek.* 20. and *Ezek.* 36. 21, 22, 31, 32. where God saith when they would not cast away their abominations, &c. that he nevertheless

Chap. IX.

thelefs *wrought for his name fake, and caufed them to go forth,* &c. fee verf. 8, 9,10,14. &c. fee the like ftory *Pfal.* 106. 8,43,45. comp. with the reft of the Pfalm. *Pf.*78.38. comp.36. the reafon of his compaffion not their goodnefs, but their mortality: verf. 39. 65. *Jer.* 30. 8. &c. comp.15. -31. 19. Nor were their children he carried into *Canaan* better then their fathers, *Ezek.* 20. 21. (for which confider that ftrange paffage, *Amos* 5. 26. (of which the modefty of *Mofes* hath faid nothing in the ftory) the fecret *carrying along* with them (befides the Lords) the effigies and *Tabernacle which they made to themfelves of Molech and Chiun, &c.*) *But yet for his name fake, &c.* verf. 22. And fee verf. 37, 40, 41. How God promifeth after the expiring of his punifhments and wearinefs of afflicting (very frequent in the Prophets) before any at leaft acceptable repentance of theirs, a reftorement of them to all his mercies and bleffings; upon which reftorement (faith he) *ye fhall remember your waies,* and *loath your felves, when I have wrought with you for my names fake, not according to your wicked waies,* verf. 43, 44. fee *Ezek.* 16. 59. &c. Not as if he did not require our repentance for to obtain the return of his favours, efpecially to challenge or expect it; which is fo effectual to haften his mercies, and cut off the remains of juftice. See *Lev.* 25. 39. *Ezek.* 6. 8, 9. But if this be not: Mans impenitence or unbelief fhall not fruftrate for ever Gods faith, promife, glory; *Rom.* 3. 3. But he will create new hearts in us rather; and we fhall repent after his mercies at leaft, when not before: and St. *Paul* fhall cry out; *O the depth* ! *Who hath firft given* unto him, *Rom.* 11. 35. For he who hath tyed himfelf upon repentance to fhew mercy; hath not tyed himfelf not to fhew it but only upon repen-

C c tance

tance. And indeed Gods judgments many times, (particularly war) making men worse; and his punishments (by our desperate malignity) increasing sin; whence could any reformation begin but from himself? who is forced at last, (when our sin contends in duration with his justice) because his mercies endure for ever, to pardon us for nothing. Nay when his favours are built upon our repentance, 'tis the same, tho not so short a way of pure mercy. We have no goodness but that some grace prevents it. It only makes its own way; 'tis only it, that invites it self; and prepares its own lodging; and if we would find out the beginning of Gods mercies we can go only from one to another in *infinitum*; who makes first that repentance, which he afterward rewards; and gives us first to ask those favors, which he gives us for asking.

§ 13.
Moses.

To return to the subject in hand. Now in this time of greatest necessity God sent *Moses*: whose law was given for a light to the feet of the sons of faith; as for a letter of condemnation to the sons of Belial. About 400 years after, *Act.* 13. 20. when the Israelites were quite declined from the pious steps of their forefathers; and *the word of the Lord* (upon it) for a long time, had *been rare and precious*,

Samuel and David.

See *Judg.* 2. 10. 1 *Sam.* 3. 1. God sent *Samuel*, *David*, &c. 500. years after this; all relapsed into idolatry; and in their captivity little amendment; see *Ezra* 9. 1. *Zech.* 7. 5. &c. just when ten forede-creed Sabbaths of years for the land (whose Sabbaths among other things by them were not observed) see *Lev.* 26. 34. 2 *Chron.* 36. 21. were run out: God for his names sake sent a restorement of their

Zerubbabel and Joshuah.

Church and government by *Zerubbabel* and *Joshua*. Near the end of 70 Sabbaths or weeks of years, i. e. 490

CHAP. IX.

490 years *Dan. 9. 25.* after this, when we know what a miserable condition the Church of God was in, from the wickedness of the High Priest; the superstition and hypocrisie, and false doctrines of the Pharisee, when there was now *hoc dignus vindice nodus;God sent his son* to reform all things *Heb.9.19.* And *His own Son.* we may gather also from *Rom.* 11.26,27,28, 29. that the last conversion of this nation, shall be only for Gods promise, not their repentance. And indeed who so considers that from God proceeds all our reformation; as well as his blessings for, and upon it; for all the effects of mercy must wholly acquiesce in him; and acknowledg all things alwaies done for his own sake; nothing for ours. These set and foremeasured times of performing these purposes of God the Evangelist hath otherwise observed in the 14 generations; that were between those great Epocha's of *Abraham* and *David; David* and the Captivity; Captivity and Christ. *Matt. 1. 17.*

§. 14

And now what can hinder Gods goodness; or decay the Church; since 'tis plain that sin cannot? God preserving it not for its holiness, but his glory. To whose power Satan is so far inferior; that tho he is permitted to work much sin in the world; yet was he never, nor never shall be, able to frustrate by sin any of the least of Gods designs. And therefore that supposition is not pious, of his assisting the Church so far as she neglects not her duty: which is only promising, that the Church shall not (if it doth not) fall away; for so doubtless it had been, long since many times over, perished: And Gods enemy have had the universal Monarchy of this lower world. But as from him only it is that the Churches faith continues; so his promise that she shall not, is also that her faith shall not, fail; see *Luk.* 22. 32.

God for ever preserving the Church not according to its perseverance in holiness; but his own eternal purpose and pleasure.

The benefits of our Saviour.

comp. with *Matt.* 16. 18. And the motives of Gods protection of Her are now the same as of old, (wherewith his servants, upon the rising of his indignation against her, alwaies conjured him); i. e. not respect to her righteousness; but the care of his *name: least it* (either the power or glory thereof) *should be polluted amongst Chrifts* spiritual *enemies*, Satan and his Angels: and temporal, Antichrist and his worshippers; whilst he seemed unable to protect her. [Hence the jealousy of Gods and Chrifts name, amongst the Mahometans now, no less then amongst the Heathen before, shall secure Christianity.] See *Numb.* 14. 16. Who is now also as jealous as ever of his honor; and faith as of old, *Pf.* 46. 10. *I will be exalted amongst the Heathen,* &c. Or the truth and faithfulness thereof should be asperfed amongst his servants; after so many promises and oaths made (for besides those latter of the new Testament, even that old one to *Abraham* (which was concerning his spiritual seed) is no way yet canceld or expired), if he should appear unready to preserve her. See *Exod.* 32. 13. And in that great judgment *Matt.* 24. 21. from which some are saved, he faith not for the righteous, but *for the elect tho 'e daies shall be shortned*: i. e. for his election of some to whom he will shew mercy: which election *Rom.* 9. 11. is of God calling, not man working; who creates repentance, as well as shews favor upon it; and who of a sudden brings an holy generation out of a corrupt. Whose omnipotency delights to exercise it self in changing even curses themselves into blessings. As we see in the curse of *Adam*; Satans mischiefs upon *Eve*, being the occasion (in cursing him) of promising the blessed seed. *Gen.* 3. 15. In the curse of *Babel*; by it peopling the world, *Gen.* 11. 8.-10. 2. &c. Of *Levi's race,*

CHAP. IX.

race, *Gen.* 49. 7. whose scattering in Israel became their preeminence in the imployment of the ministry of holy things. *Numb.* 16. 9. Of Christ, *Gal.* 3. 13. the killing of whom by Satans great plotting and malice, became the salvation of the world. The Babilonian Captivity, which ('tis observed) much advanced in the world the knowledg of the true God, and prudent laws. The prosecuting of the death of *Stephen*, and destruction of the Christians; by which the Gospel was spread over the world. *Act.* 8. 4. *Onesimus* his running away, *Philem.* 15. his conversion. Glory be unto his omnipotency and wisdom out of weakness producing strength; and good out of evil! Amen. And again whose unsearchable counsel doth not ty and restrain it self to prosper all good intentions and pious designs of those, who are zealous for propagating his Church; either by converting Heathens to the christian faith; or Heretical Christians to the truth. And this only because his preappointed *time of* mercy to such a people *is not yet come:* who for their sins are yet longer to suffer the just judgment of blindness and error; And *it is not for men* to *know the times and seasons which the Father hath put in his own power*; much less to take up the sword unbidden in his cause; being an Engine he hitherto hath not used, to promote religion. And perhaps therefore it hath been (tho I am perswaded sometimes drawn out of pure zeal to Gods honor) hitherto so unsuccesful. Witness, those many unfortunate attempts uppon the Mahometans in several parts, by Christian Princes in the Holy war: By *Lewis* 9th, by *Charles* 5th, &c. Towards which enemy of Christian religion (since he hath attained his just bounds) their defences have been wonderfully successful; not so
their

their invasions. And since the last divisions in the Church 1500. the many as unprosperous civil wars of Christians amongst themselves. As on one side the famous invasion of the *Swedes*, the attempts of the Reformed in the low-Countries; in *France*; On the other side the invasion of 88; The powder-conspiracy; the late insurrection of the Romanists in *Ireland*, &c. without any considerable advantage to that side (which ever it be) that is orthodox.

§. 15.
The eminent promulgation of the Covenant of Grace 430 years seniour to that of the law.

Neither did *Moses*, and the giving of the law annul or weaken the covenant of grace; being seniour to this promulgation of the law, (as it was renewed to *Abraham*) yet being before him also, 430 years, *Gal.* 3. 17. neither yet did the Gospel, i. e. the covenant of grace manifested and accomplisht in the times of the Gospel, annul or weaken the law. See *Gal.* 4. 21. *Rom.* 3. 31. -3. 21. And therefore the Gospel is said, as to be preached to *Abraham*,

The Gospel preached to the same people when the law was.

so also to them in the wildernes; tho *many of them it profited not*, (as also now it doth not), *being not mixed with faith in many of the hearers. Heb.* 4. 2. And first for the law Ceremonial; it was nothing but the Gospel in symbole and type; and therefore is not abolished by the Gospel when fully manifested, but only by being compleated and improved; as the Gospel in shadow by the Gospel in substance, or a child is by becoming a man. *Gal.* 4. 3. -3. 24.

The law to the children of faith, consistent with, subservient to, and no way annulled by, the Covenant of Grace; or the Gospel.

Secondly, for the law moral; it now well consists with the Covenant of the Gospel, not one title of it being expunged; but (rather) as some think much enlarged; and a stricter observance thereof then by *Moses*, required by our Saviour. See *Matt.* 5. 17, 18. comp. 19, 20. *Rom.* 8. 4. 1 *Cor.* 7. 19. And it was included and presupposed in the Covenant of grace transacted with *Abraham. Gen.* 18. 19. Why then

should

Chap. IX.

should we think that the law given at *Sinai* did not well accord with the Gospel, that was then also preached? *Heb.* 4. 2. Nay, that more perfect knowledg of Gods will, the giving of the law to *Jacob*, &c. whilst other nations walking in darkness were not so dealt with, *Pf.* 147. 19. is quoted as a great priviledg and favour to that people by the Apostle, *Rom.* 3. 2. -2. 18. -9. 4. (where the Apostle reckons among benefits not only the promises, and one Covenant, but *the Covenants* and *the giving of the law*) and rejoyced in, as such every where by the Psalmist, *Pf.* 119. -147. 20. which rendred them (I mean the sons of faith not of works) much more holy and less sinners, then generally the Gentiles were: see *Gal.* 2. 15. being a *lantern to the feet* of the children of the spirit; as a letter of condemnation to those of the flesh: and in that it is said *to bring nothing to perfection, Heb.* 7. 19. being intimated to have the power to advance men some steps toward it. For tho the law was not the Gospel; nor the ministration of the letter the same with that of the spirit; nor that of *Moses* with that of Christ; yet one was subservient and a precognitum unto the other. And it was first in order to receive the precept, to tell us what is to be performed; and then the spirit to enable us to perform it, (tho without the spirit also we never perfectly know it.) Therefore the first law-giving was to *Adam* as soon as created; and to it answered especially the divulging of the Gospel to *Abraham*: again the law was set forth again, and as it were reprinted by *Moses* at *Sinai*; and to it answered the manifestation and last edition of the Gospel by Christ coming in the flesh. Yet tho thus the law is before the Gospel in order of nature, yet not in time: for even *Adam* himself as he had an external

nal command to obferve, (which was the letter of the law) fo had he the fpirit to enable him for it; and that the fame fpirit which is to us reftored by the Gofpel.

§. 16. *Tho to the children of works a killing letter.*

The miniftration therefore of the law by *Mofes* (taken fingle and abftractively by it felf, from the miniftration of the fpirit, which was alfo adminiftred at the fame time (tho not in its great folemnity) to the children of the promife and of faith, tho not by *Mofes*), was of nothing but *the letter*; and that letter *a killing* one; impreffed in ftone but not upon the heart; the *the miniftration of death*, 2 Cor. 3. 7. *a Covenant faulty*, i. e. defective; and no falvation by it; but the promife annexed was only *He that doth, ſhall live, in them;* a fentence of condemnation (and fo it (accidentally) happened to be then, as now alfo,) to thofe who were of works and not of faith, Gal. 3. 9, 10. to thofe who had the adminiftration of the letter only, and not of the fpirit. In which fenfe taken, all things are faid in its difparagement *(the law* ceremonial *making nothing perfect,* the moral all fuller of fin); and all thofe oppofitions of the law to the Gofpel: and of *Mofes* to Chrift. See *Heb. 8. 9.* Therefore where the Apoftle makes any fuch oppofition; 'tis either of the more obfcure manifeftation of the Gofpel and promifes in the times under the law, in refpect of thofe after the incarnation of Chrift: Or of the law Ceremonial, fometimes alfo called the *old Covenant,* in refpect of its accomplifhment in Chrift; (as this occurs often in the Epiftle to the Hebrews) Or not of the book of the old Teftament, i. e. of *Mofes* and the Prophets, to the new Teftament, i.e. of the Gofpel of our Saviour, (for thus the new Teftament is alfo contained in, and proved out of the old,)

CHAP. IX.

old,) but of the law moral confidered by it felf in the old Teftament, (and abftracted there from all the promifes of Gods mercy and of grace, that are frequent in it,) only as it rigidly commands all righteoufnefs; forbids all fin; promifeth rewards to thofe that keep; denounceth punifhments to thofe that tranfgrefs it; and meanwhile changeth not, helpeth not at all mans natural pravity, and inability to obferve it. Yet thus alfo ; as the letter only, it ferved well, by fhewing men their fins and inability to perform them, to drive them forward with the rod of this *Schoolmafter* into the Covenant of grace, fee *Rom.* 3. 19, 21. -9. 32. *Gal.* 3. 22, 24. and to make them look after a Redeemer, by feeing how guilty they ftood before God; and after the fpirit promifed and procured by him, by feeing their former felf-weaknefs (which fpirit and redeemer then alfo offered themfelves to the children of faith.) Tho many of the Ifraelites abufed this intention of the law, by feeking juftification by it, rather then by faith : *Rom.* 9. 32. whilft meanwhile the miniftration of the fpirit, fee 2 *Cor.* 3. 6, 7, 8. *Rom.* 8. 2. *Heb.* 8. 10, 11. writ it upon the hearts of the faithful; by which fpirit as *the juft lived*; and had remiffion of former fins (committed againft this law) *by faith. Pfal.* 32. 1, 2. *Rom.* 4. 7, 8. So he was enabled (for the future) to walk in thofe fame laws; fee *Luk.* 1. 6. *Rom.* 8. 4. The law ftanding ftill in force as fubordinate unto grace, 1 *Cor.* 9. 21. for our works following faith and repentance ; (tho not for thofe preceding them) to which law we are alwaies to perform both fincere and univerfal obedience. Thefe two miniftrations therefore of the law and of the fpirit are oppofed, for their effect : one taken fingle, by it felf without

Yet fervice-able to drive them (made fenfible of their inability) forward into the Covenant of Grace.

The benefits of our Savior.

the other, serving only for conviction and condemnation, &c. and for the persons by whom they came; one by *Moses*, the other by Christ; but not for the time, or for the time also; but not as if in time (I mean since *Adams* fall) the one preceded the other for their absolute being, but only in respect of the clearer manifestation first of the one, then of the other; at several times. In the former times the law being more largely propounded; the promises seen a far off and darkly, as it were thro a cloud or veil; 2 *Cor.* 3. 13. The Messias expected to appear in the flesh; the gift of the spirit narrower for compass, less in intention: But the latter times, from it now visibly sent down from Heaven enjoying clearer manifestations of truth, larger effusions of grace. *1 Cor-* 9. 10. To conclude. As we find before the law from the beginning, a double generation, one sons of God; and the other of men: one righteous and the other wicked; and in Abrahams time *one born of the bond-woman, another of the free-woman* ; now those born of the free-woman are only such as are made free by Christ, see *Gal.* 4. 31. -5. 1. *one born after the flesh; the other after the spirit, or by promise.* (Now the spirit is the promise of the Gospel, as well as the Messias, and comes only by the Messias) one *ex operibus*, the other *ex vocante*, *Rom.* 9. 11. which two generations, (from the beginning) were also shewed in the opposition between *the elder* and *the younger* ; (as in *Cain* whose race was gigantick in comparison of the other. *Gen.* 6. 4. and Abel, or Seth: Ismael, Isaac: Esau, Jacob: Ham and Shem, &c. Which may be observed also in Reuben and Judah; Zarah and Pharez; Manasses and Ephraim; David and his brethren; Aaron and Moses; (And not only in

persons

Chap. IX.

perſons, but nations; ancienter and greater nations, againſt that choſen for Gods people; Iſrael and the Egyptian: Iſrael and the Canaanites: Iſrael and the Philiſtine: Iſrael and Babylon; Jew and Antiochus; Jew and Gentile; then Gentile the people of God and the Jew Apoſtate: laſtly, the Church and Antichriſt. The Elder perſecuting the younger, or the former born, the latter; but yet the latter ſtill overcoming the former; *for that which is firſt is natural.* 1 *Cor.* 15. 46.

So under the law alſo we find a twofold generation; one of faith holding of Abraham; another of works of the law, holding of Moſes, *Gal.* 3. 9, 10; and two Covenants on foot; the one the Mount Sinai; and the other the Jeruſalem-Covenant. *Gal.* 4. 25. and two explanations upon them, to guide men to which covenant they ſhould adhere; the one [*Curſed is every one that continueth not in all things written in the law to do them;* and *He that doth, ſhall live in them. Rom.* 10. 5. *Gal.* 3. 12. quoting *Deut.* 17. 26. *Levit.* 18. 5.] The other [*The juſt ſhall live by faith*]; or *Bleſſed is the man whoſe iniquities are forgiven.* See *Rom.* 3. 3, 7, 8. *Gal.* 3. 10, 12, 11. *Rom.* 4. 3. - 9. 33. quoting *Pſal.* 32. 1, 2. *Habbak.* 2. 4. *Iſai.* 28. 16. *Gen.* 15. 6: Nay ſee both theſe coming from the mouth of Moſes, who himſelf was a Son of faith. The one *Levit.* 18. 5. the other *Deut.* 13. 11, 12. explained by the Apoſtle, *Rom.* 10. 5, 6, 7. &c. The latter of which [*The word is nigh thee, in thy heart,* &c.] that is, ſaith he, the word of faith; and that ſame faith which the Goſpel preacheth, verſ. 8. And therefore as we are now referred for ſalvation to the preaching of Chriſt and his Apoſtles; ſo Abraham then (before theſe) referred Dives his brethren for their ſalvation and eſcaping of hell to the

§. 17. The two miniſtrations of the law by Moſes; and the ſpirit by Chriſt, how; and how not, oppoſed.

preaching of Moses and the Prophets. *Luk.* 16. 29, 31. And both St. Paul and St. James, treating about the point of juſtification, take their examples out of the old Teſtament; inſtancing, how it was in Abraham amongſt the Hebrews, and Rahab amongſt the Gentiles. See *Rom.* 4. 1. &c. *Jam.* 2. 21, 25. And as the other held of Adam and the law; ſo theſe latter in all ages held of Chriſt and the Goſpel: and (as we now) had alwaies the ſame Saviour, their King to conduct them; the ſame ſpirit to inſpire and inform them; the ſame Sacraments (for ſubſtance) to confirm them: Baptiſm in the Red ſea and in the Cloud, thro which ſee *Exod.* 14. 19, -13. 21. *Matt.* 3. 11. they paſſed to Canaan: and the Euchariſt; the body of our Lord in the Manna, coming down from Heaven; and his blood in the water, ſtreaming out of the rock. 1 *Cor.* 10. 1. &c. So Circumciſion was adminiſtred, and their ſacrifices uſed by them, as Baptiſm and the Euchariſt by us: (of which inſtituted by the Lord Jeſus theirs delivered to the fathers were types) for remiſſion of ſin, and conferring grace, for appeaſing Gods wrath, and thankſgiving for mercies with reference to the ſame blood of the new Teſtament, and the onely true ſacrifice. So St. Auſtin *de nuptiis & concupiſcentia.* l. 2. c. 11. ſaith *Circumciſionem ad purgationem originalis peccati valuiſſe magnis & parvis, quemadmodum nunc Baptiſmus.* And that threat *Gen.* 17. 14. *That ſoul ſhall be cut off from his people* is ordinarily underſtood; that he is cut off as well for being *extra pactum,* as being *præcepti violati reus.* And tho Circumciſion in Abraham (who was before the receipt thereof juſtified by faith) was only a ſeal of that former juſtification; as alſo the Sacrament of Baptiſm was to Cornelius (ſaith St. Auſtin *contra Dona-*

The Ancients had alwaies the ſame way of ſalvation as the latter times.

CHAP. IX.

Donatiſtas. l. 4. c. 24.) See *Act.* 10. 47. comp. 44. and is to many other. Yet this hinders not (faith Eſtius 4. Sent. 1. d. 31. ſec.) but that in *parvulis ſicut nunc Baptiſmus, ita olim Circumciſio non nudum eſſet ſignaculum juſtitiæ interioris, ſed efficax atque operatorium.* And St. Auſtin ibid. *Cur ergo ei præceptum eſt ut omnem deinceps infantem octavo die circumcideret ; niſi quia & ipſum per ſcipſum ſacramentum multum valebat?* And for this purpoſe alſo were their ſacrifices uſed. See *Lev.* 4. 20, 26. and *the Prieſt ſhall make an attonement for him as concerning his ſin and it ſhall be forgiven him. Vulgar ; Rogabitque pro eo Sacerdos & pro peccato ejus, & dimittetur ei.* See *Lev.* cap. 5. cap. 17. and *Numb.* 15. cap. and *Heb.* 5. 1. *That he might offer ſacrifices for ſins,* ſo *Job* c. 1. v. 5. *offered ſacrifice for the ſins of his ſons,* and 42. cap. 8, and v. 9. *he offered ſacrifice and prayed for the treſpaſſes of his friends, and God accepted him.* See the ſame 2 *Sam.* 24. 25. How like is that *Lev.* 4. 26. in the old Teſtament to *Jam.* 5. 14, 15. in the new, for remiſſion of ſin by the Prieſts uſing ſacred ceremonies and praier ? and that *Deut.* 34. 9. to *Act.* 8. 17. for conferring of the graces of the ſpirit ? Therefore thus St. Auſtin Quæſt. 84. in Levit. *Moſes ſanctificabat viſibilibus ſacramentis per miniſterium ſuum, Dominus inviſibili gratia per ſpiritum ſuum.* And Tract. 26. in Johan. he faith *Sacramenta Judæorum & noſtra fuiſſe in ſignis diverſa ; in re, quæ ſignificatur, paria* : quoting 1 *Cor.* 10. 2, 3. *Omnes eandem eſcam ſpiritualem manducaverant, ſpiritualem utique eandem quam nos. Aliud illi, aliud nos, ſed ſpecie viſibili, quod tamen hoc idem ſignificaret virtute ſpirituali.* To which I will add two ſayings of Leo, the one Serm. 3. de Nativit. Domini. *Non minus adepti qui in illud magnæ pietatis ſacramentum credidere promiſſum, quam*

The benefits of our Saviour.

qui fuscepere donatum. The other Serm. 1. in die Pentecost. *Cum in die Pentecostes discipulos Domini spiritus sanctus implevit, non fuit inchoatio muneris, sed adjectio largitatis. Quoniam & Patriarchæ & Prophetæ & Sacerdotes, omnesque Sancti, qui prioribus fuere temporibus, ejusdem sunt spiritus sancti sanctificatione vegetati; & sine hac gratia nulla unquam instituta sacramenta, nulla sunt celebrata mysteria, ut eadem semper fuerit virtus charismatum, quamvis non eadem fuerit mensura donorum.* Indeed the Sacraments of the old Testament considered in themselves, as separate from, or opposite to, the merit of Christ and the grace of the Gospel, were of no power for expiating sin, or conferring grace. We find the Sacrifices also instituted in Levit. for lesser sins: those of ignorance; those offending against some legal rites, and ceremonies; those damaging our neighbor in some smaller matters, joyned with restitution; but not for expiation of the great ones, murder, idolatry, blasphemy, or adultery; and for these lesser sins we may not imagine them expiatory of the guilt, or sin in it self (save as they foresignified the merits of the Sacrifice on the Cross, and thus strengthned the faith of the offerer in the promises to come: for which faith obeying Gods command in offering to him these Types thereof, the merits of the Sacrifice of the Cross was applied to him for remission of his sin, great, or little) but only of the legal immundicities, or some temporal penalties due thereto; which sacrifices therefore were of themselves *quotidiana peccatorum accusatio*, but not *solutio*, as St. Chrysostom in Heb. Hom. 17. Therefore also where we find discourse in the Prophets of remission of sin, as in *Ezekiel.* 18. chap. the legal Sacrifices are not proposed as any remedy thereof;

Chap. IX.

thereof; and many times spoken of in the old Testament as unprofitable thereunto. And what is said here of the common, and ordinary Sacrifices, is to be said for those more solemn ones, offered once a year, on the great day of expiation, which are extensible only to the same ends, and purposes, as the ordinary Sacrifices were. Again, these Sacrifices also for the expiation of the exteriour immundicity, and punishment of the lesser sins (for which they were ordained) in this came short of that all-sufficient Sacrifice of our Lord: that they neither procured such indulgence from God for any future sin of the same kind, but so many sins as were committed, so many several Sacrifices were to be slain, and offered: nor procured from him any grace, or special assistance of his Spirit for the prevention of such future sins. But left those for whom they were offered as liable to the same sins, as they were before, whereas our Lords one oblation made satisfaction for all future sins as well as past; and also procured from God the plentiful effusion of the Holy Spirit, and Grace for preventing of a relapse into sin for the future. This then was the great weakness, and unprofitableness of the Sacraments, and Sacrifices of the Law. *Heb.*7.18. Therefore the Apostle calls them but *beggarly elements, Gal.* 4. 9. and in the 9. and 10. chapter to the Hebrews *denies they could take away sin,* &c. and in many places speaks against the unprofitableness of circumcision, &c. (as also many things are said in the old Testament in disparagement of the sacrifices under the law.) But as Estius 4. Sent. 1ᵈ. 28 s. methinks well notes. *Quæ ab Apostolo* (and so I may say of those things said by the Prophets*) contra Judæos proprie dicta sunt, qui Christum solum justificato-*

rem ignorantes signa pro rebus amplectebantur; existimantes sacrificia & sacramenta veteris legis per seipsa deo accepta & propitiatoria esse, ut Christi sanguine opus non esset.

§. 18. And the same thing may be said of John Baptists baptism, which, tho certainly as relating to the blood of Christ we cannot imagine that it was inferiour, in its effects to the former Sacraments administred before or under the law to those who died not having the opportunity of receiving our Saviours after it; yet first considered in it self, and as the Jews looked upon it as an external washing only coming from John it was, as he told them, only a Baptism *of water, not of the spirit*. He administring no more then the external sign only; but Christ, that came after him, the inward Grace, for that measure thereof, that was in Johns Baptism, as in other old-Testament-Sacraments, received. Secondly, Tho in his Baptism, or other former Sacraments to the rightly prepared Grace might be and was received, yet was there no descent of the Holy Ghost, or donation of those higher gifts or Graces thereof (which externally manifested its internal presence, and therefore κατ᾽ ἐξοχὴν had the name of the Holy Ghost, see *Act.* 8. 17. *Act.* 1. 8. -10. 44. -19. 6. comp. 2, 3. of which doubtless the Baptist speaks, *Matt.* 3. 11. distributed, save extraordinarily, till the coming of our Lord and by his Missioners; the first effusion thereof being at Pentecost, and so continuing ever since more frequent in the Church as to several of these eminent gifts thereof, to and upon so many, whose hearts, and conversation are very much purified from sin; for which therefore John was sent before our Lord to prepare the world by a due repentance and reformation, our Lord not

Chap. IX.

not vouchsafing to *put this new wine save into new vessels:* for defect of which, even in these latter times of the Gospel also, the donation of the Holy Ghost taken in this sense is not so common. It must be granted then that the former Sacraments also, as they referred to Christ, yet were many waies inferiour in the benefit received by them, to those instituted by our Saviour after the mystery of our salvation accomplished. *Veteribus sublatis* (saith S. Austin) *instituta sunt nova, virtute majora, utilitate meliora, actu faciliora, numero pauciora*, and Leo (quoted before)*eadem fuit virtus charismatum, quamvis non eadem fuit mensura donorum*, and this may be the reason of those 2 Canons in the Concil. Trident. 7. Session. *Siquis dixerit novæ legis sacramenta à sacramentis antiquæ legis non differre nisi quia ceremoniæ sunt aliæ, & alii ritus externi: Anathema sit.* And again, *si quis dixerit Baptismum Johannis habuisse eandem vim cum baptismo Christi, Anathema sit.* Which was also the Ancient doctrine of the Church against the Donatists pleading from it the lawfulness of the iteration of Christs baptism. To whom St. Austin replyes *contra literas Petiliani* l. 2. c. 37. *Sicut aliud est carnis circumcisio Judæorum, aliud autem quod octavo die Baptizatorum nos celebramus: & aliud est Pascha quod adhuc illi de ove celebrant, aliud autem quod nos in corpore & sanguine Domini accipimus; sic alius fuit Baptismus Johannis, alius est baptismus Christi: Illis enim ventura ista prænunciabantur, ihis completa illa prædicantur.* Thus Calvin also Instit. l. 4. c. 14. 22. *Quin uberior etiam spiritus gratia hic* (i. e. in the Sacraments of the new Testament) *se proferat, si tempus cum tempore compares non dubium est: Nam id pertinet ad gloriam regni Christi, sicut ex plurimis locis præsertim ex* 7 capite

E e   Johan.

Johan. *colligimus*: *Quo sensu accipere oportet illud Pauli, umbras fuisse sub lege, Corpus sub Christo. Neque enim consilium est exinanire suo effectu testimonia gratiæ in quibus olim Patribus veracem se probare deus voluit, sed comparative magnifacere quod nobis datum est.* And I think no Christian hath reason to equal the benefits of their Manna or Paschal Lamb to those of the Eucharist instituted by the Lord Jesus, with annullation of the other; and a preface of *Hoc est corpus meum*, which seems needless innovation, if as much might have been said of the former Lamb. See Bishop Forbes de Eucharist. l. 1. c. 1. s. 26. *Haud dubie prisci fideles ante Christi incarnationem carnem Christi spiritualiter edebant in Manna, & rebus aliis figuratam, & sufficienter pro statu œconomiæ illius ad salutem* 1 Cor. 10. *&c. sed nihilominus per communicationem carnis Christi in Eucharistia multo altius & solidius nos Christianos incorporari Christo quam priscos fideles, qui Christi incarnationem præcesserant*: And again. *Eadem fuit Judæorum & Christianorum esca quoad significationem, non autem quoad rei significatæ & figuratæ præsentiam & exhibitionem. Haud absurde igitur dicitur Agnum paschalem, Mannam, petram &c. fuisse Sacramenti Eucharistiæ typos & figuras, &c.* And if any one think to equal the benefit of the new Sacraments with those old ones because salvation was also had under them, He must also deny any profit thereof also now to people formerly penitent and beleevers: because these also prevented of the actual reception of these Sacraments may attain eternal life. Thus 'tis confessed the former Sacraments to be in many degrees inferiour to the new instituted by Christ. The Schoolmen go yet further in depressing them. *Non valuisse sacrificia vetera, &c. ad expia-*

Chap. IX.

expiationem peccati quoad culpam & pœnam Gehennæ, nisi quatenus signa quædam erant protestantia fidem in Christum. Non justificasse vi sua (as the new ones do) *sed ex fide & devotione suscipientis, quæ fides nunc non efficit gratiam sacramentalem, neque dat efficaciam sacramentis, sed solum tollit obstacula. Instituta esse primo & per se ad significationem fut.rorum* (according to that of St. Austin *non dantia salutem, sed promittentia salvatorem*) *non ad efficiendum aliquid nisi per accidens, quatenus in eorum susceptione erat protestatio fidei, &c.* Yet (to conclude) How ever be it *per se,* or be it *per accidens,* 'tis granted by all that the same effects for remission of sin, and grace necessary to salvation according to the œconomy of those imperfecter times, were wrought in the receiving of those Sacraments as since in the new. So Aquin. part. 3. 62. q. 6. art. confesseth *per Circumcisionem Gratiam fuisse collatam quantum ad omnes gratiæ effectus, sicut in Baptismo non tamen ex virtute ipsius Circumcisionis sicut per Baptismum.* And Bellarmine. *Meritum Christi nobis applicatur per sacramenta, Hebræis autem per solum fidem*: But he adds *quæ tamen fides requirebat sacramenta vetera ut conditiones sine quibus non fides operabatur.* Yet since more abundance of grace and salvation comes by the new, more immediatly and properly instituted by our Saviour for such an effect; Therefore were the new much desired by (and we are not to doubt) with much benefit administred, to those who had formerly received the other; which were also the types and figures of these. And Blessed ever be God who hath made our times partakers of these his more excellent benefits and dispensations.

The same way of salvation ; first; by remission of sin past, &c. *Ps.* 32. 1, 2. upon repentance. Second- §. 19. ly,

The same justification and sanctification. ly, by obedience for the time to come: the children of faith being guided by the same Evangelical precepts, regenerated by the same spirit; and this spirit operating the same purity and sanctity in their hearts, under the old Testament, as under the new. Neither may we think that the latter Saints more illuminated differed from the ancient more oreshadowed, in the perfection of any new parts of obedience, but only in the perfection of degrees. Nor (for degrees) was their illumination so small (and consequently their obedience so *The same obedience then required and performed.* impure), in comparison of us as some imagine. Which thing, after first having taken notice, that the two greatest Commandements which indeed contain all the rest whatsoever *Rom.* 13.10. are quoted by our Saviour out of ehe law and Prophets. *Deut.* 6. 5. *Lev.* 19. 18. see *Matt.* 22. 37.-7. 12. We may the better discern by running over the strictest precepts of our Saviours Sermon, *Matt* 5. &c. and seeing how far those of the Law and Prophets have advanced towards them, tho the supine negligence or hypocrisy of the Jewish Doctors took notice only of some places (for the outward expression) of less restraint; as Thou shalt not kill, commit adultery, forswear thy self, &c. without considering others at all that were of greater.

§. 20.
The Parallel precepts under the law, to those under the Gospel.   The parallel precepts given under the law, to those of our Saviour; *Matt.*5. vers.21. see *Eccles.*7.9. *Psal.* 3.7,8. *Exod.* 22. 28. *Psal.* 39. 1. *1 Pet.* 3. 9. [*not railing*] confirming it from *Psal.* 34. 13. and the practises of David, 2 *Sam.*16.10. and of Moses *Numb.* 16. 4. and the censure of Nabal for calling David a runaway. 1 *Sam.*25. 14. And indeed the general precept of the law [*loving our neighbour as our self, and doing only to him, what we would he should to us*] suffici-

CHAP. IX.

sufficiently involves the prohibition. To our Saviours, *Matt.* 5. 27. see *Prov.* 6. 25. *Job.* 31. 1. *Prov.* 5. 8. where advised to *turn another way*. *Jer.* 5. 8. Is our Saviours stricter then *Prov.* 23. 31, 33. And lastly the 10th Commandement; from which we may argue; If (now) the eye look, &c. without coveting, 'tis innocent: if with it, then also this was a sin. To those *Matt.* 5. 33. see the third Commandement; and our Saviours reason for not swearing, *Matt.* 5. 37. Which reason [*of its coming of evil*] argues that it was never lawful; and (consequently) alwaies forbidden; either by the positive, or the natural, divine law. Now tho we find not in the positive law [*swear not at all*] (which precept is in no times to be understood absolutely); yet we find that we shall *only swear by the Lords name Deut.* 6. 13. -10. 20. (for *swearing by him was his honour*, *Esai.* 65. 16. *Jer.* 2. 16.) and again that *we shall never take his name in vain*. Therefore *they might not swear at all*; unless upon necessary and just causes; But so also we may now swear. And see this in St. Paul not unfrequent. To that *Matt.* 5. 38. see *Prov.* 20. 22. -24. 29. *Lev.* 19. 18. *Tooth for tooth* (for publique revenge) is still lawful; but private never was. See *Numb.* 35. 24. And see *Lam.* 3. 30. *Esai.* 30. 6. answering to *Matt.* 5. 39. To *Matt.* 5. 43. &c. See *Exod.* 23. 4, 5. and *if his Oxe*; then if a thing much dearer to him; then also if Himself. See *Rom.* 12. 20. quoting it out of the old Testament. *Pro.* 25. 21,22. *Psal.* 7. 4. *Job.* 31. 29, 30. *Lev.* 19. 17. *Prov.* 24. 17, 18. Tho some enemies there were devoted to destruction, to whom they might shew no mercy. *Deut.* 7. 16. As also now some enemies of God we may not pray for, 1 *Jo.* 5. 16. and some acts of charity there were, in which they were obliged only to

their

their brethren. *Deut.* 15. 3. -23. 20. But so also 'tis now, *Gal.* 6. 10. Now concerning these precepts above quoted we may not think that they were unknown or unpractised till the time wherein we find them registred. For we find not only the morals of Moses, but even many of the ceremonials, observed before his times; As *paying tithes, Gen.* 14. 20. *Purifying, cleansings, changing their garments. Gen.* 35. 2. *Holocausts, Gen.* 8. 21. *Peace-offerings, Exod.* 24. 5. *Clean and unclean beasts. Gen.* 7. 2. *The birds in sacrifice not divided. Gen.* 15. 10. comp. *Lev.* 1. 17. *Not eating the blood, Gen.* 9. 4. *Not marrying with unbeleevers* as may be gathered from *Gen.* 6. 2. comp. 1. And so Polygamy seems then prohibited. See *Matt.* 19. 4, 8. comp. *Gen.* 6. 2. and 4. 19. *Raising seed to their brother. Gen.* 38. 8, 10. But they happened rather to be registred and set down by parts, what the Holy Ghost alwaies on the same manner dictated to the faithful; as those sins also were by them strictly avoided. Else the holiness of ancient Noah and Job would not have run parallel with that of Daniel, *Ezek.* 14. 14. which in the 10 Commandements were only reductively prohibited. This publication of the divine laws being still more and more perfect; Moses more illustrating, and commenting, as it were, upon the former patriarchal Traditions; and the Prophets upon those of Moses; and Christ again upon those of the Prophets; he compleating and fulfilling all things.

§. 21.
The same sufferings, and mortifications, &c. required and undergone.

3. The same way of salvation anciently, (as now) was by sufferings. Self-denial, taking up the Cross, mortification, affliction, as they are the portion of the godly under the new, so were they under the old Testament: and the same promises of protection, deliverance, temporal happiness and prosperity,

Chap. IX.

rity, that were to the righteous under the old, are also to the Saints under the new. And as the present state of the wicked is observed to be prosperous since our Saviours coming, but endless destruction after it; so it was before. And they are Gods constant waies, from the beginning never changed; first affliction, then deliverance; first evil, then good to the godly: first prosperity, then ruin; first good, then evil, to the impious. But who so will universally discern these paths of God by his experience, must first perfectly see the goodness and wickedness of the heart (where their chief seat is) to distinguish between the good and the bad; and then must see the joyes and afflictions of the heart (where their chief seat is) to distinguish between the truly temporally happy, and the miserable. Besides these he must see to what place the soul goes when it leaves the body; and to what place also the body goes when it leaves the grave: for t e reasons, *Matt.* 16. 26. *Luk.* 12. 20. *Rev.* 18. 7. And then for the better considering of temporal judgments and mercies he must live the time of 3 or 4 generations. Till which let his ignorance say with the Wise man, *Eccl.* 9. 1. *Homo nescit utrum amore an odio dignus sit.* Meanwhile to see the unity of the doctrine of the two Testaments concerning these: 1. And first for self-denial, mortifications, &c. Generally we learn from those ancienter Saints, sackcloth, dust, and ashes, fasting, lying on the ground, &c. (see Davids humiliations, 2 *Sam.* 12. 16.) so far as some that will hold only on the liberty of the new, reject these as humiliations proper only to the old Testament. The austerities of the Prophets were very great: the self-denial of Abraham and Moses, &c. not to be parall'd. 2. That temporal afflictions

Consider the old Testament mortifications.

ons were the portion of piety under the old Testament; and that this book taught men so; see the witness that the new bears to it, chusing rather to recite it as an old, then teach it, as a new credend. See *Heb.* 12. 5. quoting *Prov.* 3. 11. *Rom.* 8. 36. quoting *Psal.* 44. 24. *Jam.* 5. 11. chusing an example of sufferings out of *Job*. And now for the history of old times. Consider how that old-Testament-Piety began in *Abel*; and how it ended in those mentioned, *Heb.* 11. 35. &c. How the *children of promise* were at first the servants of their Brethren, as at last their Masters. So that as the Apostle *Gal.* 4. 29. faith, as then, so it is now; we may lawfully convert it in saying, as now, so it was then. See *Abrahams* leaving his country *Act.* 7. 5. the complaint of *Jacob, Gen.* 47. 9. Consider the afflictions of *Moses* (yet those chosen by him) of *David*; and those not less after, then before, his coronation. See *Psal.* 39. 12. see the sad complaint of *Psal.* 44. notwithstanding verf. 17. lastly, consider the design of holy *Jobs* history divulged most early to lesson all posterity, not to adjudge prosperity only to the godly, nor affliction to the wicked. But it was so with single persons, but not so with nations; because they had promises of temporal happiness then upon holiness, first: and have they not so still? Doth not God still temporally bless both persons and nations that fear and serve him? the preachers tell them so. And for righteous men are there none now that may say with *David, Psal.* 16. 6? But if temporal prosperity be the promise of the law, and affliction the lot of the Gospel; then, as then we argue *Israel* Gods people, when prosperous, we must argue them so still: because now most distressed. Nay further, them then not to be Gods people, because no nation

Temporal afflictions of the godly.

Of single persons godly.

Of nations godly.

CHAP. IX.

on seems to have suffered more then the Israelites, (not to a final extirpation of them, for whom mercy is in the last place reserved, but for all manner of tyranny and oppression over them) if we do but together with their short felicities in Joshua's, and Davids, and Solomon's time, &c. consider their condition in Egypt, after in the wilderness; in the time of the Judges; under the invasions of the kings of Syria, Babylon, Egypt, Antiochus, Romans. For as the temporal prosperity of those, who are Gods people, depends only on the continuance of their holiness (God judging here those more, whom he will not judge hereafter; and visiting the sins of his servants almost alwaies with temporal afflictions, tho he deals not so with others, because reserved for future and greater punishments) so they never continuing long without offending God, it comes to pass that they never long abide temporally happy. And we see the very life of holy men not unoften ending in the temporal punishment of some sin, as good Josiah's and Moses's, and the Corinthians 1 *Cor.* 11. 30. comp. with 32. Only the certain comfort to these whether men or nations, is; that Gods judgments alwaies end to them in mercies; mercies everlasting. And Gods proceedings with them are alwaies such as are described, *Psal.* 89. 32. and *Esai.* 54. 7, 8. yet that moment contains their sufferings at this day as appears by v. 9. &c. and speaking of their last conversion. 3. That prosperity was observed under the old Testament to be the ordinary inheritance and portion of the wicked, see those many expostulations we find every where in the ancient Scriptures. See *Jer.* 12, 1, 2. *Job.* 21. 1. &c. and whose friends were reproved by God, for maintaining throout that discourse,

Temporal prosperity of the wicked.

F f   the

the contrary *Job.* 42. 7, 8. *Pſal.* 73. 1. &c. *Mal.* 3. 14. *Pſal.* 17. 14. which wonderment is as much now, as it was then; and proceeds not from a right ſuppoſition of any promiſe God made either then or ſince of perpetual proſperity to the godly, and adverſity to the wicked; but from an human, ſhort-ſighted, non-conſideration of the future endleſs happineſs of the one, and deſtruction of the other: which only is the word of the Almighty and ſhall ſtand faſt for ever. But we will needs conceive their end already paſt; when they are but entring upon an eternity of being. 4. That temporal proſperity under the new Teſtament is not to be denied to the godly, ſee *Mark.* 10. 30. 1 *Tim.* 4. 8. *Matt.* 5. 5. comp. *Pſal.* 37. 11. from which it ſeems to be taken. *Jam.* 5. 11. Where the Apoſtle propoſeth Job's re-proſperity for an example to Chriſtians; And that long life promiſed to obedience to parents; and bleſſings not only upon themſelves, but their children, to thoſe who obey Gods Commandements, are ſince the Goſpel, antiquated; and theſe events altered, who dares to affirm? Or what good man is there that hath not long ſtories of Gods ſeveral temporal mercies to him in this world? And when I conſider the temporal condition of the greateſt ſufferers; (tho 'tis true 1 *Cor.* 15. 19. to the eye of men, and the little enjoyment of any good things of this life, *they are of all men moſt miſerable*) yet in ſuch condition, for the preſent, alſo they ſeem of men the moſt happy (only if you ſuppoſe their hopes to be true): for I find them, tho not freed from adverſities; yet alwaies ſure of protection in, and deliverance from, them. See S. Pauls words 2 *Cor.* 1.10. and 2 *Tim.* 4. 17, 18. agreeing with the doctrine of *Pſ.* 37. and *Pſ.* 34. 19. So that his bonds aſſured with ſuch

Under the new Teſtament temporal proſperity in ſome ſenſe to the godly.

CHAP. IX.

such mercies made others bold, and *Phil.*1.12.&c. and their joyes solid and true and not counterfeit, and far exceeding, and making them even senseless of their sorrows: see 2 *Cor.* 1. and when I look on their life ending in a violent, painful, and ignominious death, yet when I consider the wages for it; it seems that it ought not to be called an affliction, but an extraordinary service; undertaken for to attain a greater reward eternal, then others shall have who take not the same pains. See *Heb.* 11. 35, 26. But concerning temporal prosperity of Saints two things we must note. 1. That it is not for the most part so constant as the wicked's is (see the reason before) because all men sinning; the just God punisheth in this world those of his servants, &c. (the reason of this because he punisheth them not hereafter:) but (according to the qualification inserted *Mark.* 10. 30.) interlined with afflictions; and consists more in protection in and deliverance from, then vacancy of, all crosses (yet which things make it to them infinitely more pleasant; as war and conquest is, then a constant peace: and hunger and a feast then constant satiety): and that it is a happiness as succeeding evils; so succeeded by them, like the condition described, *Psal.* 106. but good and peace alwaies the last. *Ps.* 37.37. 2. That when it is, it is more secret, and within, and less discerned; whereas that of the wicked is more external, and specious, and obvious to the eye. So that the world sees much more of the one and much less of the other then indeed there is. To conclude this point from the premises I think we may safely pronounce. 1. That a constant prosperity (excepting some evils of no moment) hath sometimes happened to the wicked; but never to any good

good man. 2. That conſtant adverſity never happened either to evil or good. Not to the evil, becauſe they purchaſe evil to come only by the pleaſures of ſome preſent ſins: nor to the good becauſe God delivers as he afflicts. 3. That to the good, more worldly diſſatisfaction, then worldly content, either from his not having, or at leaſt his not uſing and enjoying, its good things, 1 *Cor.* 7. 29. hath alwaies happened. 4. That for the people and Church of God in general; ever ſince the beginning, the latter afflictions thereof have been and ſhall be ſtill greater; greater therefore under the times of the Goſpel, then of the law; ſee *Matt.* 10. 34. and greater ſtill the deliverances; all Glory be to the infinite wiſdom of our God!

§ 22.
3 The ſame rewards eternal then promiſed.

Thus much of the ſame obedience and ſufferings, required alwaies of the children of faith, under the times of the law and Prophets; as ſince under the times of Chriſt; even the ſame from the beginning. Next, theſe required alwaies upon the ſame rewards promiſed and puniſhments denounced, i. e. eternal bliſs, or torments: which that they were alwaies believed, hoped, feared by the moſt of men (for now alſo ſome there are who believe them not) we may learn from the ancient univerſality of this opinion (for ſo much as concerns the ſoul) even amongſt falſe religions; which muſt either be borrowed from the relations of it made to the Church, (as all falſe religions were but ſeveral corruptions of the true): or from the common light of nature (as ſuch a thing there is, *Rom.* 2. 14, 15.) For indeed how could at any time right reaſon allowing only a God; and reward and puniſhment; for virtue and vice; as 'tis, *Gen.* 4. 7. argue otherwiſe? For they ſeeing the wicked many times here proſpe-

Puniſhments eternal threatned.
The common belief of all nations concerning theſe.

CHAP. IX.

prosperous; and the righteous suffer; even the first good man murdered by his own brother: and then holding after death no second state, there remains no punishment, &c. for temporal death, passing upon all, can be no punishment of any ones sin, except Adams, any more, then it is of the sins of all. Now the light we find amongst the ancient Heathens we may not deny to have shined much more in the Church. But secondly, That not only future bliss and pains, but a resurrection also was commonly believed in the Church before our Saviours times, encouraging the good, affrighting the wicked, see 2 *Maccab.* 12. 44. *Wisd.* 4. 16. and all the 5th cap. 2 *Maccab.* 7. 9, 36. which tho not Canonical yet are convincing, to shew the Jews ancient opinion in this point; and the last place seems to be verified by the Apostle, *Heb.* 11. 35. see *Martha's* ready answer, *Jo.* 11. 20. and the opprobrium of the Sadduces for denying it. *Matt.* 22. 23, 29. Of whom, note, that they were a Sect not numerous; counted generally Hereticks among the people (as the Pharisees the Orthodox) that, for the evidence of these truths therein they were forced to reject the writings of the Prophets, and were told also by our Saviour that they understood not the writings of the law. *Matt.* 22. 29. And again that this belief amongst them was of no later date, see *Heb.* 11. 12. &c. whence may be collected the quality of that faith mentioned verf. 6. which (compared with the end of the 4th verf. and beginning of 13.) must needs be believing God to be a rewarder after this life, or else is nothing worth, see verf. 35, 40. verf. 26. *of the reward* i. e. eternal; else Egypt was to be preferred before the Wilderness. See *Luk.* 1. 54, 72. *Rom.* 3. 21. -1. 2. Next let us consider the old Testament,

Of the Ancient Church concerning a resurrection of the body.

The benefits of our Saviour.

The scriptures of the old Testament concerning a resurrection. ment, and the many places therein declaring this truth (tho the cleer light we have of these things since the Gospel, makes us fancy the darkness of former times to be far greater then it was). Concerning which our Saviour chides the Sadduces not only for not knowing the point, but *not knowing the scriptures,* Matt. 22. 29. (as the Apostle likewise doth the Corinthians 1. ep. 15. 34. *I speak it to your shame*) and quotes *Exod. 3. 6.* for the proof of it : as also St. *Peter* 2 *Ep.* 3. 13. for the new creation quotes *Esai.* 65. 17. See for this day of judgment and new Creation, *Esai.* 66. 15, 22. -51. 6, 8. *Psal.* 102. 25. -50. 1. &c. And the righteous living after it. *Psal.* 102. 28. comp. 26. *Esai.* 51. 6. -66. 22. There-

Concerning eternal bliss after it of the faithful. fore is *God* also *himself* said *to be their reward. Gen.* 15. 1. *Psal.* 73. 26. -142. 5. *Eccles.* 11. 8, 12, 14. *Eccles.* 2. 3. See first then that clear expression, *Dan.* 12. 2, 3, 13. *Esai.* 13. 12. where note that the term of *sleeping* for *death* used so frequently in the new, see 1 *Thess.* 4. 13. is borrowed from the old, Testament ; and not only intimated rest, but argued a rewaking; whence also the resurrection is called *the morning,* *Psal.* 49. 14. 2 *Pet.* 1. 19. and *seeing light again, Psal.* 16. 9, 10, 11. spoken of the resurrection *Act.* 13. 35. in the first place of Christs, but also of Davids, by him. *Psal.* 17. 15. comp. with 14. and with *Psal.* 16. 11. *Psal.* 49. 15. comp. with 14. *Psal.* 73. 24, 26. *Psal.* 36. 8, 9. comp. with the rest. *Job* 19. 25. &c. *Job* 13. 15. *Esai.* 26. 19. opposed to 14. *Hos.* 13. 14. *Esai.* 25. 8. -51. 6, 8. quoted 1 *Cor.* 15. 54, 55. *Exod.* 32. 32. *Ps.* 69. 28. comp. with *Phil.* 4. 3. *Rev.* 20. 12. *Luk.* 10. 20. where keeping this memorial of them, is upon their being first by death removed out of sight, see *Mal.* 3. 16, 13. where this registring of them differenceth the righteous from the prospering wicked. Add to these

CHAP. IX.

these Enoch's assumtion to another life before, Elias under, the law ; as Christ after it. Add the raising of several other to life. 2 *King.* 8. 5. -4. 35. *Heb.* 11. 35. Arguments to the old world both of Gods power and purpose. *Esai.* 13. 9, 10, 11, 12. comp. with *Matt.* 24. 29. Enough of the resurrection of the just to life ; but what of the wicked to eternal torments? First these seem to follow necessarily upon concession of the other ; sins being our own, more then righteousness is ; and therefore if this in us obtains a reward, the other will punishment. Again this punishment is not a temporally miserable life, (as appears before) ; oftner undergon by the good then the bad ; nor can it be a temporal death ; because there is no more undergon by the profanest, then the holiest ; and is so far from deterring the unbelievers of future torments, from sin ; as 'tis made an argument for it. [*Let us eat, &c. to morrow we dy, Esai.* 22. 13. 1 *Cor.* 15. 32.] I may go further, Neither could the loss of a pleasure to come tho greater, yet unknown and a far off, sufficiently sway most men to loose and forego a pleasure present and acquainted ; (the worth of the one being counterpoised by the nearness of the other.) Yet more ; Neither could the danger of incurring of some future pains make men forbear the pursuit of some present delights ; if all their joy must be bought with some sorrow ; It seeming to them no wisdom to be in pain to avoid it. Tis therefore the wisdom, and also mercy of the Lawgiver, to appoint a penalty so high, as may abundantly serve to deter men from the fault : and this can be only future pains; not only great, but eternal. The severity of which, by how much it seems to us super-proportioned to sin, so much more

Eternal punishment of the wicked.

The benefits of our Saviour.

is it neceffary and juftified; fince neither the fear thereof can yet keep the moft men from fin, and many alfo for fear of thefe efcape fin here; and attain to heaven; who upon a lefs penalty would have entertained the enticements of vice; and loft the promifed reward, and voluntarily as it were contracted for prefent delight a future mifery, had it not been fo unmeafurably great.   2. Tis plain, that the wicked of the old world fuffer eternal torments, fee *Matt.* 11. 22, 24. 2 *Pet.* 2. 9, 10. comp. with 5, 6. and with 1 *Pet.* 3. 19. *Jude* 7. where the unclean falfe teachers are threatned with the fame deftruction to come, as the divels, the old world, or the Giants, Sodom, Cain, Core, &c: And hence it follows that either from the evidence of Confcience, or of Tradition, or of Scripture, thefe were fufficiently made known unto them. For tho' Gods bounty may be greater then his engagement, yet not his punifhments then his threats; leaft he fhould feem to hide the hook of our mifery, only to make us fwallow the bait of fin. But thirdly, *Did not Ifrael know,* &c. Yes, See *Luk.* 16. 29. Abrahams anfwer to Dives in thefe torments: who it feems having not believed, till felt them himfelf would fain have fome warning of them fent to his Brethen; and the Patriarch anfwered him *they have Mofes and the Prophets.* And indeed we fcarce find any, or no expreffions of thefe future pains in the new Teftament but taken out of the old. *Matt.* 5.22. Gehenna or *the valley of Hinnon*; a pleafant vale near Jerufalem; in which was *Tophet* a place where children were burnt alive to the honor of the idols; 2 *King.* 23. 10. *Jer.* 7. 31. taken out of *Efai.* 30. 30. where *Tophet* is fet to fignify thefe eternal pains. *Mark.* 9. 43. *fire unquenchable* and *never dying worm* (alluding to that of the grave)

Chap. IX.

grave) out of *Esai.* 66. 24. *Rev.* 19. 20. out of *Gen.* 19. 24, 28. comp. with *Jude* 7. And these, and many other expressions are used also in the old Testament; not to signifie but the same thing, as they are in the new: which the better to discover, we are to take notice; 1. That all the expressions mentioning *going down into darkness ; into Hell ; and the pit ; the place of Giants ; the place of the uncircumcised ; of the slain ;* under, or *into the lower parts of the earth ;* (where (in the inferiour spatious concavity thereof, the Diameter of its body amounting at least to 7000 miles) in all likelyhood, is the place of those torments. It being farthest from light, and the mansion of the Blessed : which place seems to be intimated *Luk.* 8. 31. where the Divels desire they may *not be sent into the deep,* but live on the earth, *Mark.* 5. 10.) *going into destruction ; death gnawing upon them ; their* grave-worms *never dying ; never seeing light ; perishing like the beasts ; their iniquity being upon their bones ;* being had *no more in remembrance ;* and being *blotted out of the book of the living, &c.* signify not simply the common lot of the grave (where the righteous are said to *sleep, Esai.* 57. 2. comp. 1.) or only a suddainer descent thither, by an untimely death ; (for the righteous also many times have an early decease,) but the place of a prison and torment. 2. That the frequent threats there of Gods coming to judgment, are often not meant of some particular temporal executions of his wrath upon the living ; but of that last general, that shall be upon all the world : called by the Baptist *the wrath to come, Matt.* 3. 7. as appears by the quotations of them in the new Testament, applyed to that day. See 2 *Pet.* 3. *Rev.* 20. 21, 22. chap. compared with the last chapters of *Esai. Ezek. Zech.*

The benefits of our Savior.

Zech. &c. *Esai. 13. 9.* comp. *Matt. 24. 29.* 3. That the future misery of the wicked, as it is expressed in some places by the *pæna sensus,* so not unoften by the *pæna damni*; only by privation of light, of life, i. e. future, of remembrance, &c. see *Psal. 73. 18, 20.* [*awakest*] i. e. in the morning of the resurrection, as *Psal. 39. 14.* and *Psal. 17, 15.* comp. with *24. 4.* and with *Job 21. 13.* [*in a moment,* i. e. without such languishing pains as Job had] *32.* where they are intimated to dy without much pain, as well as live in much prosperity. If therefore after such pleasures their destruction means only death; death many times peaceable and easy: what preeminence over them at any time hath the Godly? why may he not then bless himself? and others also praise his providence? *Psal. 49. 18. Psal. 49. 14, 19, 20.* where by *perishing like beasts,* and *death gnawing upon them;* and *never again seeing light,* is expressed their *pæna damni,* their condemnation to utter darkness; and non-restorement to life eternal; as appears comparing them with vers. *15.* and *Psal. 16. 11.* And such are those expressions, *Psal. 9. 5, 17, 7, 8.* chiefly intending the last day of judgment and vengeance. See *Psal. 69. 27, 28.* comp. with *Exod. 32. 33.* and *Phil. 4. 3. Psal. 17. 11. Esai. 26. 14.* comp. *19.* But for their opinion of *pæna sensus* too; See the opinion of latter times, *Wisd. 4. 20.* comp. with *5. 1. -6. 6, 8.* of the former; in the ancientest testimony in the world, that of Enoch the Prophet. *Jude 14, 15.* He speaketh so early of the last judgment: frequently appeal'd to in the old Testament tho mistaken, see *Ps. 2. 9.* compar'd with *Rev. 2. 27. -19. 15.* See *Esai. 30. 33. -33. 14.* comp. *16. -66. 24.* These compared with *Job. 26. 5, 6.* where the Vulgar and Diodat [*Ecce gigantes gemunt sub aquis*

Pæna damni.

Pæna sensus.

CHAP. IX.

& *qui habitant cum eis*] and *1 Pet.* 3. 19. and *Esai.* 14. 9, 12. *suscitavit tibi gigantes,* 15, 18, 19. *Prov.* 2. 18. and 9. 18. *The dead,* the Giants as in the other i. e. the wicked of the old world; and condemnation to the place where these are, is the future punishment of the unchast; and signifies not death or the grave; but *hell* and torment. See the like expressions, *Ezek.* 32. 18, 19. &c. 28. 10. -31. 18. *Prov.* 7. 26, 27. *Esai.* 10. 18. *Psal.* 63. 9, 10.

Thus in all times the same way of salvation; the same God never changing his counsels, the same Son of God Patron of the Church; the same Spirit illuminating and sanctifying it; the same Covenant of Grace; the same Gospel; the same benefits; by looking forward *(* as of old *)* upon the seed promised; or looking backward *(* as in these latter times, *)* upon the promise fulfilled. And as *Heb.* 8. 8. shews that the Gospel was a Covenant of the latter daies, in respect of Christ exhibited; so *Gal.* 3. 16, 17. shews it was of the former, in respect of Christ promised. And those places where we read of *new* and *better Covenants, Heb.* 8. 9, 10. better *promises, Heb.* 8. 6. better *Hope, Heb.* 7. 19. *&c.* are not so to be understood; as if there were now produced and made known some way of salvation to the world, when as there was none before; or some new way of salvation, when as there was another before; But are opposed, either not to the former times in general; i. e. in respect of all persons, and of all Covenants made with, and promises made to, them: but only to those times, in respect of the covenant of works; which then by the errour of many of the Jews (the children of works) was generally more looked after, then the Covenant of faith, which had then but few followers: see *Rom.* 9. 31, 32.

§. 23.
Conclusion.

when also the one Covenant was more largely and legibly drawn in great Characters; the other put forth more obscure, and in a lesser Print, and a veil drawn over it, *2 Cor.* 3. 14. *till the fulness of time was come.* Therefore also the former times had the denomination of the *times of the law*; the latter *of the Gospel.* And again, in respect of the literal promise (under the law) of felicity in the earthly Canaan. Therefore where the Apostle saith [*established on better promises*] understand there those typical ones, of earthly Canaan, made to Israel at the promulgation of the law. Or opposed to those times in general: but this only; first, in respect of the diverse administrations of the former times with · many troublesome ceremonials and types to be afterward abolished: and of the degrees of the greater manifestations, in the latter times, of the way of salvation; being void of shadows, types, and figures: all these now being brought to perfection and accomplishment in the incarnation of the Son; effusions of the Spirit; enlargement of the Church; promulgation of an Heavenly country instead of an Earthly Canaan; and from these greater manifestations many more of the children of works becoming now the children of faith: And from its stronger beams as well those illuminated, *who* before *sate in darkness, Luk.* 1. 79. and midnight; as this light increased to those, who had before some dawnings thereof. And secondly, in respect of the accomplishment of those promises to the faithful of the former ages: which are made thro Christ, spoken of *Heb.* 11. 13, 14, 16. In which they could not be compleated and perfected before the times of the Gospel: neither in respect of the body, they waiting for the restorement of that, till those of the Gospel are

Chap. IX.

are glorified with them; nor (according to the reverend opinion of Antiquity) in respect of the soul, they not having the kingdom of heaven laid fully opened unto them till our Saviour was first entred in thither. See *Eph. 1. 10. Col. 1. 20. Heb. 11. 39, 40. -12. 23.* For indeed the performance and perfection of the mystery of mans redemtion was a thing only received in the last daies. And tho the virtue of Chrifts incarnation is communicated alwaies to all men; yet not the latter times on the former, but the former depend on the latter, for the substance and ground of their hope and salvation, Jesus Christ come in the flesh. These having the *body*, of which body coming toward them the other had the *shadow* ; *Col. 2. 17.* And in these respects the times of the Gospel are said to have so much advantage of those of the law: we seeing *in a clear glass* Gods glory, they thro a *thick veil;* we *2 Cor. 3. 13.* standing in a clear, whereas the best of them in a dim, light; and the most of them in utter darkness. See *Matt. 13. 17. -11. 11. 1 Cor. 2. 10.* &c. *2 Cor. 3. 7.* &c. Here note that the oppositions of the times that are used in the other heads preceding (in which I follow only the phrase of the Holy Scriptures) are by these limitations so to be interpreted, as that they no way contradict the doctrine of this last chapter.

F I N I S.